OUTBACK GHETTOS

To Norm Etherington and those long dinnertime conversations

Studies in Australian History

Series editors: Alan Gilbert, Patricia Grimshaw and Peter Spearritt

Steven Nicholas (ed.)   *Convict Workers*
Pamela Statham (ed.)   *The Origins of Australia's Capital Cities*
Jeffrey Grey   *A Military History of Australia*
Alastair Davidson   *The Invisible State*
James A. Gillespie   *The Price of Health*
David Neal   *The Rule of Law in a Penal Colony*
Sharon Morgan   *Land Settlement in Early Tasmania*
Audrey Oldfield   *Woman Suffrage in Australia*
Paula J. Byrne   *Criminal Law and Colonial Subject*

OUTBACK GHETTOS

ABORIGINES, INSTITUTIONALISATION AND SURVIVAL

Peggy Brock

DEPARTMENT OF ABORIGINAL AND INTERCULTURAL STUDIES
EDITH COWAN UNIVERSITY

CAMBRIDGE
UNIVERSITY PRESS

Published by the Press Syndicate of the University of Cambridge
The Pitt Building, Trumpington Street, Cambridge CB2 1RP, UK
40 West 20th Street, New York, NY 10011-4211, USA
10 Stamford Road, Oakleigh, Melbourne 3166, Australia

Printed in Hong Kong by Colorcraft

National Library of Australia cataloguing in publication data
Brock, Peggy, 1948–
Outback ghettos.
Bibliography.
Includes index.
ISBN 0 521 43435 1.
ISBN 0 521 44708 9 (pbk.).
1. Koonibba Mission Station – History. 2. Nepabunna Mission – History. 3. Poonindie Mission (Poonindie, S. Aust.) – History. [4]. Aborigines, Australian – South Australia – Cultural assimilation. [5]. Adnyamathanha (Australian people. [6]. Aborigines, Australian – Missions – South Australia – History. I. Title.
305.8991509423

Library of Congress cataloguing in publication data
Brock, Peggy, 1948–
Outback ghettos: A history of Aboriginal institutionalisation and survival.
Peggy Brock.
p.   cm.   (Studies in Australian history)
Includes bibliographial references and index.
ISBN 0-521-43435-1. ISBN 0-521-44708-9 (pbk.)
1. Australian aborigines – Government policy. 2. Australian
aborigines – Cultural assimilation. 3. Australian aborigines – Social
conditions. 4. Social integration – Australia. 5. Acculturation –
Australia. 6. Australia – History. 7. Australia – Politics and
government. I. Title. II Series.
GN666.B75 1993
306'.0899915–dc20   93-16329
                                                        CIP

A catalogue record for this book is available from the British Library.

ISBN 0 521 43435 1 hardback
ISBN 0 521 44708 9 paperback

Contents

List of maps/illustrations   vi
Abbreviations   viii
Note on currency and measurements   ix
Acknowledgements   x

1   Introduction   1

2   Legislation and policy: The context of outback ghettos   11

3   Poonindie, home away from 'country'   21

4   An established community and its destruction   43

5   Koonibba, a refuge for west coast people   63

6   Institutional upheaval and adjustment   89

7   Dispersal and the end of the mission era   103

8   Adnyamathanha, survival without institutionalisation   121

9   Nepabunna mission   138

10   The ghetto experience and survival   156

Select Bibliography   168
Index   176

List of maps/illustrations

List of maps

Australia showing South Australia and mission locations 15
Poonindie region 22
Koonibba region 64
Flinders Ranges 123

List of illustrations

Poonindie

St Matthew's Church, Poonindie 27
Portrait of Samuel Kandwillan, a pupil of the Natives' Training Institution, Poonindie, South Australia, by J. M. Crossland, 1800–58 30
Farm machinery and implements, late 19th century, Poonindie 33
Poonindie Mission, mid-1860s 38
Adults and children, Poonindie, c. 1885 47
A photograph that was probably taken about the time Poonindie closed in the 1890s 57

Koonibba

Christmas at Koonibba in the first years of the mission 70
Koonibba workers, c. 1901 75
Six young women on the verandah of the Children's Home, c. 1914 81
Koonibba church on the day the Children's Home was opened 83

Koonibba mission buildings, *c.* 1914   84
A group of children on the verandah of the Children's Home, *c.* 1914   94
Mr F. M. Linke with confirmation class, Koonibba, between 1909–15   97

Nepabunna
Rufus Wilton with Mavis Patterson, late 1930s   133
Nepabunna Mission   140
Stone hut with pressed kerosene tin roof, Nepabunna, late 1930s   142
Hut made of lime mortar on chicken wire, Nepabunna, late 1930s   143
Fred McKenzie, late 1930s   147
An Aboriginal camp with women in mourning, North Flinders Ranges   151
Donkey team pulling car body, Nepabunna, late 1930s   165

Abbreviations

AL	*Australian Lutheran*
AMB	Aboriginal Mission Board of the Evangelical Lutheran Church of Australia
CL & I	Crown Lands and Immigration
GRG	Government record group, Public Record Office of South Australia
LKA	*Der Lutherische Kirchenbote für Australien*
PRG	Private record group, Mortlock Library of South Australiana
SAPP	South Australian Parliamentary Papers
SAPRO	South Australian Public Record Office
SRG	Societies record group, Mortlock Library of South Australiana
UAM	United Aborigines Mission

Note on currency and measurements

Currency
In the currency used during the period dealt with in this book, there were 12 pennies (d.) in one shilling (s.), and 20 shillings in one pound (£).

The sum of 10 shillings and 6 pence could be written as 10s 6d or as 10/6. A farthing was a quarter of a penny, and a guinea was £1 1s.

When Australia changed to decimal currency in 1966, $2 was equal to £1.

Mass
1 ounce (oz) = 28.3 g
1 pound (lb) = 454 g
1 stone = 6.35 kg
1 ton = 1.02 t

Area
1 acre = 0.40 ha
1 square mile = 2.59 km²

Length
1 mile = 1.61 km

Volume
1 pint = 0.57 L
1 gallon = 4.55 L
1 bushel = 0.036 m³ = 36.4 L

Acknowledgements

This book could not have been researched and written without the cooperation of many people. First I would like to thank the Aboriginal people and communities with whom I worked for their cooperation and interest in researching their history. In particular the Adnyamathanha, who participated in numerous field trips and the Koonibba Community Council for their invitation to research their history. Also Doreen Kartinyeri, a descendant of the Poonindie people, who produced genealogies which link present-day Aboriginal people with the history of Poonindie. The Aboriginal and non-Aboriginal people I interviewed for this study are too numerous to mention, but I thank them all for their willingness to work with me and for the information they contributed.

I would also like to acknowledge the support of the Aboriginal Heritage Branch of the Department of Environment and Planning in South Australia, for its support of my research and its foresight in recognising the importance of post-contact history to the heritage of Aboriginal people of South Australia. Vlad Potezney of the Aboriginal Heritage Branch drafted some of the maps reproduced in this book, others were drawn up by the graphics department at Edith Cowan University and I thank them for their assistance.

The staff at the Mortlock Library of South Australiana and the South Australian Record Office have assisted me over many years and I would like to acknowledge their help. Also, I would like to thank the archivist at the Lutheran Archives for his cooperation in making Koonibba records available and arranging for the transcription of records in the old German script into spoken German. I would like to acknowledge C. V. Eckermann's assistance in introducing me to the Lutheran Archives, correcting some of my German translation and challenging my interpretation of Koonibba history from his own deeply committed perspective.

Professor Fay Gale and Dr John Young supervised the PhD thesis on which this book is based and I thank them for their interest in my research over many years. Finally I thank my husband, Norman Etherington, for his unflagging interest and enthusiasm in this project and his invaluable critical comments on final drafts.

1

INTRODUCTION

it is very hard for us to think of our dear old homes and white people living there and we've got to pass by like strangers . . .[1]

We battle ourselfs we dont want to be chased about from place to place . . . The minister dont want us on the Mission station & from there he hunt us away . . . And when we are in Ceduna, they get the Policeman to hunt us away from here. We dont know where to go they chase us like wild dingoes . . .[2]

Could you please come up here and see how we are kicked around. I am likely to be kicked off the [Copley] Common at any time. I am not the only aborigine receiving this treatment.[3]

These are pleas for help and sympathy from Aborigines forced off missions in South Australia by economic and political circumstances. Having left the communal and institutional life with which they grew up, they struggle in a hostile world. This book will consider the institutional experiences and their impact on Aboriginal people in southern Australia. It identifies strategies used by Aborigines to reinforce existing community identities or form new ones centred on permanent, institutional settlements. It illustrates that these Aboriginal communal identities are not based purely on a distant, 'traditional' past, but are historical constructs, which change over time.

The institutions which isolated Aborigines in rural settings had a double-edged character which recalls the ghettos of early modern Europe as well as the twentieth-century ghettos of American cities. The word ghetto is used specifically to evoke the ambiguous relationship between Aboriginal people and these institutions. Like the ghettos of other lands, outback missions simultaneously oppressed and nurtured the communities they confined. These institutions offered a haven from the hostile, outside world and a basis for community solidarity and consolidation in contrast to that world.

1

Louis Wirth's description of Jewish ghettos, encapsulates many Aboriginal institutional experiences:

> The world at large was cold and strange . . . but within the ghetto he felt free. Within the circle of his own tribal group he received that appreciation, sympathy and understanding which the larger world could not offer. In his own community, which was based upon the solidarity of the families that composed it, he was a person with status.[4]

But there the similarities end. There is no intention to demonstrate the existence of underlying structural similarities between Aboriginal missions and places called ghettos elsewhere in the world. The operation of Aboriginal missions and government stations, with their paternalistic/dictatorial non-Aboriginal administrative structures, were very different from the largely self-administered urban ghettos.

The context of research

This study is situated in the context of a considerable body of previous research. Two of the most influential schools of thought on Aboriginal history stand almost diametrically opposed to each other. One, which reflects nineteenth- and early twentieth-century attitudes, views white, colonial authority as all powerful, dominating technologically and culturally 'primitive' Aborigines, who are unable to cope with the challenge of European 'settlement'.[5] The other insists that Aboriginal people have made their own history, first by heroically resisting the white invaders and subsequently battling to 'survive in their own land'. The second, more recent school predominates today, but has not obliterated the legacy of the first.[6]

In the past Aborigines were commonly portrayed as helpless victims and this view is perpetuated through the language which continues to be used to describe the colonial situation. There is the convenient myth that the act of 'settlement' was swift and not resisted by Aborigines and that superior technology rightfully predominated over people with outmoded, 'primitive' crafts. Australian history has thus ignored the presence and displacement of Aborigines. This historical interpretation of the past is reinforced by the legal doctrine that Australia was 'terra nullius', even though it is known that the continent was inhabited at the time of British colonisation.[7] This legal and political fiction presents the land as 'settled' by 'settlers', rather than invaded by a colonial power which unsettled Aborigines and provoked them into periodic violent resistance. In the colonial state 'protection' took on a new meaning. The accepted definition 'to defend or guard from injury or danger; to shield; to keep safe, take care of; to extend patronage to'[8] was supplanted by new connotations of isolation, discrimination, institutionalisation and invisibility. 'Protecting' Aborigines meant removing them from the sight and awareness of the general Australian population, restraining them within carefully defined lands, maintaining them as unproductive, dependent communities which could act as labour pools in times of labour shortage, singling out Aborigines as different from the rest of the population. Aboriginal attempts to deal with this process of 'protection' and institutionalisation and Aboriginal responses to it will be extensively examined in this book.

The strategies Aborigines developed to aid their survival can only be understood when the detailed circumstances of their oppression are exposed. This exposure is occurring now on many fronts: through Aboriginal political activity, which has become increasingly vocal and visible since the Second World War; through Aboriginal writers and dramatists who articulate their people's experiences for a wider audience and reveal the double standards that have applied in the treatment of Aborigines;[9] and also through the growing awareness of non-Aboriginal writers and social scientists that most Australians falsely perceive their past.[10] This view acknowledges that, despite the oppression of the colonial situation, Aborigines were active agents in their interaction with the colonisers. Within the context of this current research, this book seeks to determine as precisely as possible which constraints were most important in inhibiting Aboriginal action and which strategies were most effective in ensuring survival, self-respect, community cohesion and economic well-being. Three case studies are used to illustrate these historical circumstances of Aborigines. Each case demonstrates that Aborigines were making choices about the direction their lives would take. Often their preferred line of action was blocked or huge obstacles were put in the way of their progress, but there is evidence of great perseverance in the face of these impediments.

One option which faced many Aborigines was the possibility of aligning themselves with a mission or government station. This study will consider how the decision to move on to an institution affected Aboriginal ability to survive. Survival in this context is not defined by the maintenance of a gene pool, but by the persistence of a communal identity.[11] The unplanned effect of protective government policies and institutionalisation was to create strong, sedentary Aboriginal communities with close-knit but extended kinship networks. While the assimilation and integration policies of the post-war era reversed some of the worst restrictions of protectionism, they have also been criticised as highly destructive of Aboriginal society, because their aim was to break up these communities and assimilate individuals into mainstream society.[12]

American Indian and Aboriginal history—contrasts and parallels

There is a substantial literature on the subject of agency and options for survival in American Indian (also referred to as Amerindian) history and anthropology which helps to define some key issues. Amerindian history was established earlier in the USA and Canada than was Aboriginal history in Australia. As a result, many of the issues which are only now being professionally investigated in Aboriginal history have previously been broached in the USA and Canada. The research and writing of Amerindian history began in the late 1940s and 1950s, stimulated by the legal battles over land claims based on treaties signed by specific Indian groups.[13] Twentieth-century descendants of these people had to prove in court that they were the descendants of the signatories, so they employed anthropologists and historians to justify their claims.[14] But even before this legal tussle, anthropologists had begun studying cultural change among Amerindians in an historical context—looking at change over time.

Early anthropological thinking on both sides of the Atlantic had been dominated by evolutionary assumptions. Franz Boas in America (and the functionalists in Britain) were the first to look at the cultures of indigenous peoples as 'neither moral examples nor living fossils but simply different and equally valued'.[15] But this new generation of anthropologists wanted to study these indigenous cultures in their pure, unchanged state before colonial intervention. Cultures that existed prior to and at the point of European contact were deemed to be within the anthropologist's field of interest. Changes, which occurred after contact, fell within the historian's area of expertise: 'What happened to the California Indians in the years following 1849—their disruptions, losses, sufferings, and adjustments—fall into the purview of the historian rather than of the anthropologist whose prime concern is the purely aboriginal, the uncontaminated native.'[16] It was not until the 1930s and 1940s that there was a change of emphasis from 'how culture is received to how it is created'[17] and historical perspectives were incorporated into anthropological theory and practice.

Ralph Linton was a major influence in bringing about this shift of emphasis in anthropology. In 1940 he edited a book which considered seven Amerindian tribes and their process of 'acculturation'.[18] Linton defined acculturation as 'comprehend[ing] those phenomena which result when groups of individuals having different cultures come into continuous first hand contact with subsequent changes in the original culture patterns of either or both'. This definition implies a voluntary two-way process, but he goes on to discuss directed cultural change whereby the dominant group tries to control its own environment: a situation of relevance to colonial conditions.[19] The case studies in Linton's book document changes in seven Indian communities as a result of the influence, direct and indirect, of Europeans and show how the Indians responded to these forces of change. Indians are presented in Linton's work as active agents in their own historical development, adopting some European innovations, rejecting others, or adapting them to their own purposes.

An instructive contrast can be drawn between Linton's work and that of his Australian contemporary, A. P. Elkin. Elkin, an influential figure in Australian anthropology and the first Australian to occupy a chair of anthropology in Australia, was heavily influenced by evolutionary assumptions. He believed that hunter-gatherers had to progress through predictable stages before they could become assimilated into the colonial society and culture. Writing ten years after Linton, Elkin still perceived Aborigines from a superior colonial viewpoint: 'The general picture all over Australia from 1788 onward is that on first contact with definite settlement the Aborigines are usually shy and harmless.'[20]

Elkin believed Aborigines were moving on a set course from the unchanging traditional past towards assimilation into European society. He developed a paradigm of Aboriginal reaction which suggested Aborigines ultimately had only two options in the face of European domination: assimilation or 'return to the mat' through breakdown of their society and disillusionment.[21] Elkin characterised Aborigines as lacking curiosity, only adapting to the pastoral economy (he generalises from a narrow data base)[22] out of necessity, not a desire to change. These 'intelligent parasites' did the minimal amount of work to sustain their communities, they only gave the appearance of adapting, their 'real' life was 'their own world of traditional security, mythological depth, social warmth, ritual and technical efficiency'. 'Acculturation' was not possible in this rigid, unchanging traditional world. The only alternative to assimilation was disintegration.[23]

Anthropologists interpreting Amerindian society within a changing historical context moved beyond this concept of the ethnographic present long before some of their colleagues in Australia.[24] Edward H. Spicer writing in the early 1960s criticised Elkin's 'invariant sequences' of reaction suggesting they were meaningless without statements of the conditions of contact between indigenous people and Europeans.[25] Spicer built on the groundwork laid by Linton, distinguishing between directed and non-directed cultural change among American Indians, though asserting that change can be directed in one period and non-directed in another. He presented the Mandan as an example of non-directed cultural change. Their first contact with Europeans was through the fur-traders in the eighteenth century. They adapted their economy to these new trade possibilities, adopting aspects of European technology that suited them and rejecting others. But in the nineteenth century Mandan numbers were decimated by several epidemics and their situation changed dramatically.[26] The Yacqui, of the south-west, on the other hand experienced directed change through the presence of Jesuit missionaries who proselytised among them. The missionaries were accepted as authoritative figures within Yacqui communities, where they established a programme and organisation to implement change.[27] Spicer's point is that there is no invariable inevitable series of changes resulting from the colonisation of indigenous peoples as Elkin insisted, but that changing circumstances require changing strategies by the colonised if they are to survive.[28]

The emphasis in Amerindian ethnohistory on cultural change and the agency of Indians is still evident today. One of its foremost proponents is James Axtell, whose article on the ethnohistory of missions is of direct relevance to this study. He asks what are the criteria for judging success or failure of a missionary programme?[29] He suggests that generally this question has been answered using the *missionaries'* criteria of number of baptisms and similar indicators, rather than considering the question from the Indian viewpoint and asking the supplementary question, why did Indians convert to Christianity? The answer to this question must be that Christianity provided solutions to urgent social and religious problems that Indians faced at that point in their cultural history.

Axtell takes as a case study the 'praying towns' of New England established by an English missionary, John Eliot.[30] At the time Eliot was proselytising, the eastern Massachusetts had been decimated by disease and faced the alternatives of revitalising or dying. Large numbers chose to convert, which entailed wholesale cultural change but preserved their ethnic identity. Axtell suggests that the success or failure of missions from an Indian perspective is premised on whether they assist ethnic survival. The conversion of the Indians must be seen as a tragic loss if the pre-contact Indian is seen as the only true Indian, but if ethnic survival is the yardstick, then the missions were a success. Axtell concludes that the Indians, not the missionaries, decided the rate and timing of their conversion. They chose to establish a 'praying town' to maintain the communal life of the group where it was threatened with disintegration, but when their cultural resources and sovereignty were unimpaired they chose selectively from the missionaries' offerings. The Indians were making active choices about how they would best survive.[31]

Similar issues arise in Aboriginal history. Axtell's conclusions about the Massachusetts and their use of the 'praying towns' have parallels in Aborigines' use of missions in their strategies for survival. Marshall Sahlins has characterised this view of cultural change as 'externally induced, yet indigenously orchestrated [and is] present everywhere in human experience'.[32]

The three Aboriginal communities which will be considered are from distinct but overlapping historic periods in different parts of South Australia and represent very different Aboriginal experiences. They also have much in common. The three communities survived the devastation caused by colonisation, but in different ways. They experienced institutionalisation on missions, but in different eras and for differing lengths of time. The first community was established by people who went to Poonindie Anglican mission on southern Eyre Peninsula, north of Port Lincoln. The mission was established in the first assimilationist period by Archdeacon Mathew Hale in 1850 and closed in the 1890s. The initial members of this institution were Aborigines who had first contact with the colonisers around Adelaide and along the Murray River.

The second community was on the west coast of South Australia where Aborigines encountered Europeans later than the people of the Adelaide Plains and Murray River. Pastoralists came to the area in the 1860s and agriculturists in the 1890s. A Lutheran mission, Koonibba, was established in 1898 introducing the first experiences of institutionalisation to Aborigines in the region. This mission opened only a few years after the closure of Poonindie, at a time when government was again taking an active role in Aboriginal affairs following decades in which its role was limited to making rations available for distribution.

Finally, the fortunes of the Adnyamathanha of the Flinders Ranges will be traced. These people had a long experience of interaction with non-Aboriginal people through the pastoral industry and spasmodic mining in the Ranges stretching back to the 1850s. It was not until the depression years in 1930 that they first experienced mission life. This came at a time when assimilationist policies were once again gaining some currency, although their implementation in the 1950s had much less impact on the Adnyamathanha than upon the west coast people. For a variety of reasons, which will be analysed later, the Adnyamathanha had a less intense experience of institutionalisation than the other communities under study. The mission did not form the community as at Poonindie and Koonibba; rather, the missionaries attached themselves to a strongly self-identified group. Oral testimony as well as written records clearly testify to the people's use of the mission as a means of survival.

Several themes recur throughout this work. A major issue is the segregation and institutionalisation of Aborigines. This must be understood against the background of government policies and community attitudes towards Aborigines in the last 150 years, which will be discussed in the next chapter. Few Aboriginal communities have escaped the experience of institutionalisation in southern Australia. In South Australia, for instance, of the 14,000 people in the State who identify as Aboriginal today, the vast majority have experienced institutionalisation or are descended from people who have.

One must conclude from this that institutionalisation, while discriminatory and often harsh, has been a major factor in the survival of Aboriginal communities.[33]

A parallel can certainly be drawn here with the role of ghettos in the survival of a distinctive Jewish identity and strong kinship and communal networks. This Jewish identity has been maintained long after the abandonment of the ghettos, but in a climate of continued discrimination:

> When the ghetto walls do finally crumble, at least sufficiently to permit the escape of some of the inmates, those that get a taste of the life in the freer world outside and are lured by its colour are likely to be torn . . . On the one hand there is the strange and fascinating world of man; on the other, the restricted sectarianism of a little group into which he happened to be born, of neither of which he is fully a member. He oscillates between the two until a decisive incident either throws him headlong into activities of the outer world . . . or else a rebuff sends him bounding into his old familiar primary group, where life, though puny in scale, is rich and deep and warm.[34]

The *raison d'être* for the establishment and maintenance of Aboriginal institutions has shifted many times. Initially they aimed to segregate Aborigines to facilitate their training, education and Christianisation;[35] later in the nineteenth century segregation was advocated to protect Aborigines from the destructive interaction with a 'superior civilisation'.[36] By the twentieth century Aborigines were removed from the general community so that they would not contaminate it by their proximity;[37] and most recently it was argued that special homes be provided to train Aborigines of mixed descent to become assimilated into Australian society.[38] Yet, whatever the professed aim, the long-term outcomes were certainly not planned by those who established the institutions. The Aborigines used the institutions as a base for the establishment of communities with strong identities.[39] The people at Poonindie became Poonindie people and many of their descendants today identify their ancestry as Poonindie, rather than Murray River or Adelaide plains. People who came from Koonibba are also likely to claim it as an identifying label, rather than using pre-existing language groups such as Kokatha or Wirangu as communal identities. Even the Adnyamathanha, who had formed their modern identity before the missionaries appeared, refer to the mission settlement, Nepabunna, as 'their home'.

Other themes which recur throughout the book are the role of Aborigines in the labour force, education and the effects of the natural and manmade environment on Aborigines. The historical record indicates that while Aborigines from the three regions under study were prepared to incorporate themselves within the money economy, the mainstream society was determined to keep them out, except where it depended on Aboriginal labour to maintain the economic viability of particular enterprises.[40] Training and education of Aborigines illustrate the non-Aboriginal Australian's double standards in relation to Aborigines. Prior to the 1960s, attempts to train and educate Aborigines were spasmodic as well as futile. The aim of education could only be to train them for a role in the general community, while other policies ensured that they remained segregated in institutions.[41]

Another factor affecting Aboriginal responses to European invasion of their lands was the local environment and its gradual alteration. The rugged terrain of the Flinders

Ranges or the dense mallee on Eyre Peninsula offered the Aborigines refuge from European attacks, unlike the open plains in other regions. The dense urban development of Australia's large cities elicited very different responses from local Aborigines than did pastoral or agricultural development elsewhere.

The major impetus of this book stops with the disbandment of the missions and the end of segregation and discriminatory government policies and legislation towards Aborigines, although it may be argued that the segregationist attitudes of the late nineteenth and early twentieth century have taken a new guise in the late twentieth century. This is shown, for example, in high rates of imprisonment to which Aborigines have been subjected as they move into the general community.

Notes

1 PRG 275/130/207, Mortlock Library of South Australiana.
2 GRG 52/1/1945/63, SA Public Record Office.
3 GRG 52/1/1948/36.
4 Louis Wirth, *The ghetto*, Chicago, 1928, p. 26.
5 For example, Kathleen Hassell, *The relations between the settlers and Aborigines in South Australia, 1836–1860* Adelaide, 1966 (published MA thesis from 1921).
6 For example, see Anne Bickford, 'Contact history: Aborigines in New South Wales after 1788', *Australian Aboriginal Studies*, no. 1, 1988. This convenient misconception reflects views held by colonists in North America, 'Another approach was to ignore indigenous people altogether. In a symbolic sense their land was vacant and therefore available. This mythconception appears in early as well as recent writing. One advocate of English colonization wrote in 1662 that, "to us they cannot come, our land is full; to them we may go, their land is empty . . . their land is spacious and void, and there are few and do but run over the grass, as do also the foxes and wild beasts" ' (Cushman 1963 [1622]:91) William S. Simmons, 'Culture theory in contemporary ethnohistory', *Ethnohistory*, 35(1) 1988, pp. 2–3.
7 Julie Cassidy, 'The significance of the classification of a colonial acquisition: the conquered/settled distinction', *Australian Aboriginal Studies*, no. 1, 1988.
8 *The Shorter Oxford English Dictionary.*
9 For example, Jack Davis, Colin Johnson (Mudrooroo Narogin), Oodgeroo Noonuccal (Kath Walker).
10 Humphrey McQueen, *A new Britannia*, Melbourne, 1982, p. 18; R. White, *Inventing Australia*, Sydney, 1981, p. 70.
11 The Lumbee of North Carolina in the USA are an extreme example of the potency of this point. They are defined and define themselves as Indians even though it is impossible to trace any Indian antecedents, but they have a strong identity based on a communal past stretching back over many decades: Karen I. Blu, *The Lumbee problem. The making of an American Indian people*, New York, 1980.
12 Mudrooroo Narogin is a strong exponent of this view. He is critical of Aboriginal people who do not maintain a strong group identity. In his recent book *Writing from the fringe* (Melbourne, 1990, pp. 149, 159) he criticises authors such as Ella Simon, Sally Morgan and Glenyse Ward for being individualist or assimilationist and not putting the concerns of the Aboriginal community first.
13 Harold Hickerson, *The Chippewa and their neighbors: a study in ethnohistory*, New York, 1970, pp. 7–8.
14 A comparable situation did not arise in Australia until the *Land Rights (NT) Act*, 1976.
15 Simmons, 'Culture theory', p. 3.
16 Simmons, 'Culture theory', pp. 3–4, quoting Alfred Kroeber, 'The nature of land-holding groups in Aboriginal California' in Robert Heizer (ed.), *Aboriginal California. Three studies in culture history*, California, 1961 [1954].

17 Simmons, 'Culture theory', p. 4.

18 Ralph Linton (ed.), *Acculturation in seven American Indian tribes*, Gloucester, Massachusetts, 1940.

19 Linton (ed.), Acculturation, pp. 501, 504.

20 A. P. Elkin, 'Reaction and interaction: a food gathering people and European settlement in Australia', *American Anthropologist*, 53, 1951, p. 166.

21 Elkin, 'Reaction and interaction', p. 178.

22 Heather Goodall, 'An intelligent parasite: and white perceptions of the history of Aboriginal people in New South Wales', unpublished paper presented at the Australian Historical Association conference, 1982, p. 18.

23 Elkin, 'Reaction and interaction', pp. 169, 170, 176.

24 Bruce Trigger regarded this attitude as belonging to the nineteenth century, where change was interpreted as a process of cultural disintegration or assimilation. He went on to say that it was now clear that indigenous cultures did not begin to change as a result of the arrival of the first Europeans, but that change had been a characteristic of Amerindian cultures since they arrived in the western hemisphere: Bruce G. Trigger, 'Ethnohistory: problems and prospects', *Ethnohistory*, 29(1), 1982, pp. 11–12. Of course Elkin's attitudes cannot be generalised to all Australian anthropologists of the time, for instance W. E. H. Stanner's postwar work took cognisance of change over time, for example, W. E. H. Stanner, 'Continuity and change among Aborigines' (1958), *White man got no dreaming: essays 1938–1973*, Canberra, 1979.

25 Edward H. Spicer, 'Types of contact and processes of change' in Edward H. Spicer (ed.), *Perspectives in American Indian cultural change*, Chicago, 1969, p. 541.

26 Spicer, 'Types of contact and processes of change', in Spicer, *Perspectives*, p. 522; Edward M. Bruner, 'Mandan' in Spicer, *Perspectives* (first published 1961), pp. 205, 208–9.

27 Spicer, *Perspectives*, p. 522.

28 One commentator has gone so far as to describe Spicer as primarily a historian rather than anthropologist. See William Y. Adams, 'Edward Spicer, Historian', *Journal of the South West*, 32, 1990.

29 James Axtell, 'Some thoughts on the ethnohistory of missions', *Ethnohistory*, 29 (1), 1982, pp. 35–6.

30 Axtell, 'Some thoughts', pp. 36–9.

31 Axtell, 'Some thoughts', p. 39.

32 Marshall Sahlins, *Islands of History*, Chicago, 1985, viii, quoted in Simmons, 'Culture theory', p. 7.

33 Figure from 1986 census. Jane Jacobs points out that the Kokatha who did not use Koonibba as a permanent base, but moved along the Transcontinental railway line or from mission to mission, were not able to maintain such close community links and this affected their social organisation: Jane Jacobs, 'Aboriginal land rights in Port Augusta', MA thesis, University of Adelaide, 1983, pp. 215–16.

34 Wirth, *The ghetto*, pp. 289–90. It is interesting to note that the language Wirth uses here to describe the warm familiarity and depth of ghetto life is echoed in Elkin's description of Aboriginal traditional life—'traditional security, mythological depth, social warmth . . . ': 'Reaction and interaction', p. 170.

35 The original rationale for the establishment of the Native Training Institution at Poonindie.

36 This was the aim of most institutions which existed from the late nineteenth until the mid-twentieth century, including the first years of Koonibba mission.

37 The protective institutions also fulfilled this function, for example, Koonibba, Point Pearce, Point McLeay and other missions in the south of the State. The government stations in Western Australia such as Moore River Native Settlement were notorious for their role of protecting the general community from contamination of Aborigines: see Anna Haebich, *For their own good. Aborigines and government in the Southwest of Western Australia, 1900–1940*, Perth,1988, pp. 304–6.

38 For example, St Francis Boys Home, Colebrook Home in Adelaide.

39 C. D. Rowley suggested that most Aboriginal ties in eastern Australia were not 'tribal', but common traditions of an institutionalised sub-group: C. D. Rowley, *Outcasts in white Australia*, Victoria, 1972, p. 169.

40 Similar attitudes are evident in other parts of Australia, for example, Anna Haebich, *For their own good*, pp. 74–5, 162, 354–5; P. E. Felton, 'Aboriginal employment problems in Victoria', in Ian G. Sharp and Colin M. Tatz (eds), *Aborigines in the economy*, Melbourne, 1966, p. 91; Barry Morris, 'From underemployment to unemployment: the changing role of Aborigines in a rural economy', *Mankind*, 13 (6).

41 Albert Namatjira is a tragic example of an Aborigine who was successfully trained in European skills, but rejected by European/Australian society; another example is David Unaipon from Point McLeay.

2

LEGISLATION AND POLICY: THE CONTEXT OF OUTBACK GHETTOS

All aspects of Aboriginal life since colonial occupation of the Aborigines' lands have been overwhelmingly influenced, not only by the physical presence of the colonists, but also by European preconceptions of Aborigines as primitive and inferior, and by their determination to claim ownership of their land. These late eighteenth- and nineteenth-century attitudes towards Aborigines in Australia have precedents in European attitudes towards Indians in North America from first contact in the sixteenth century:

> In implying that Indians were not yet 'men' the Europeans meant one of three things. The first meaning was that the natives were the children of the human race, their passions still largely unrestrained by reason. The second . . . [r]ather than innocent children, the Indians in this view were little better than animals, incapable of reason and enslaved by the most brutal passions. The third and by far most prevalent meaning, however, was simply that the Indians had not mastered the 'Arts of civil Life and Humanity'.[1]

Similarly, Europeans in claiming rights to Aboriginal land were repeating claims made to Indian land: '. . . John Winthrop decided that the New England natives "inclose noe Land, neither have any setled habytation, nor any tame Cattle to improve the land by", and so were devoid of legal claim to their territory.'[2]

Government policies and legislation towards Aborigines, influenced by similar attitudes, have controlled the lives of Aborigines since colonisation. These policies and legislation have varied from colony to colony and State to State, but their impact on Aborigines has been very similar. Some colonies (for example, Western Australia, South Australia, New South Wales) in the mid-nineteenth century experimented with assimilationist policies in the belief that Aborigines, if given the opportunity of a Christian education, could be incorporated into European society. But these isolated experiments were overwhelmed by a high level of violence against Aborigines as colonists appropriated their land, and the refusal of Europeans to accept Aborigines as equals. Disease and dislocation further contributed to the disruption of the Aborigines' lives.

By the latter half of the nineteenth century governments had lost interest in trying to ameliorate the condition of Aborigines, restricting government activities to providing rations for the young, sick and aged. At the same time, in newly colonised regions such as northern Queensland and the Kimberley in Western Australia, levels of violence between Aborigines and non-Aborigines remained high. In Queensland a deliberate policy of 'dispersal' was adopted, which aimed to break up or disperse groups of Aborigines, but became an official euphemism for attacking and killing Aborigines.[3]

In 1897 the Queensland government introduced a protectionist Act, which was to be the blueprint for similar legislation in Western Australia, South Australia and the Northern Territory. There had been previous attempts to control the exploitation of Aboriginal workers through legislation, but the *Aboriginal Protection Act* of 1897 was the first to try comprehensively to control the lives of Aborigines. The protectionist era survived well into the second half of the twentieth century in some parts of Australia. Aborigines were segregated on reserves, their economic, social and sexual lives were strictly regulated and they were denied freedoms taken for granted by other Australians. Victoria and New South Wales did not follow the protectionist trend and were forcing Aborigines off reserves at the time segregation was being practised elsewhere.[4]

Since 1937 the State and Federal government ministers and administrators responsible for Aboriginal affairs have met periodically to discuss policy. The first meeting supported assimilation policies, but it was not until 1951 that they agreed to repeal protection/segregation legislation. It took some States sixteen years to update their legislation.[5] In 1961 the conference of Federal and State ministers reaffirmed their policy of assimilation:

> All Aborigines and part Aborigines will eventually attain the same manner of living as other Australians and live as members of a single Australian community with the same rights and privileges and responsibilities, with the same customs and influenced by the same beliefs and loyalties. Therefore any special measures taken for Aborigines and part-Aborigines are regarded as temporary, and not based on colour but to assist in the transition from one stage to another.[6]

In 1967 a national referendum gave the Federal government the power to legislate in the area of Aboriginal affairs. Previously Aboriginal affairs had been a purely State matter under the Australian Constitution. The Federal government only had direct control of Aboriginal affairs in the Northern Territory, where it took over legislative and administrative control from South Australia in 1911. The 1967 referendum also enabled Aborigines to be counted in the national census, acknowledging that they were part of the Australian population. These new federal powers were not fully utilised until the Whitlam Labor government came to office in 1972 and dramatically increased the budget for Aboriginal affairs. Labor also attempted to bring the administration of Aboriginal affairs largely under the control of the Federal government.[7] While the Federal government is now responsible for funding government and semi-government programmes in Aboriginal affairs, the State governments continue to have a major influence on the implementation of policy.

The history of Aboriginal/non-Aboriginal contact varies considerably from State to State and region to region. There are also broad similarities. The legislative and administrative background to Aboriginal/non-Aboriginal relations in South Australia will be discussed to establish the context of institutional life there. Although the history of European occupation of this State differs in some dramatic ways from the colonisation of other regions, attitudes towards and treatment of Aborigines share features common to the entire continent.

South Australia has often been characterised by historians as influenced by a different colonial ethos than the other States:

> In the founding of South Australia there was a greater measure of idealism than in that of the other Australian colonies. It was not a colony but a 'province', and transportation of convicts was to play no part in its history . . . Radical politicians, systematic colonizers, non-Conformist bankers, and 'reforming' speculators all played a part in its establishment, and some of them settled there.[8]

By the 1960s South Australia was once again seen to be in the forefront of social experimentation. A major innovation was the liberalisation of legislation and administration affecting its Aboriginal population. Despite this apparent liberal treatment, the Aboriginal experience in South Australia resembles that of other States. The implementation of policies may not have been as draconian as in Western Australia or Queensland, nevertheless, South Australians held similar perceptions of Aborigines and were very much products of their time in their racial attitudes.

South Australia

> Whereas that part of Australia which lies between the meridians of the one hundred and thirty-second and one hundred and forty-first degrees of east longitude, and between the Southern Ocean and twenty-six degrees of south latitude, together with islands adjacent thereto, consists of waste and unoccupied lands which are supposed to be fit for the purposes of colonization: . . . Be it therefore enacted by the King's most Excellent Majesty . . . to establish one or more provinces . . . and that all and every person who shall at any time hereafter inhabit or reside within His Majesty's said province or provinces shall be free, . . . subject to and bound to obey laws, orders, Statutes, and Constitutions as shall from time to time, in the manner herein-after directed, be made, ordered, and enacted for the Government of His Majesty's province or provinces of South Australia.[9]

With this document of 1834 began the colonisation of the indigenous people of South Australia, although this Act proclaiming the establishment of the colony did not recognise the existence of the indigenes, whose land was 'waste and unoccupied'. Notwithstanding, they did exist and had, prior to 1834, been in contact with Europeans. French and British ships had surveyed the coast; men hunting seals and whales in the Southern Ocean had taken women and Captain Charles Sturt encountered many people along the Murray River during his expedition in search of the mouth of the river in 1829–30. In the *Foundation Act* of South Australia the colonisers suited their language to their purposes.

The 1834 Act was drawn up by a private company, the South Australian Colonisation Commission, and rushed through the British parliament. In many respects it ran contrary to government policy administered by the Colonial Office. This policy tried to ensure the rights of the Aborigines over their land in the colony by insisting on the appointment of a government official to protect the interests of Aborigines, and issuing Letters Patent which included a clause protecting Aboriginal rights to land.[10] But the 1834 Act prevailed and Aboriginal rights to land were ignored, thereby setting the pattern for Aboriginal/European relations for the next century and a half.

The peoples who occupied the territory which became South Australia were affected by the process of colonisation in different ways depending on where they lived, when they encountered the full impact of colonisation and how they responded to it. In general terms, those who occupied the southern part of the colony confronted the colonisers first and had to contend with heavier concentrations of them than peoples of the north, who were the last to experience the impact of the intruders.

Government policies and community attitudes towards Aborigines

Thus, the *Foundation Act* establishing the Colony of South Australia ignored both the existence of the indigenous people of the region and the express wishes of the British Colonial Office. Aboriginal rights to land were never enshrined in legislation, mainly because they would have interfered with the commercial interests of the South Australian Colonisation Commission. The prevailing view among the colonists was that Aborigines 'wandered over the land', erected no permanent structures on it and, therefore, did not occupy it. While they acknowledged the country was not empty, they considered it unoccupied.

In 1842 the *Waste Lands Act* enabled the Protector of Aborigines to establish reserves for Aborigines. But these reserves were small, reflecting the prevailing but shortlived policy which anticipated that Aborigines would be 'civilised' and trained to live like Europeans. The intention was that Aborigines would settle down on them and 'cultivate the soil'.[11] When this did not occur most of the reserve lands were leased to non-Aboriginal farmers.

By the late 1850s any remaining idealism about State obligations to Aborigines had been defeated by concern to cut spending and by a strengthening conviction that 'primitive' Aboriginal culture would crumble before the onslaught of European 'civilisation'. These attitudes were reflected in the Report of the Select Committee of the Legislative Council on the Aborigines in 1860, which noted that the number of Aborigines was decreasing rapidly and recommended the appointment of a Protector and sub-protectors to watch over their interests.[12] This minimal involvement suited the governmental purse and for the next fifty years government involvement did not go beyond distributing food and blankets to those Aborigines who were considered aged and infirm.

The vacuum left by the government's withdrawal from financial and administrative responsibility for Aboriginal affairs was partially filled by philanthropic and church groups. A number of missions sprang up in the second half of the nineteenth century, whose aim was to segregate and protect the Aborigines in their declining years.[13] Of these, two were established in the salt lakes area in the north: Killalpaninna and Kopperamana (1866); the other major missions were in the southern part of the State: Poonindie (1850),[14] Point McLeay (1859), Point Pearce (1868) and, at the turn of the

Australia showing South Australia and mission locations.

century, Koonibba (1898). Aborigines who were not associated with one of the mission stations either lived independently from white people, obtained casual work on farms and stations, or received the rations distributed by pastoralists and the police. During this period the police were generally the only government representatives in outlying areas. Their work in relation to Aborigines included not only law enforcement but also ration distribution, census taking and implementation of government directives.

By the early twentieth century attitudes towards Aborigines were changing. It was acknowledged that Aborigines would not solve the problem of their administration by disappearing, and that their numbers were, in fact, increasing. In 1860 it was evident to observers that Aboriginal death rates were very high, while birth rates were low.[15] But at that time there were very few people of mixed descent. By the twentieth century the number of people of mixed descent was rapidly increasing and a new era of racial policy-making began. The mixed descent population increased despite protective government policies and mission attempts to prevent miscegenation.

Aboriginal children, whatever their genetic make-up, were integrated into existing Aboriginal communities. Europeans on the other hand, ascribed profound meaning to racial mixture, making ludicrously fine distinctions. They measured descent in terms of 'blood' and the racial terminology of 'fullblood', 'halfcaste', 'quadroon', 'octoroon' became common in the twentieth century. Aborigines now suffered under the double burden of being perceived, not only as low on the evolutionary scale, but disadvantaged by genetic mix. Although they were constantly exhorted to rise from their 'primitive' state to a 'civilised' standard, their potential for progress was generally thought to be limited by their various degrees of genetic inferiority. On the basis of this genetic determinism a 'fullblood' was held to be inferior to a 'halfcaste', and an 'octoroon', who only had an eighth Aboriginal 'blood' was superior to both. Government policy and legislation reflecting these attitudes in the early twentieth century aimed to prevent a 'race' of nearly white people living like Aborigines.[16]

In 1911 an Act, based on the 1897 *Queensland Aboriginal Protection Act* was passed. Its stated aim was to provide 'for the better Protection and Control of the Aboriginal and Halfcaste Inhabitants of the State of South Australia'. Under the Act 'an aboriginal' was defined as 'an aboriginal native of Australia' or 'a halfcaste' married to an 'aboriginal native' or habitually associating with them, or a 'halfcaste' child under 16 years. Under section 10 of the Act the Chief Protector was the legal guardian of all Aboriginal children under twenty-one 'notwithstanding that any such child has a parent or other relative living'. With such powers the Protector could take charge of all 'halfcaste' children found 'wandering and camping with aborigines' and put them under the control of the State Children's Department.[17]

The Act also gave the Chief Protector enormous authority over adults. Under section 17 of the Act he could move them to a reserve or institution, or from one reserve or institution to another. Under section 31 he could remove them from camps in towns and specify where they could camp in proximity to towns. Under section 35 he could 'undertake the general care, protection and management of the property of any aboriginal or halfcaste' and '[t]ake possession of, retain, sell, or dispose of any such property, whether real or personal . . . '. He could also act on behalf of an Aborigine to recover money or property owing to him. Although these clauses were described as protective, they were custodial; every aspect of an Aborigine's life was open to control by the state from the time she or he was born. There were also protective clauses which controlled those who might harm Aborigines. For instance, it was illegal to remove certain classes of Aborigine (especially women and children) from a district or reserve without authority (section 12). The only section of the Act which might have positively helped Aboriginal people establish themselves independently was section 18 which allowed a block of Crown land 'not exceeding one hundred and sixty acres' to be allotted to Aborigines or suitable land to be purchased for them.

The passing of the 1911 Act was followed by a Royal Commission on The Aborigines which made a progress report in 1913 and a final report in 1916. The Royal Commission echoed the general view of white South Australians that there should be more direct government involvement in Aboriginal affairs. While in the past the administration of Aborigines had made little distinction between people of full descent and mixed descent on the assumption that they were all going to disappear, the Commission now recommended that these distinctions should be made the basis for appropriate policies. The specific concern which had led to the establishment of the Royal Commission was the administration of two missions, Point Pearce and Point McLeay. Therefore the first report dealt mainly with these two institutions.

But the main thrust of the Royal Commission's final report was to distinguish between 'fullbloods' and 'halfcastes'. It recommended that 'fullbloods' be separated from 'halfcastes' and that each live in a separate community and that 'halfcastes', 'quadroons' and 'octoroons' be compelled to go outside their communities and become self-sufficient (recommendations 15 and 17). It also recommended that 'neglected' children continue to be taken into care and 'that the board have power to take control of any children at the age of 10 years whose environment is not conducive to their welfare . . .' (recommendation 21).

Although legislation and policy were fairly consistently segregationist and paternalist, there was occasional acknowledgement that these policies were preventing Aborigines from becoming independent and self-supporting. This ambivalence continued well into the twentieth century. The 1911 Act confirmed in legislation existing policies, including the removal of children of mixed descent from their parents. The protective sections of the legislation segregated Aborigines without protecting women from non-Aboriginal men and then took the mixed descent children of these illicit unions away from their Aboriginal families.

By the 1930s the emphasis of policy had begun to shift from segregation and control towards assimilation of people of mixed descent into the general population, but the implementation of this policy did not gather momentum until the 1950s. Assimilation was proposed on both racial grounds (through interbreeding Aboriginal 'blood' would disappear) and social grounds (Aborigines would be brought up to the 'standard of western civilisation').[18] The clear implication of an assimilation policy was that the people to be assimilated would have to be treated similarly to the general population but this took two decades for administrators, legislators and the general public to grasp. Releasing Aboriginal people into the community without housing, education and financial assistance forced them to live in camps on the edges of towns in conditions that were socially unacceptable to the rest of Australian society.

The *Aborigines Act Amendment Act 1939* while still basically protectionist, foreshadowed the assimilation policy. Among its amendments was one which assisted the process of assimilation by bringing all Aboriginal people under one definition:

4.(1) Every person –
(a) who is of the full blood descended from the original inhabitants of Australia; or
(b) who being of less than full blood is descended from the original inhabitants of Australia' (section 5).

Having brought all Aborigines under one definition the Act went on to make exceptions by exempting some through a new clause 11a (section 14):

In any case where the board is of the opinion that any aborigine by reason of his character and standard of intelligence and development should be exempted from the provisions of this Act, the board may, by notice in writing, declare that the aborigine shall cease to be an aborigine for the purposes of this Act. Any such declaration may be made by the board whether or not an application is made by the person to whom the declaration refers.

An exemption could be unconditional and irrevocable, or conditional for up to three years.

The exemption system, like earlier methods devised for separating people of full descent from people of mixed descent, ignored Aboriginal familial and social ties. It also ignored cultural, linguistic and historic differences between Aboriginal and non-Aboriginal people. It caused great social dislocation and trauma, splitting families and communities (a reversal of the effects of the older 'protective' policies). Exempted people could drink alcohol legally; but were prohibited from living on an Aboriginal institution or from 'consorting' with Aboriginal women, other than a wife. They could receive Commonwealth social services but no assistance from the Aborigines Protection Board in the form of rations or blankets etc. Many exempted people found themselves caught between two societies and not legally a full member of either.

Another clause in the 1939 Act which caused Aboriginal people great grief was the insertion of 34a:

> Any male person, other than an aborigine, who, not being lawfully married to the female aborigine (proof whereof shall lie upon the person charged)—
> (a) habitually consorts with a female aborigine; or
> (b) keeps a female aborigine as his mistress; or
> (c) has carnal knowledge of a female aborigine, shall be guilty of an offence against this Act.

This meant that 'exempted' men could not associate with Aboriginal women. There were also provisions under the *Police Offences Act* which made it illegal for Aborigines to associate with non-Aborigines.[19] These provisions ensured that if people attempted to follow the path of assimilation they were cut off from family, friends and associates and had to carry a piece of paper as proof of their new racial identity.

By the 1950s the South Australian government was actively assisting Aboriginal people to move away from missions and reserves by providing housing, education and other services, which might enable Aboriginal people to raise their standard of living. In 1954 the first government housing was built for the Department of Aboriginal Affairs for an Aboriginal family, and by June 1959 sixty houses had been constructed.[20] The department also advanced money to Aboriginal people so they could furnish and equip their houses. Increasing numbers of children were accepted into the State school system. Changing expectations of Aboriginal living standards put great pressure on privately run Aboriginal institutions. Subsisting with minimal government support, these institutions lacked the financial resources to improve living conditions. Their housing was inferior, education often failed to meet Education Department standards and vocational training was non-existent. The private organisations' inability to improve living standards and changing public expectations of government responsibility for Aboriginal affairs led the South Australian government to assume financial and administrative responsibility for all Aboriginal institutions in the 1960s and 1970s.

By the late 1960s the assimilation policy of social absorption, which had been adopted at the national level, had been modified. In South Australia three Acts were passed in the 1960s allowing Aboriginal people increased autonomy and control over their own affairs. These Acts were the harbingers of dramatic changes in Aboriginal affairs throughout Australia over the next two decades. These changes of the 1960s were based on a policy of 'integration' rather than assimilation, a policy 'which recognizes the right of a person to decide his own future and enables him to make the transitional stages at his own pace'.[21] The policy emphasised consultation with Aboriginal people, self-help and self-determination.

The *Aboriginal Affairs Act* was passed in 1962 and amended in 1966 and 1968. Its stated aim was to 'promote the welfare and advancement' of Aborigines. Most of the old 'protective' clauses disappeared from the legislation, but the exemption system lived on in the form of a Register of Aborigines from which names could be removed as Aboriginal people became 'capable of accepting full responsibilities of citizenship' (section 17 (i)). Like previous legislation, the Act allowed the allocation of land to Aborigines and made special assistance available to Aboriginal people to help them establish themselves in 'primary, mechanical or business pursuits'. The 1962 Act included provisions to legalise the drinking of liquor by Aborigines by allowing proclaimed areas not to fall under sections 172 and 173 of the *Licensing Act 1932* (which made it illegal for Aboriginal people to be supplied with or drink liquor). By 1965 Aboriginal people were able to drink legally throughout the State.[22]

The 1966 amendment allowed Reserve Councils to be set up thus empowering Aboriginal people to run their own institutions and regulate entry to their lands. For the first time since 1836 Aborigines in South Australia were legally able to run their own communities. In the same year the *Aboriginal Lands Trust Act* was passed, giving some Aborigines some control over their own lands. The Trust, a completely Aboriginal body with a non-Aboriginal adviser, had all Aboriginal reserve lands transferred to it, but could only 'sell, lease, mortgage or otherwise deal with land vested in it ...' if the Minister consented.

Thus the 1960s saw a dramatic change in the legal status of Aborigines and in governmental involvement and financial commitment to Aboriginal affairs, both at the State and Federal level.[23] There were changes in the administration of Aboriginal health, welfare, housing and education. In this period of liberalisation many Aboriginal people moved away from segregated communities and into towns and cities, where they could now obtain housing and an education for their children.

Notes

1   James Axtell, 'The invasion within. The contest of cultures in colonial North America', in James Axtell, *The European and the Indian. Essays in the ethnohistory of colonial North America,* New York, 1981, p. 45.

2   Axtell, 'The invasion within', p. 51.

3   Noel Loos, *Invasion and resistance. Aboriginal-European relations on the North Queensland frontier 1861–1897,* Canberra, 1982, p. 22.

4   Nevertheless the Act under which NSW Aboriginal communities were being broken up was called the *Aborigines Protection Act 1909.* Peter Read, 'Breaking up the camps entirely: the dispersal policy in Wiradjuri country 1909–1929', *Aboriginal History,* 8(1), 1984.

5   Federal government 1953, Victoria 1957, South Australia 1962, Western Australia 1963 and NSW 1967: from M. S. Brock, 'A comparative study of government policies towards Aborigines and Africans in South Africa', unpublished BA (Hons) thesis, University of Adelaide, 1969, p. 47.

6   Brock, 'Africans and Aborigines', p. 47.

7   See Scott Bennett, *Aborigines and political power*, Sydney, 1989.

8   Russel Ward, *Australia*, Sydney, 1969, pp. 52–3.

9   *An Act to empower His Majesty to erect South Australia into a British Province or Provinces, and to provide for the Colonization and Government thereof, 1834.*

10 Henry Reynolds, *The law of the land*, Ringwood, Victoria, 1987, pp. 103, 107, 110.

11 SAPP 1860, no. 165, p. 4.

12 Report of the Select Committee of the Legislative Council upon the Aborigines, 1860, p. 3. When the previous Protector, Matthew Moorhouse resigned in 1856, his position lapsed and no new appointment was made.

13 Fay Gale, *A study of assimilation: part Aborigines in South Australia*, Adelaide, 1964.

14 Poonindie was the only mission to survive from the early period of Aboriginal administration, with government financial support which was withdrawn in 1860.

15 For instance, at Poonindie between 1850 and 1856 of 110 Aboriginal youths and young adults admitted to the institution 29 had died and there had been no live births: Peggy Brock and Doreen Kartinyeri, *Poonindie. The rise and destruction of an Aboriginal agricultural community 1989*, Adelaide, p. 23.

16 Protector of Aborigines' Report, 30 June 1911, Adelaide, p. 1.

17 Protector of Aborigines' Report, 30 June 1909, p. 3. The *Western Australian Aboriginal Act 1905*, the *Northern Territory Aboriginal Ordinance 1911* and the *Queensland State Children's Act 1911* all made the Protector of Aborigines legal guardian of Aboriginal children and gave him the right to remove them from their parents, these Acts were aimed at children of mixed descent: Richard Broome, *Aboriginal Australians. Black response to white domination 1788–1980*, Sydney, 1982, p. 134.

18 Brock, 'Africans and Aborigines', p. 44.

19 Christobel Mattingly (ed.), *Survival in our own land. Aboriginal experiences in South Australia since 1836*, Adelaide, 1988, p. 47.

20 GRG 52/1/1959/147, SAPRO.

21 Brock, 'Africans and Aborigines', p. 30.

22 Fay Gale, 'The History of Contact in South Australia', University of Adelaide Publication 19, 1969, p. 13; SA *Government Gazette* 25/7/1963, 16/4/1964, 1/4/1965, Adelaide.

23 In 1967 a referendum gave the Federal government power to legislate for and administer Aboriginal affairs and it subsequently took over primary responsibility for Aboriginal affairs from the States.

3

Poonindie, Home Away from 'Country'

The non-Aboriginal population of South Australia increased very rapidly from 1836. In 1840 the first official census recorded 14,160 Europeans in South Australia. Over half of these lived in the City of Adelaide (6,557) and on the Adelaide Plains (1,600); the rest had moved to rural areas (5,414). By 1851 the non-Aboriginal population was 63,700 of whom nearly 30,000 lived in and around the city of Adelaide.[1] Twenty-six thousand one hundred and fifty hectares of land were under cultivation and there were a million sheep and 100,000 cattle in the colony. Large copper mines were being developed on Yorke Peninsula, at Kapunda in the Barossa Valley and Burra.[2] There are no accurate estimates of the number of Aborigines on the Adelaide Plains in 1836, but it is likely there were less than 1000 and they would have been almost immediately overwhelmed numerically by the intruders on their lands.[3]

Aboriginal life along the Murray River was also disrupted very early in the life of the colony, not by dense European settlement but by overlanders bringing stock into South Australia along the river from New South Wales, and later by pastoralism. By 1855 both banks of the river in South Australia were under pastoral lease.[4] The disruption of Aboriginal life on the Murray and the Adelaide Plains resulted in the death of many Aborigines (some documented, most undocumented) and dislocation,[5] but it also created opportunities for changing patterns of Aboriginal movements. Prior to European encroachment there appears to have been little reciprocity between the people of the upper Murray in South Australia and those on the Adelaide Plains. Now people from the upper Murray took advantage of the new order to visit Adelaide. By 1842 there were reportedly so many River Murray people in the town that the local people, the Kaurna, moved away.[6]

The continued existence of the Kaurna and to a lesser extent the people of the upper Murray was under serious threat by the mid-1840s and the options for survival few.

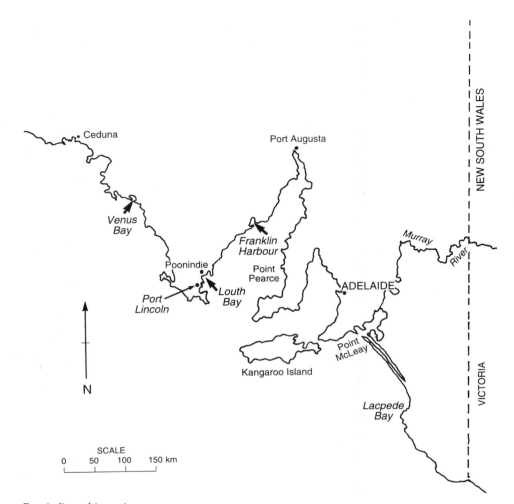

Poonindie and its region.

Matthew Moorhouse, the Protector of Aborigines, reported in 1843 that all children between 5 and 10 years old 60 miles to the north and south of Adelaide along a 10-mile strip east-west had had some schooling and knew the alphabet; some could also read, write and do arithmetic.[7] As the average attendance at the Aboriginal school in Adelaide was between ten and thirteen pupils between 1840–42, these figures suggest there were very few children left on the Adelaide Plains seven years after the arrival of the colonists. There are no documented accounts of massacres of Aborigines and not many accounts of individual Aborigines being killed around Adelaide, although it is likely that some killings went unrecorded despite the rule of law.[8] Many Aborigines did die from introduced diseases and the effects of alcohol and trauma associated with being displaced by the colonists.[9]

The Kaurna were so overwhelmingly outnumbered that they faced two options, either cooperate and associate with the intruders or move away from their traditional lands to join people with whom they had previously had a reciprocal relationship. There is little documentation on those who moved away from Adelaide, but it is possible to follow the careers of some who decided to throw in their lot with the colonists.

In contrast, violence was endemic along the Murray River throughout the period. There were gratuitous killings, as well as planned battles between Aborigines and Europeans.[10] There is also evidence that smallpox infected Aborigines on the Murray before any direct contact with Europeans. Charles Sturt saw evidence of smallpox during his expedition down the river in 1830.[11] This disease would have killed large numbers of people as the Aborigines had no previous immunity, devastating cultural and social life. Life along the Murray, therefore, had been seriously disrupted since the late 1820s through disease and violence. In 1841 the government decided on a policy of pacification as an alternative to confrontation, appointing E. J. Eyre Sub-Protector of Aborigines and distributor of rations at Moorundie on the upper Murray. This strategy seems to have been effective as violence along the river diminished after the depot was established, although there are reports of pastoralists and other Europeans killing Aborigines long after the overlanders stopped using the river route into South Australia.[12] In 1849 Aborigines from Encounter Bay were reported to have come to Adelaide with the intention of driving the Murray River people out of the town, but were prevented from doing so by the intervention of the Mounted Police.[13]

The Murray people had a wider range of options open to them than the Kaurna of the Adelaide Plains. Large numbers of Aborigines congregated at Moorundie at ration distribution times and then most dispersed until the next distribution. Eyre reported that many of the Aborigines from Moorundie would travel south to Adelaide out of curiosity and to collect further rations and blankets.[14] Some were persuaded to leave their children at the Aboriginal boarding school. Others adapted to the changing circumstances in their own country. They were not forced off their lands in the same way that the Kaurna were pushed aside by urban development. Yet by the late nineteenth century there were few Aborigines left along the Murray.[15]

Aboriginal children were encouraged to assimilate into European society by the Protector of Aborigines, and missionaries interested in converting Aborigines to Christianity. A major expression of the assimilationist ethos of this early period of colonial rule was the establishment of schools for Aboriginal children in Adelaide. In 1838 William Wyatt, the Protector of Aborigines, established the Native Location on the north side of the River Torrens, opposite the site where the Adelaide Gaol was built and where the previous Protector, Captain Bromley lived. The Location was to consist of a school and twelve huts and it became a general meeting place for the Kaurna.[16]

In October 1838 two German missionaries, Christian Teichelmann and Clamor Schürmann, arrived in Adelaide in the same ship as the new Governor, George Gawler. They had been sent out by the Dresden Mission Society, with the support of George Fife Angas, and lived at the Native Location. They worked with the Aborigines building houses and establishing gardens and learning their language. In 1839 they established a school for Aboriginal children, teaching them in their own language. Children attended the school attracted by regular meals, which they took back to the Aboriginal camps at night, or because their parents sent them there in exchange for blankets. No healthy adults could receive blankets unless their children attended school.[17] Nevertheless, attendance was erratic. When native foods were plentiful the children would move away from Adelaide with their families. If there were other activities in the colony which interested them more than school, they did not attend. The arrival of a new ship in port, where children might get handouts from new arrivals, proved far more attractive than school.

In December 1842 it was reported that all but six of the Kaurna children left the school because their people had moved away from Adelaide on the arrival of a contingent from the upper Murray. There were tensions in the school between the six remaining Kaurna children and the River Murray children. In March 1843 the Kaurna returned to Adelaide and in June the school became a boarding school with eleven pupils. In April 1844 a separate boarding school was established for the River Murray children at Walkerville. This school was run and controlled by the government with a government teacher who taught in English. In July 1845 the two schools were amalgamated at a new site, the Native School Establishment centrally located off North Terrace, on Kintore Avenue.[18]

After 1843 attendance at the boarding schools was made compulsory, but could not be enforced as the children still left to join their people from time to time as they moved camp. When the children graduated from school, Moorhouse found positions for many of them in Adelaide on the assumption that they would assimilate into the European community.[19] But their families had different expectations. They did not consider they had committed their children permanently to European society, but rather had substituted one form of childhood training for another. They assumed that when the children were ready for adult responsibilities they would return to their people, take part in initiation ceremonies and marry when appropriate. Moorhouse thought there was a simple solution to this 'problem' and that was to anticipate these demands on young adolescents by arranging marriages for the children at an early age (14 for girls, 16 for boys) to prevent them returning to their people. But parental consent was needed to allow minors to marry and the Advocate-General would not approve any exceptions.[20]

In 1848 the first Anglican Bishop of Adelaide, Augustus Short, arrived in the colony with his Archdeacon, Mathew Hale. Both were concerned about the condition of the Aborigines and the ineffectual efforts to Christianise and 'civilise' them. Hale believed if the children from the Adelaide school were sent away to a training institution removed from their own people and the corrupting influences of low life in Adelaide, education and Christianisation would be accelerated.

Hale was an independently wealthy man with influential friends. He was thus very different from the German missionaries, who were regarded as outsiders by the general community and continually struggled to maintain themselves on meagre grants from the mission societies and the government. Hale received a £600 loan from the government, £200 of which would be paid back after eighteen months, to establish his project, and £300 per year to pay the wages of a schoolmaster, matron and labourer.[21]

He proposed to establish a mission ghetto in an isolated place away from Adelaide for Aboriginal children with some initial education and training. He chose Boston Island, an uninhabited island off the coast from Port Lincoln. Moorhouse, who had a group of children graduating from the school in Adelaide, was anxious for the Training Institution to be established quickly so that these children could continue their training and not revert to life in the bush. He sent them off in couples of males and females to Port Lincoln ahead of Hale to work as servants for local white residents. There is no evidence that these young people were coerced into going to Port Lincoln, although some incentives must have been offered to make them leave their familiar environment. But it is probable that they volunteered to go, for few tried to leave Poonindie once they were there.

Hale left for Boston Island in September 1850, but was unable to find fresh water to maintain his community so he applied for land at Poonindie north of Port Lincoln. Although this site was not so isolated, there was land already set aside as an Aboriginal reserve and only two sections of thirty-five surveyed in the area had been purchased. Hale proposed that these thirty-three sections be resumed and that the Society for the Propagation of the Gospel buy the other two.[22] He later bought an adjoining pastoral lease with £1000 of his own money to maintain the isolation of the mission from the influence of white farmers.[23]

The 'Christian village'

The Native Training Institution at Poonindie was supported by a small section of Adelaide's white settlers who regretted the effects of their presence on the Aborigines. They viewed the problem from a position of assumed superiority and sought to alleviate the Aborigines' appalling situation by teaching them European ways. Although they never fully articulated their vision of the place they hoped educated Aborigines might assume in South Australian society, Hale and Short had fairly precise ideas about how Poonindie should develop. In 1872 Bishop Short recalled that Hale's grand idea had been 'a Christian village of South Australian natives, reclaimed from barbarism, trained to the duties of social Christian life and walking in the fear of God, through knowledge and faith in the love of Christ Their Saviour; and the Power of His Spirit'.[24] On another occasion he pointed out:

> The natives were taught to read, write and cypher [at the Adelaide school]. They were put in possession of the signs of ideas, without having acquired the ideas themselves. They could do a sum in addition, but knew not practically the value or proper use of money. They were not educated to be labourers or mechanics. Their play-hours were spent in practising throwing the spear, or in dancing 'Corobbery'.[25]

So the principles on which Hale proposed to proceed were 'isolation, industrial education, as well as the usual schooling; marriage, separate dwellings, hiring and service for wages; gradual and progressive moral improvement based upon Christian instruction, Christian worship, and Christian superintendence'.[26]

This vision was thoroughly in keeping with the philosophy of social experimentation that pervaded South Australia in the first days of white settlement. Hale and Short did not want to impart the values and lifestyle of the average European. Instead, they strove to remove the Aborigines from the 'bad influence' of the majority of Europeans, who did not lead moral, Christian lives.

What Hale did succeed in creating was an Aboriginal village, an Aboriginal community which long outlasted his involvement. It did not, however, conform to the original utopian vision of a holy Christian village. Over the years it was transformed by European superintendents into an institution dominated by custodial rather than humanitarian thinking. Those in charge increasingly employed the language of the asylum and the prison rather than the Anglican parish. They referred to themselves as 'overseers' and 'matrons'. However, while superintendents, teachers and overseers came and went, a core of Aboriginal people stayed and grew into a close-knit community. Their self-confidence and self-sufficiency continued to develop until the 1890s when their lands were seized by Port Lincoln whites singularly lacking in Christian charity.

Poonindie operated from 1850 to 1894. These years can be roughly divided into three phases: the first, idealistic period when Hale established the institution with a small group of Aborigines and Europeans and Dr Octavius Hammond took over from him; second, the period from the early 1860s to the mid-1880s when the institution was well established and attitudes fairly typical of institutionalised life set in both among staff and residents; and a last phase which was marked by instability as the local Port Lincoln whites lobbied to have Poonindie closed and the land subdivided.

Poonindie, 1850–68

Once the site for the mission had been chosen at Poonindie a great deal of work was required to establish a farm and training institution. Houses and farm buildings were built, land cleared, fenced and sown with crops. (The church still stands and continues to be used for services.) This pioneering work was largely undertaken by the Aborigines under supervision of white staff. The Aborigines were quick to learn both skilled and unskilled work.[27] As early as 1852 Poonindie shearers were working on neighbouring properties as the goldrush had enticed most white labour away from the district.[28]

Hale clearly defined his recruitment policy. He only took young people who had been to a European school and had a knowledge of reading, writing and Christianity. His was a training institution; he did not want raw recruits. Although he preferred to take his Aborigines from Adelaide to isolate them from their relatives, as early as 1850 he was considering taking young people from Port Lincoln (presumably only those who had been through the Port Lincoln school established by the Lutheran missionary Schürmann).

Then in 1852, only two years after the mission was established, Hale altered his policy. After a large intake of children from the Adelaide school in 1852, the seven children remaining there absconded to return to their people on Yorke Peninsula. The school was temporarily closed for lack of children and there were so few children in Adelaide in the ensuing months it never reopened. Hale's main source of recruits was cut off. In the same year the Protector of Aborigines decided to close down a school in Port Lincoln, established by the Lutheran missionary, Clamor Schürmann, and transfer its function to Poonindie.[29] In addition, Hale was informed that if he wanted continued government support he would have to take any children of mixed descent sent to him by the Protector.

St Matthew's Church, Poonindie.
(Courtesy of Public Record Office, South Australia.)

The government turned Hale's original policies on their head. No longer was Poonindie to be isolated from both Europeans and Aborigines. In 1852 a despatch from the Governor stated that it was intended to use the training institution to prevent misery and crime in the Port Lincoln district and stop conflict between Aborigines and whites by firstly, educating and training Port Lincoln Aborigines at Poonindie and secondly, using Poonindie as a distribution point for rations. This directive was in response to the high level of violence between Aborigines and Europeans on lower Eyre Peninsula.[30] Hale accepted this change in the role of his institution and in June 1853 decided to encourage local Aboriginal adults to work at the mission. He employed ten to fifteen men for four months. The experiment was so successful he decided to continue employing them.[31] He treated what he called the local 'wurley natives' quite differently from Poonindie residents:

> All those who were enrolled as inmates had to conform strictly to the habits of civilised life. They had to all be in their own proper sleeping places at night; they had to attend prayers in the house, take their breakfast, dinner etc. at the proper time, and attend prayers again at night—over the outside or Wurley natives . . . I did not attempt to exercise any control, and when I employed them it was always by the job, not by the day.[32]

By this time Hale had accepted three major intakes of Aborigines from the Adelaide school.[33]

These founding members of the Poonindie community were, in a sense, human guinea pigs in a cross-cultural experiment. Many of them volunteered, or at least were easily coerced, into participating in the experiment, perhaps sensing that it was a chance of survival. In the long term they were proved correct, not about their own personal survival, but the survival of an Aboriginal community with roots traceable to the Adelaide and upper Murray districts.

The cultural dislocation that must have been suffered by the early Poonindie residents has not been documented, but there are reports of daily life which indicate they rapidly adapted to European living conditions and work practices. Biographical details recorded for many of these people suggest that the social dynamics between the couples were tense, sometimes violent and unhappy, most likely because these marriages were not arranged with regard to Aboriginal kinship structures or group affiliation. People seem to have found it easier to adapt to the new work routine than the marriages which were arranged for them.

Early residents at Poonindie

The following biographical sketches of couples and individuals give an indication of how these first residents adapted to their new life and each other.

Among these earliest inhabitants were Neechi and his wife Kilpatko. They were the first to be sent to Port Lincoln, arriving ahead of Hale, and were married by Bishop Short in the presence of Governor Young. They worked for a local settler, as shepherds for eleven months before Hale went to Boston Island. At Poonindie, Kilpatko worked as a baker and Neechi as a butcher.[34] But by July 1852 there were tensions between them and Neechi asked if he could go to an outstation as a shepherd as a break from his bad-tempered wife. She died in 1853 and in June 1854 he married Moonya who like him was from the Murray district. He was an enthusiastic convert to Christianity and when he died on 18 August 1855 he told his wife he was going to heaven.[35]

Another couple sent ahead of Hale were Narrung and Manyatko. They worked for Captain Bishop who later became a trustee of Poonindie. Hale married them on 17 October 1851. (He commented later that they lived together for twelve months before they showed any real attachment to each other.) Both had studied at the Adelaide school before going to Port Lincoln. When most of the European shepherds left Poonindie in 1852 Narrung took over their responsibilities and established an outstation as a base for the shepherds. Manyatko died in May 1852.[36] Her death, according to Hale, increased Narrung's commitment to Christianity and he and his brother, Toodko (who joined Poonindie a few months after Narrung) evangelised both among the Port Lincoln Aborigines and their own people on the Murray River. Toodko persuaded some of the Aborigines, who had returned to the bush after leaving the Adelaide school, to go to Poonindie.[37] After working a few months at the outstation, Narrung came back to Poonindie at his own request and cared for the horses. He lived with some of the older, more trustworthy single men in one of the stone cottages.[38] He died in October 1853 followed by his brother, Toodko, in January 1856.[39]

Kandwillan and Tandatko were another couple who joined Hale on Boston Island and adapted readily to the new work routine but had domestic problems. Kandwillan had been at the Adelaide school a considerable time and could read and write well. He had been a quiet and conscientious student. Tandatko had also been a competent student at the school, could read and write, and was a good needlewoman and washerwoman.[40] Hale at first worried because these teenagers, whose marriages Moorhouse and he had arranged, did not behave like European couples but remained segregated. Hale thought this undesirable pattern of behaviour was the result of the long time it had taken to get established and build separate cottages for each couple, rather than a reflection of Aboriginal patterns of behaviour. He noted one day in January 1851 that the couples were strolling along the beach in pairs and was relieved to see them conforming to his social standards.[41] Kandwillan and Tandatko were married at the same time as Narrung and Manyatko.

Kandwillan was one of the most highly regarded Aborigines at Poonindie in the early years and Hale gave him more responsibility than most. However, in August 1852 Tandatko went to Hale about something Kandwillan had done (Hale does not reveal even in his diary what it was) which Hale thought so immoral as to merit dismissal. Kandwillan was in Port Lincoln at the time, so Hale

> sent two boys to detain him on the other side of the River and prevent his crossing over. He came at sundown I then mustered all the lads and accompanied by Mr Haslop crossed over with the whole body and made them draw up on the burial ground. His dismissal was most affecting many of the boys shed tears, nor could Mr Haslop or I refrain from doing same ourselves.[42]

The next day Hale recorded in his diary:

> My sense of grief and suffering has been very great over Kandwillan. His poor wife was inconsolable, she sat out of doors in the cold and wet nearly the whole day. There was also a silence and sadness about the natives . . . Seeing how much punishment had been felt by all and hoping that enough had been done as warning. I received joint petition of all boys together I consented to receive him back.[43]

After this episode Kandwillan conformed to the morality of the mission. He and Tandatko were baptised by Bishop Short with many others on his visit to Poonindie in 1853. That same year Kandwillan was sent by Hale to have his portrait painted in Adelaide by the well-known painter, J. M. Crossland.[44]

Tandatko died in December 1856. Kandwillan subsequently married a woman only listed as Maria, who died in August 1858. Kandwillan died in May 1860.

The preceding biographical sketches describe people who were able to make a successful transition to life at Poonindie despite hardship, cultural dislocation and isolation from all that was familiar to them. Their feelings are expressed most articulately by one of the early residents, probably Mudlong or Tartan:

> Whenever I take my walks abroad
> How my poor I See
> What shall I render to my God for all his gifts to me
>
> Not more than others I deserve
> yet God hath given me more
> for I have food while others starve
> or beg from door to door

Portrait of Samuel Kandwillan, a pupil of the Natives' Training Institution, Poonindie, South Australia, by J. M. Crossland, 1800–58.
(Oil on canvas, Rex Nan Kivell Collection, National Library of Australia.)

The poor wild Natives whom I meet
Half naked I behold
While I am clothed from head to feet
And covered from the cold

While some poor wretches Scarce can tell
Where they may lay their head
I have a home within to dwell
And rest upon my bed

While others early learn to swear
And curse and lie and steal
Lord I am taught thy name to fear
And do thy holy will

And these thy favours day by day
To me above the rest
Then let me love thee more than they
And try to serve thee best[45]

Others found the transition more difficult. Nantilla and Peltungal (known as Popjoy) came to Poonindie in late 1850. He was an exception to Hale's rule as he had had no schooling before he came to Poonindie and was about ten years older than the others. He came from Lake Bonney on the River Murray and was a good worker, but he never 'settled'. He had a violent temper and Hale had difficulty controlling him. He twice assaulted his wife, Nantilla, so Hale reported him to the Port Lincoln government resident. Nantilla had been to the Adelaide school. She and Popjoy initially worked as servants in Hale's house in Port Lincoln. She was the first woman to become pregnant at Poonindie, but after a painful and protracted labour her child was stillborn. Popjoy was dismissed from the institution and returned to Adelaide where he died of consumption eleven months later.[46] Nantilla married Thomas Dicks in January 1853.

Another person dismissed in the early days was Monaitya. Although he had spent five years at the Adelaide school, he was not happy at the mission. Initially he was to be married to Maria, but she left the institution. Then it was decided he should marry Puiscumba who had been left at the institution by a European shepherd, who had been living with her and had promised to marry her or leave her with Hale. The shepherd appears not to have come back to claim her. Monaitya refused to commit himself to Puiscumba and there were complaints about his behaviour: he was said to be a disruptive influence on the mission. He was dismissed in April 1851.[47] He went back to Adelaide and then returned to the bush.

Maria spent only four months at Poonindie. She had worked for many years at Government House as a servant, where Bishop Short encountered her:

We have a native girl in the house. She has been here five years; and makes a very good servant. She does our washing, and I am told gets up linen very well; but I have not yet seen her performance. If she is treated harshly, or offended, she will walk off for a day or two, and then come back. And I am told, when the weather is very hot, she will leave her clothes and throw a blanket over her shoulders and go into the bush.[48]

After leaving Government House she fell 'into disreputable habits of life'. Hale initially hoped she might 'retrieve her character and become a respectable woman' at Poonindie, but he soon dismissed her, while keeping her mixed-descent baby son, Charlie. Hale claimed that she had left her son willingly, but entries in his diary suggest she may not have been as happy with the arrangement as he indicated. Charlie stayed at Poonindie until his death in a boating accident in 1872.[49]

Relatively few absconded from the institution. This is surprising as the mortality rate in the first ten years was very high. Mempong was one of the few who left. She joined Poonindie in mid-1851 and in November married Keure, who had come a few months earlier. She worked as a laundress while he did a variety of jobs including shepherding. Keure physically abused Mempong and Hale reported him to the government resident. He remained unrepentant until he had to appear in court.[50]

He died of consumption in Adelaide, surrounded by his family. Two days later Mempong went into the town to buy some material and did not return. Moorhouse, the Protector of Aborigines, was most upset, claiming she had been taken by a former lover against her will. He threatened the Aborigines camped on the Adelaide Parklands with expulsion if they did not find her and bring her back. They said she would be on the Murray in the hot weather. Scott, the Sub-Protector at Moorundie, found Mempong at Lake Bonney and forcibly took her away, creating such a hostile reaction among her people that he was afraid to send her on to Adelaide because of the violence that might result. When he eventually sent her she was in tears on hearing she was to be sent back to Poonindie, claiming she would sicken and die if she returned. Moorhouse relented and returned her to Moorundie.[51]

Although Moorhouse had the authority to send Aborigines to Poonindie, he believed that if they were taken against their will they would pine away and die.[52] Pressures were no doubt applied to 'educated' Aborigines to go to Poonindie, but they were never physically forced to go. When it was found Mempong had voluntarily absconded, she was allowed to return to her people.

Daily life

Day-to-day life was occupied with establishing a mission settlement and farm. Land had to be cleared, ploughed and fenced, stock shepherded, buildings erected, people fed, trained and educated. There was much movement between Poonindie and Port Lincoln until Poonindie became established. Some extracts from Hale's diary give an idea of how work was allocated and what was done:

20/3/51   Wollaston [the farm overseer] and I marked out a well and waterhole near the stockyard and set Nylchie [Neechi] and Konwillan [Kandwillan] to work.
27/3/51   Narrung came to my hut this morning to tell me that Pilpane having now kept the cattle a fortnight which he had undertaken to do, wished to give them up and that he would keep them with Charlie.

In March 1852 Wollaston left Poonindie to go to the goldfields and Hale was left to teach himself and the Aborigines how to farm.

10/3/52   After breakfast had two bullock teams yoked up, our original team in the dray and Tucknott team at plough. This attempt at ploughing with the natives only as agents I look upon as a most important event in its probable bearing upon our future operations. Ngullar ngullar (sic.) was the ploughman and Charley the driver and the result was such as to satisfy my expectations fully.
13/3/52   I wanted to determine something about shifting the yards or forming a new station for the natives by whom flocks are to be shepherded when Jones and Punch [white men] leave. Found on our return that Ngullar ngullar and Charley had got to work on the plough of their own accord.
17/3/52   Popjoy commenced ploughing as a learner and got on remarkably well.
26/3/52   After breakfast I made Mannera yoke up 2 teams of bullocks viz original team to be driver himself hauling wood. 3 bullocks for ploughing Tartan and Yorrock being in Port with the third team. Put Neriud upon the bullock and ploughing department—today is his first attempt quite as good as some of the others.

10/4/52   Narrung takes one flock [to Colombo outstation], Keurie [Keure] is to take the other flock and Pathera is to go up with them to remain during the daytime at the hut that the women [Narrung and Keure's wives?] may not be left at home alone.

18/5/52   Day wet again. Put Williamy to plough, which did not remain long in the paddock . . . Ploughing did not go very well after the rain. Williamy did not perform well.

3/6/52   Today I measured and marked off what had been a sheep yard for the boys garden. Divided it into 6 plots of 1½ rods each.

2/7/52   I got Yorrock and Mudlong and others to dig a water course from the well to the river.

3/7/52   The principal features of this period have been that the country being wet and boggy our operations have been circumscribed and shaped accordingly. The boys have worked more in a large gang . . .

14/7/52   Tartan went to the Peninsula to relieve Pitpowie and the latter came home. The cowboys did not crop over the other side this evening because of the strength of the current [of the Tod River]. This has been the first occasion on which they have missed cropping after prayers.[53]

In 1859 two outsiders observed the mission and wrote about their impressions with quite different interpretations of the scenes they observed. A visitor to Poonindie in November 1859 described the daily routine:

On Monday morning, at seven o'clock, the bell was rung for prayers, at which most of the people attended, when a chapter from the Old Testament and a selection of prayers from the Liturgy were read. After breakfast the men and boys went about the business of the farm. Most of them were employed in cutting hay, which was carted home during the week, the whole being done by them without any superintendence. At eleven o'clock the women and children assembled in the

Farm machinery and implements, late 19th century, Poonindie.
(Courtesy of Mortlock Library of South Australiana.)

schoolroom for instruction . . . I heard them read from their lesson books, and also from the New Testament. In the afternoon they again met to be taught sewing, in addition to reading and writing. The evening school conducted by Mr Hammond, was well attended by men and boys . . . At about half past eight the bell was rung, when the adult population assembled in the schoolroom for evening prayer. The same course of procedure is gone through daily, except during shearing time, when the school is necessarily interrupted.[54]

Another visitor to Poonindie in March of the same year gave a less glowing report of his visit. He was Edward Hitchin who had been requested by Francis S. Dutton, the Commissioner of Crown Lands and Immigration, to report on the mission.[55] Hitchin found at that time of year only a few of the men were regularly employed—three shepherds, one cook, and two horsebreakers; and two women as domestic servants. He believed all the men could be given regular employment and the land made more productive. He also described the daily routine:

the European workman has to really labor for ten hours daily, and take his uninviting meals from his wallett; the blackfellow is roused from his slumber by the ringing of a bell shortly after 6 o'clock; after the expiration of a waking and dressing hour (and then not without a good deal of bell-ringing), those who choose attend morning prayers; immediately after which, breakfast is served, consisting of freshly-baked bread, hot meat, and capital tea, followed by pipes of tobacco; at 9 o'clock their employment ostensibly begins; to be succeeded by other similar meals at mid-day and early in the evening.[56]

Poonindie population

Poonindie had been established in 1850 with eleven Aborigines from the Adelaide school. By 1856 one hundred and ten Aborigines had been admitted to the institution, but of these 29 had died, 11 had been dismissed, 5 had left on their own initiative, 9 were temporarily absent, which left fifty-six.[57]

At the end of 1856 there were 61 residents at Poonindie; between 1856 and 1860, 7 babies were born, 20 people admitted and 44 died so that in 1860 there were only 44 remaining. In the mid-1860s the population at last stabilised and, although the death rate was probably still high by nineteenth-century standards, the number of deaths per year had reduced to one or two by 1863. These deaths tended to be babies and young children, rather than young adults in their prime. Most of them resulted from chest complaints, mainly consumption (tuberculosis). Of 44 deaths between 1856 and 1860, 28 were ascribed to tuberculosis. Hale claimed that, while he was at Poonindie, all deaths, bar one, resulted from chest complaints; many may have started with influenza, the infection then moving to the lungs.[58]

It is perhaps surprising that so few people left voluntarily in the face of such a high incidence of disease and death. Hale believed that the high mortality turned many of the people to Christianity and this appears to be borne out by the rate of conversions in the first years. There was only one death at Poonindie in the first year and little interest in Christianity and baptism. By 1853 when the Bishop visited Poonindie eight had died at the mission and eleven were ready for baptism.[59] News of the deaths travelled back to Adelaide and the Murray and deterred many prospective residents. Others continued to come, possibly because they had nowhere else to go and felt secure at Poonindie, a sense denied to them both in Adelaide, where very few Kaurna survived and the River Murray where old patterns of life had been disrupted.

From 1850–52 most Poonindie residents were taken from the Adelaide school, but only a few of these were Kaurna people. Hale claimed that of sixty-seven Aborigines sent to him from Adelaide only six were Kaurna.[60] Most of the people sent from Adelaide had originally come from the upper Murray. People from the lower Murray around Wellington and the Lakes refused to go. In the late 1850s George Mason, the Sub-Protector of Aborigines at Wellington, had been asked to round up some girls from this district to send as wives for men at Poonindie. He reported

> there is no probability of inducing the young Native females of the Lakes or this part of the Murray [Wellington] to leave their friends for the purpose of locating themselves at 'Poonindie'. They say 'the young men at "Poonindie" belong to distant tribes, with whom they have never associated, and that when they are in want of husbands, they will not require to go so far in search of them.'
>
> At the request of Mr Moorhouse when that gentleman was Protector of Aborigines—I endeavoured to get a number of Native Boys and Girls to attend the Adelaide or Poonindie Schools, but never could induce them to leave the Murray, in consequence of the dread they have of Natives of strange tribes, and of being such a distance from their friends.[61]

In 1852 three girls were sent from Schürmann's Port Lincoln school to Poonindie to marry three boys brought over from Adelaide. Soon after, Schürmann's school was closed and Poonindie took over the education and training of the people of the lower Eyre Peninsula. By 1854 there were twenty-seven people from the Murray, twenty-two from Port Lincoln and four from Adelaide at Poonindie.[62]

There were also increasing numbers of people of mixed descent coming to the institution following the government's change of policy in 1852. In 1860 six 'half castes' were at Poonindie and in 1862, ten.[63] Two families of boys of mixed descent were brought to Poonindie in the 1850s. They were some of the very few to survive from these early years. The only other people who appear in the early records and were (or had descendants who were) still at Poonindie in the later years were James Wanganeen, who originally came from the Murray, Louisa Roberts, a woman of mixed descent and her first husband, Frederick Milera, from Port Lincoln. The boys of mixed descent were Tom and Tim Adams who were brought to Poonindie in 1855, and John, Emanuel and George Solomon. George came in 1858, John in about 1860–61 and Emanuel in 1870. Both the Adams and Solomons were products of formal marriages between white men and Aboriginal women. Thomas Adams (senior) was the first white man to marry an Aboriginal woman in South Australia. When Kudnarto, Thomas Adams' wife, died in 1855 after seven years of marriage, and Rathoola, George (senior) Solomon's wife died in 1858, neither man could support his children, so they applied to send them to Poonindie.

When Octavius Hammond, a qualified medical practitioner, became superintendent in 1856 he was appalled at the insanitary conditions. Sheoak huts described picturesquely by Bishop Short in 1853 had badly deteriorated.[64] The dirt floors had worn away so that in winter, people were sleeping over large puddles in their huts, or, as they preferred in these circumstances, outside.[65] The fences and woolshed had also deteriorated. Hammond built new brick and stone cottages, replaced the fencing and the woolshed and established a large garden to supply fresh vegetables to the community. However, his improvements did not have an immediate effect on the health of the people. During his first years in charge, the mortality rate reached the previously mentioned new heights with 50 per cent of the population dying between 1856 and 1860. The mortality rate dropped dramatically in the latter part of this period and several healthy children were born. Only one baby had survived prior to 1856.[66]

Poonindie after Hale

In 1856 Hale left Poonindie to become the first Bishop of Perth in Western Australia and Octavius Hammond took charge. Hammond lacked Hale's administrative ability and flair for public relations. The building programme he established put the institution into debt and there was dissatisfaction among local whites and in government circles at his administration and the productivity of Poonindie. Edward Hitchin was appointed in March 1859 to investigate the mission and produced a critical report. As a result the government cut its grant and appointed a farm overseer responsible to the Commissioner of Crown Lands and Immigration.[67] In 1861 the Poonindie trustees sold the lease of the Toolilee Run and its stock to John Tennant, and with the proceeds paid off their debt to the rural agents, Elders, whose loans had helped support the institution.[68] Henceforward, Poonindie was self-supporting. By 1862 Alexander Watherston, the government-appointed overseer, had increased the number of sheep to 9300 and cattle to 400. Believing the Aborigines to be lazy and untrustworthy he employed a number of white men, taking all responsibility and initiative from the Aborigines. In 1860, apart from Hammond and Watherston, there were five white employees: an assistant-overseer, a cook and three shepherds, a retrograde step from 1852 when Hale had run Poonindie with virtually all Aboriginal workers.

Before departing, Hale called the residents together to tell them that all the stock and land at Poonindie belonged to them and that they should look after the property.[69] Hammond had continued Hale's policy of respecting the Aborigines, acknowledging their abilities and allowing them some autonomy which enabled them to continue to feel that Poonindie belonged to them. It is not surprising that the Aborigines resented the advent of Watherston; they felt that Poonindie was theirs. Watherston reported to the Commissioner of Crown Lands that his authority was being undermined by a concerted campaign:

> my time having been fully occupied in looking for lost Sheep, at the present moment there are betwixt 200 and 300 amissing for the last fortnight I have done nothing else but look after lost Sheep and I find it no use sending the Natives to find them . . . . they never find any—with all their former faults I can't believe they have ever acted as they are doing now it appears to be a combination amongst them to do no work. . . . Stopping their dinner or supper will have a great effect in getting work done—at least I will try it. I have been offering them extra Tobacco if they would find lost Sheep, a remedy I have never known fail but here . . . .What with one thing and another I am nearly a fit patient for the Lunatic Asylum.[70]

Watherston's appointment marked the end of the idealistic period. Gone were the days when an Aboriginal worker could come to the superintendent and say he was tired of shepherding and would like to try some other work. Now he was told what to do and how to do it and was threatened with removal of basic requirements such as food or with dismissal if he did not cooperate. It was reported in parliament in 1860: 'Mr. Watherston is now in charge of the property of the institution and the labour of the natives and has a policy to win the natives over to useful work, or failing winning, to compel them to duty, where they are capable of it, by refusing all supplies'.[71]

Neither was Watherston interested in the Aborigines' moral or educational development. Hammond continued in charge of these aspects of the mission as well as the physical health of the residents, but he was no longer the dominant authority. He maintained a role at Poonindie until his death in 1878 and was the longest-serving white man at the mission, but his responsibilities continued to be whittled away. In 1868 a new missionary, William Holden, took over as Superintendent and by the time of his death, Hammond was only responsible for the medical condition of the Aborigines.[72] Thus this early period of Poonindie history is characterised by idealism and compromise on the part of the European founders, and pragmatism and adaptation on the part of Aborigines.

Achievements in the first period

Hale had attempted a social experiment at the Native Training Institution. He claimed that educating Aborigines in total isolation had not been tried in Australia before and that all other attempts to 'civilise' and Christianise Aborigines had failed because of this. Isolation implied separation from Europeans and Aborigines with whom residents had familial or community ties.

The early history of Poonindie suggests that the Aborigines went there without coercion and stayed voluntarily. The mission must therefore have had attractions for them. It provided regular meals and security in contrast to the unpredictable pattern of their lives since Europeans moved on to their lands. Many had been forced to move from their ancestral lands, or if they still had access to them they found their sacred sites desecrated, their ceremonies interrupted along with sources of food and water. Most of the early residents were young and more willing to experiment than their parents and older members of Aboriginal society. This seems to have been a common pattern in Aboriginal communities; the older people who had won seniority and power through experience and age did not want to adapt to a new pattern of life.[73]

Aborigines carefully weighed up the pros and cons of accommodation with the colonists. When they assessed it to their advantage they accepted interference in their established patterns of life, but if adequate rewards were not forthcoming they withdrew. Schürmann claimed the Pangkala round Port Lincoln were willing to send their children to his school, and the children were willing to stay as long as they were well fed, but when meat was withdrawn from their rations, they all absconded.[74] In 1852 the three eldest girls at Schürmann's school were sent to Poonindie as prospective wives for the single men. The children remaining at the school were worried at the possibility that they might also be sent to Poonindie and attempted to leave on several occasions. When they learnt the school was to be closed and they were all to be transferred, they ran away.

Poonindie Mission, mid-1860s.
(Courtesy of Mortlock Library of South Australiana.)

They were obviously prepared to subject themselves to European education in return for regular, good quality rations, but they were not prepared to live in an institution with people they did not know.[75]

Hale's experiment, based on the model of an English village, gave the Aborigines the farming skills of an English labourer and educated them to a level as high, if not higher than a labourer. Hale's primary aim as a missionary, to convert them to Christianity, seems to have been achieved. Some of the Aborigines became devout Christians. Narrung, Todbrook and later James Wanganeen became evangelists. Kandwillan took services at Poonindie in Hale's absence and Wirrup and Wanganeen often assisted with services and prayers.[76]

Hale also made an impact on the personal lives of the Poonindie residents. He made them conform to the European notion of the nuclear family. He built a cottage for each couple and encouraged them to socialise as couples. He was most concerned at having a surplus of single men and did his best to find wives for them. Communal responsibility for orphaned and deserted children was not encouraged; they were housed separately in dormitories and supervised by the superintendent, his wife or a matron.

The people were inducted into the money economy by being paid for their services. Men were paid wages according to the level of skill required. Women who worked as servants for the Europeans or did extra washing or cooking were also paid wages. The men were responsible for the family finances.

Hale did not believe the Aborigines had the stamina and application to work as long hours as English labourers, so he modified the number of hours the men worked each day. They were, nevertheless, encouraged to attend evening classes. By today's standards their day was very long and they were expected to conform to a strict routine quite at variance with their previous mode of life.

The Aborigines picked up western work skills and leisure activities very quickly. Many of the men became first-class shearers and ploughmen and the women excellent needlewomen. The men learned cricket and western athletics. Several of them also became competent musicians. Three men learned to play the classical flute, a decidedly middle-class accomplishment.

Using James Axtell's criteria for the success of missions, Poonindie would rate high. For the Aborigines Poonindie was a means of survival, although not in the narrow or individual sense, for many died in these early years. Rather it was the basis for the establishment of an Aboriginal community, which over the years would grow. Physical force was not used to recruit the Poonindie inhabitants, although many who went there had no other practical choice and children had no say in where they were sent. An example of the lack of coercion is the relationship which developed between the mission and the local Pangkala people. They were encouraged to join the institution from 1853 on. Some did but many did not, but nonetheless, they regularly visited and camped nearby to collect rations or obtain casual work. Then, when food became plentiful in the interior they moved away to return again when food was scarce.

The Aboriginal community that grew up at Poonindie had no roots in any particular pre-European society. In this respect it was quite unlike Point McLeay on the lower Murray established for the Ngarrindjeri, or Killalpaninna, established for the Diyari, in the far north. Poonindie was definitely not based on the local Pangkala population. Recruitment policies worked against development of a community which might adopt a particular traditional Aboriginal belief system or kinship structure.

The Aborigines at Poonindie could not relate to the land in a traditional Aboriginal sense as most were recent immigrants.[77] The land is a basic foundation of traditional Aboriginal religious life. The Pangkala people who joined Poonindie made a conscious decision to leave the land. There is no recorded evidence that they maintained their religious links with their people, although perhaps they may have done so behind the authorities' backs. If they did maintain religious links with their people it would not have been at the institution.

The mission policy in the early years stressed European education and Christianity. Residents lacked the human resources and knowledge, which can only be gained from the elders in a specified manner, to maintain a ceremonial life. All the recruits were young. Few, if any, would have passed through initiation ceremonies; those who reached that level of maturity were regarded as lost souls by Hale and the Protector of Aborigines. Hale seems, from the available evidence, to have succeeded in his aim to create an environment free of tradition. The decision to take children of mixed descent ensured a generation would grow up at Poonindie who remembered no other cultural life. Their children knew no other home.

The community which evolved at Poonindie was, in many senses, a new Aboriginal community. It started with nothing and over the years built up a thriving farm. It became self-supporting and offered friendship to its inhabitants out of which a new set of family and extended family relationships developed.

Notes

1 T. Griffin and M. McCaskill (eds), *Atlas of South Australia*, Adelaide, 1986, pp. 11, 12. Compare these figures with a European population of 23,000 in Sydney and 77,000 in the whole of NSW in 1836 (48 years after the arrival of the First Fleet): Griffin and McCaskill, p. 5.

2 Griffin and McCaskill, *Atlas*, pp. 12, 18.

3 T. Gara, 'Mullawirraburka: "King John" of the Adelaide tribe', unpublished typescript, n.d., p. 1, quoting *Southern Australian*, 11 January 1842, which estimated the Kaurna (Adelaide people) to have been between 600–700.

4 Griffin and McCaskill, *Atlas*, p. 13.

5 GRG 52/1/1858/514, SAPRO; Report of the Select Committee of the Legislative Council upon 'The Aborigines' minutes of evidence, p. 5, Adelaide.

6 Gara, 'Mullawirraburka', pp. 2, 13; J. M. Hunt, 'Schools for Aboriginal children in the Adelaide district 1836–1852' unpublished BA (Hons) thesis, University of Adelaide, 1971, p. 44.

7 Protector of Aborigines quarterly report 1843 in Hunt, 'Schools for Aboriginal children', p. 45.

8 It is more likely that in outlying areas unlawful killings went unrecorded as police had to patrol huge areas and were themselves implicated in killings, but in the Adelaide area which was relatively heavily populated this is less likely to have happened.

9 There are no accurate data on Aboriginal death rates or their causes, but the example of one known family suggests that these causes of death were major contributors to the rapid decline in Aboriginal population. Mullawirraburka, also known as King John, who cooperated with the colonists and was closely associated with them, died eight years after their arrival at the age of 35, two of his wives and six of his children had already died, none of them had been murdered: Gara, 'Mullawirraburka', p. 16.

10 See S. Hemming, 'Conflict between Aborigines and Europeans along the River Murray from the Darling to the South Bend, 1830–1841', unpublished BA (Hons) thesis, University of Adelaide, 1982.

11 N. Butlin, *On our original aggression. Aboriginal populations of south eastern Australia*, Sydney, 1983, pp. 24 and 27.

12 R. Foster, 'Feasts of the full-moon: the distribution of rations to Aborigines in South Australia 1836–1861', *Aboriginal History*, 13(1), 1989, p. 68; Fay Gale, 'Roles revisited: the women of southern South Australia' in P. Brock (ed.), *Women, rites and sites. Aboriginal women's cultural knowledge*, Sydney, 1989, p. 121; G. Woolmer, *Aborigines of the past: an Aboriginal history of the Barmera region*, Barmera 1976, p. 11. For reports of the later killings see Foster, 'Feasts of the full moon', p. 75; Woolmer, *The Riverland Aborigines of the past*, pp. 17–19.

13 GRG 52/7, 18/5/1849.

14 Foster, 'Feasts of the full moon', p. 75.

15 Woolmer, *Aborigines of the past*, pp. 17–19.

16 Protector of Aborigines quarterly report, 1/7/1838 (SAA 787), as quoted in Hunt, 'Schools for Aboriginal children', pp. 24–5.

17 GRG 52/7, M. Moorhouse to Chief Protector, Port Phillip, 10/5/1849.

18 Hunt, 'Schools for Aboriginal children' , pp. 44, 54, 57.

19 When 14 years old the boys were apprenticed in a trade—2 tanners, 4 blacksmiths, 6 joiners, 4 messengers, 4 gardeners, 2 to man Harbour Master's boats and 2 as sailors. GRG 52/7, M. Moorhouse to Chief Protector, Port Phillip, 10/5/1849.

20 Protector of Aborigines quarterly report 12/1/1846, 5/10/1846, in Hunt, 'Schools for Aboriginal children', pp. 61, 62.

21 P. B. Walsh, 'The problem of native policy in South Australia in the nineteenth century. With particular reference to the Church of England Poonindie mission 1850–1896.' Unpublished BA (Hons) thesis, University of Adelaide, 1966, pp. 62 and 77.

22 Augustus Short, *The Poomindie Mission described in a letter from Lord Bishop to Society for the Propagation of the Gospel*, Adelaide, 1853, p. 10.

23 J. D. Somerville, vol. 1, Chief Secretary's Office, 2493, 1784/50, 13/8/1851, Mortlock Library of South Australiana.

24 Augustus Short, *A visit to Poonindie and some accounts of that mission to the Aborigines of South Australia*, Adelaide, 1872, p. 11.

25 Short, *The Poomindie mission*, p. 10.

26 Short, *The Poomindie mission*, p. 11.

27 SAPP, no. 3, 1859, p. 2, Report from Octavius Hammond, Adelaide.

28 Somerville, vol. 1, pp. 392 and 413.

29 Schürmann was asked by the government to establish a school for Port Lincoln Aborigines in 1850, it opened with fifteen children on 1 May 1850: SA *Government Gazette*, 18/7/1850. The closure of Schürmann's school was first promulgated in April 1852: Somerville, vol. 1, Chief Secretary's outward letterbook, 1237, 17/4/1852. The school was closed in February 1853: Somerville, vol. 1, Chief Secretary's Office, p. 490.

30 Somerville, vol. 1, p. 363, Despatch from the Governor of SA, 7/5/1852. The level of aggression was so high that Europeans had contemplated leaving the district a few years earlier. They continued to be vulnerable to Aboriginal attacks until the mid-1950s.

31 Somerville, vol. 1, p. 447, CSO no. 1521, 22/6/1853.

32 Mathew Hale, *The Aborigines of Australia being an account of the institution for their education at Poonindie, in South Australia*, London, 1889, p. 66.

33 PRG 275, 130/190, 12/10/1850, Mortlock Library of South Australiana; PRG 275, Mathew Hale's diary, 28/6/1851.

34 Somerville, vol. 1, p. 326, CSO 3684, enclos. Dec. 1851.

35 PRG 275, 22/7/1852; PRG 275, 130/149; Somerville, vol. 2, SA *Government Gazette*, 27/12/1855.

36 Hale, *The Aborigines of Australia*, p. 58; PRG 275, Hale's diary, 8/4/1852.

37 Hale, *The Aborigines of Australia*, p. 58: Somerville, vol. 1, p. 33, CSO no. 1000, 24/3/1856.

38 Hale, *The Aborigines of Australia*, p. 58.

39 PRG 275, Hale's diary, 19/1/1855; PRG 275 130/149.

40 PRG 275, 130/195.

41 PRG 275, Hale's diary, 19/1/1851.

42 PRG 275, Hale's diary, 20/8/1852.

43 PRG 275, Hale's diary, 21/8/1852.

44 PRG 275, 130/200.

45 PRG 275, 130/224.

46 Somerville, vol. 1, p. 413, CSO 216 31/12/1852; PRG 275 130/195; PRG 275, Hale's diary, 3/8/1852; Hale, *The Aborigines of Australia*, p. 50.

47 PRG 275, Hale's diary, 4/3/1851 and 18/4/1851.

48 Bishop Short, quoted in Hale, *The Aborigines of Australia*, p. 24.

49 Hale, *The Aborigines of Australia*, p. 25; PRG 275, Hale's diary 16/2/1851.

50 PRG 275, Hale's diary, 22/6/1852.

51 PRG 275, 130/198; 130/199; 130/203.

52 PRG 275, 130/199.

53   PRG 275, Hale's diary.

54   Mr Goodman, quoted in Hale, *The Aborigines of Australia*, Appendix B, p. 86.

55   SAPP, no. 30, 1859, Report on Poonindie Mission, Adelaide. This investigation of Poonindie is dealt with in more detail later.

56   SAPP, no. 30, 1859 Report on Poonindie Mission, p. 6.

57   SAPP, no. 193, 1856, p. 5.

58   Somerville, vol. 2, p. 445; PRG 275 130/160.

59   Short, *The Poomindie mission*, p. 18; PRG 275 130/149.

60   PRG 275, 130/56.

61   Somerville, vol. 2, p. 234 Crown Lands and Immigration 376/1859, George Mason, 27/5/1859.

62   SA *Government Gazette*, 24/3/1853; Somerville, vol. 1, p. 474, CSO 395, 16/1/1854. In 1860 Hammond reported most of the people came from the Murray River, Adelaide and Mount Barker, and a few from Guichen Bay and Encounter Bay. This seems to contradict other information, for instance, he does not mention people from Port Lincoln: see Somerville, vol. 2, p. 445, Crown Lands and Immigration, 1280/1860.

63   Somerville, vol. 2, p. 311, CL & I 248/1860; 508 Public Works 799/1862, 24/2/1860.

64   'The married couples have each their little hut, built of the trunks of the she-oak set up in the ground, the interstices being neatly plastered and whitewashed, roofed with broad palings.' Short, *The Poomindie Mission*, p. 14.

65   Somerville, vol. 2, p. 160, SAPP 150, 164.

66   SAPP no. 177, 21/12/1858.

67   Somerville, vol. 2, p. 261, CL & I, outward letterbook 1038/1859, 8/12/1859

68   Somerville, vol. 2, p. 480, CL & I 1144/1861; Hale, *The Aborigines of Australia*, p. 79.

69   Somerville, vol. 2, p. 283, CL & I 123/1860, 27/1/1860; SAPP, no. 30, 1859, 11.

70   Somerville, vol. 2, p. 283, CL & I 123/1860, 27/1/1860.

71   SAPP, no. 96, 1860.

72   Somerville, vol. 3, 265, Yearbook 1879, Appendix S. Hammond had to move out of the superintendent's house when Holden took over. He moved to the property where Boston House currently stands in Port Lincoln.

73   For example, H. Reynolds, *The other side of the frontier. Aboriginal resistance to the European invasion of Australia*, Ringwood, Victoria, 1982, pp. 128–32.

74   SA *Government Gazette*, 30/1/1851, in Somerville, vol. 1, p. 242.

75   SA *Government Gazette*, 24/3/1853. There are other documented instances in which Aborigines dictated the terms on which they were willing to join a mission, for example, at Framlingham in Victoria Aborigines refused to go to Lake Condah mission when the government closed the mission at Framlingham in 1867, and it was reopened: J. Critchett, *Our land till we die: a history of the Framlingham Aborigines*, Warrnambool, 1980, p. 14; also C. Anderson, 'A case study in failure: Kuku-Yalanji and the Lutherans at Bloomfield River, 1887–1902' in T. Swain and D. B. Rose (eds), *Aboriginal Australians and Christian missions*, Bedford Park, South Australia, 1988, pp. 321-37.

76   Augustus Short, *A visit to Poonindie*, p. 7.

77   Hans Mol, *The firm and the formless. Religion and identity in Aboriginal Australia*, Ontario, 1982, p. 6.

4

AN ESTABLISHED COMMUNITY AND ITS DESTRUCTION

After the early years of high death rates the population of Poonindie gradually rose to a peak of between eighty and ninety inhabitants. A core of individuals and families lived at the institution or made it their home base; although many left the mission for long periods, they always returned.[1] Like the ghettos it offered communal solidarity, and sympathy and understanding from their own kind.

Most of the young adults at Poonindie married there. Generally there was a surplus of men, so girls of marriageable age who came to the mission were quickly paired off. Marriage was strongly encouraged by the authorities. Amelia McDennett, Amy Sterling and another girl were sent from Western Australia in 1870. Both Amy and Amelia received offers of marriage within months of their arrival but refused, much to the consternation of William Holden, the missionary. He complained several times that Amy turned down two good offers of marriage and if she was too fussy she would miss out altogether. After resisting these pressures for three years, Amy married Andrew Hamilton from Point McLeay in 1873.[2]

Most Poonindie residents came from the southern part of South Australia: Eyre Peninsula, Port Augusta, Yorke Peninsula, Adelaide, the River Murray and the south-east.[3] Children were sent from Venus Bay in the west and from the Aboriginal school at Lacepede Bay until it closed in 1876. Mathew Hale, who was then Bishop of Perth, arranged for recruits to be sent from an Aboriginal school in Albany in Western Australia run by a Mrs Camfield.[4]

In 1869 the superintendent of the mission, William Holden, went on a recruitment drive for the mission. This seems to have been one of the few periods when Poonindie suffered from a shortage of men. Holden knew many Aborigines on the River Murray from his days as a missionary in Victoria. First he went to Port Augusta and to the north and west of the town where he found that most of the people were either employed on stations or not interested in leaving for Poonindie with a stranger.[5] He then travelled to the upper Murray from Wentworth to Blanchetown with Daniel Limberry, a Poonindie Aborigine who had originally come from that region. They met many Aborigines they knew, and although Holden claimed they would have been quite happy to go with him, they would not commit themselves to Poonindie. They were fearful of leaving their country permanently and going across the sea (the gulf) to Port Lincoln. They had heard of the many deaths at Poonindie in the early years and were afraid they would be going there to die.[6] Here again is an indication that people were not forced to go to Poonindie but chose to go because of their own calculations of their chances of survival. When, as in the case of these River Murray people, they assessed their chances of survival were worse at Poonindie than in their current situation, they stayed put.

The rise of institutionalised attitudes and life

In this period there was still much illness at Poonindie but it no longer stood out from the general population of South Australia which was much more subject to infectious diseases in the nineteenth century than in the twentieth. During various epidemics which afflicted Poonindie, white staff and their families, as well as Aboriginal residents, became sick and died. In 1872 the institution escaped a diphtheria epidemic in the Port Lincoln district, due, it was thought, to its good sanitation and the healthy diet available to residents. In 1875 there was a measles epidemic at Poonindie. Seventy-five cases were reported and there were ten deaths in a population of about ninety. In 1878 there were forty cases of typhoid fever (described as enteric fever) among white and Aboriginal residents and six deaths. However, Dr Octavius Hammond pointed out that the Poonindie death rate was roughly equivalent to the mortality rate for the disease in England (13.3 per cent). In 1881 several children, including the superintendent's were suffering from whooping cough; and tuberculosis continued to claim victims, although not at the rate it had in the 1850s and early 1860s.[7]

Dismissals from the institution also produced fluctuations in Poonindie's population. Dismissal was the major tool the white authorities used to maintain their control. Anyone who disobeyed the regulations or did not conform to the strict Christian morality of the institution could be dismissed temporarily for one or more months, depending on the severity of the misdemeanour and the mood of the superintendent or farm overseer. A large percentage of the men and a few women were dismissed at some stage of their lives at Poonindie. New residents were expelled if they could not conform to institutional life. Several of the men Hale sent from Western Australia were dismissed. John Lush, for example, who came to Poonindie in 1869, refused to attend prayers and was 'insubordinate'. The superintendent first stopped his rations to try to make him conform and finally dismissed him in July 1870 when he refused to get up or work for two weeks and claimed 'I am not going to work for I came to Poonindie because it was a Natives' home and we have no right to work only when we like'. Similarly, Sam Stubbs, who was often cited among the good workers, was condemned for having the 'wrong' attitude, and eventually dismissed for drunkenness.[8]

The weapon of dismissal was most effective against longer term residents. New arrivals had no stake in the place while most long-term residents of Poonindie had no other permanent home, so dismissal meant having to leave family, friends, home, work and income. Even for a short period such as a month this could have a devastating effect on a person's life. The treatment of the Limberrys is an example of how the interference of white authorities could dominate and ruin the lives of Aboriginal people who did not conform to their circumscribed view of mission life.

Daniel Limberry came to Poonindie some time in the 1860s. He was originally from the upper River Murray. In 1869 he accompanied William Holden on his unsuccessful recruitment trip up the Murray. Holden was most impressed with his hard work and the respect he commanded along the river. In November 1869 Daniel married Mary, who had come from Point McLeay where she had been known as Agnes Hooper, married (de facto) to Jack Hooper. Agnes, of mixed descent, had an unhappy childhood brought up by a 'vile' white woman. She went to school for twelve months at Point McLeay in 1860–61 when she was 15 or 16 years old, by which time she had already been married once. In 1869 she deserted Jack Hooper while living in Strathalbyn in the Adelaide hills and went to Poonindie, where she met Daniel Limberry. As Mary had not been legally married to Jack Hooper she was baptised at Poonindie and married Daniel. While Holden remained at Poonindie, Limberry was one of the most trusted and highly regarded workers. He was not one of the top shearers, but an excellent boundary rider and stockman. In August 1873 he decided to go shearing for a few months, breaking a verbal undertaking with the farm overseer, Newland, to do boundary riding. Newland took him to court for breach of contract.[9] By November, Limberry was back at Poonindie and a hut was built at the Poonindie gates so he and his wife could act as gate-keepers. This meant they were not under the direct supervision of the superintendent and overseer, an indication of the high regard in which they were held. Daniel was also responsible for droving sheep north to a run the mission acquired at Moonabie near Franklin Harbour.

After Holden's departure the Limberrys were at loggerheads with the authorities for a number of years. Daniel was dismissed in November 1877 for not revealing the names of people who had supplied him with a bottle of brandy. His wife, Mary, had left Poonindie in June after clashing with the matron, Randall. She became a pawn in the tensions between Randall and Newland: Randall stopped her rations; Newland gave her meat; Newland wanted her back at the station; Randall refused to take her. Randall implied Mary was drinking as she was camped close to the North Shields hotel.[10] She tried to have Mary sent back to Point McLeay but the missionary, Taplin, refused to take her saying she was now a resident of Poonindie. Mary heard Taplin had written critically of her and wrote a letter of complaint,

> . . . I was surprised to here that you gave me shuch a bad character and so you have been my enemy and not a Dear friend please will you be so kind as to tell me how many childrens I head without husband which you worte and told Mrs. Randell bout me if I had been wild when I was a girl . . . and if I was a siner . . .[11]

From this period the Limberrys were on and off the station. Mary was banned for long periods, or confined to the Moonabie outstation out of contact with the rest of the community and separated from her children, whom she generally left on the mission. Daniel still worked at Poonindie driving sheep up to Moonabie and frequently requested permission for his wife to be allowed to return. In 1879 Mary had an affair with one of the young single men, James Ilkabidnie, and was again banned from the mission, despite her husband's pleas to have her back. In 1881 Daniel had an affair with a married woman, Emma Donnelly.[12] The Limberrys finally separated some time later. In 1888 Daniel applied for Native section 173 at Encounter Bay on the south-east coast where he took up farming. Previously he had worked as a tracker at Port Augusta. He subsequently joined the Salvation Army for a short time and later worked as a stock-man.[13] By the 1890s he was living near the Lakes in the south-east. Mary seems to have continued in disastrous relationships, although still legally married to Daniel. In 1895 she was living with a man on Yorke Peninsula who mistreated her. She wanted to escape and move on to a mission again but did not get a sympathetic hearing from the Protector of Aborigines, who disapproved of her morality.[14]

Recent recruits to Poonindie who were dismissed for misconduct dispersed to many different places, but long-term residents who were temporarily dismissed, or had volun-tarily left because of sickness or disagreements, stayed in the Port Lincoln district. Many obtained work on nearby properties or camped on Poonindie land. In 1878 several fam-ilies were camped a short distance from the Poonindie gates in wurleys and tents. They included: Sam Rankine's family, who had been dismissed from Poonindie after Sam was gaoled for supplying liquor to other Aborigines; the Wowindas, as Fred had been dis-missed for drunkenness; Mary Limberry and her children, who had left Poonindie because of conflict with the matron; and the Newchurch family, who left to avoid the typhoid fever which had been sweeping through Poonindie.[15] This indicates the close-ness of their ties with Poonindie. They could keep daily contact with family and friends, while avoiding conflict with the white authorities. No doubt they also obtained food as they had no means of support and their rations would have been stopped when they left the institution.

Daily life on Poonindie was carefully regulated and busy. Apart from its function as a mission, Poonindie was a prosperous farm supporting as many as ninety or one hundred people. Regulations drawn up by the three trustees were displayed at Poonindie:

1. All able bodied men, women and youths will be required to maintain themselves by their own labour; rations being supplied in part payment thereof.
2. The Incurables, Orphan Children and Confirmed Invalids will be provided with Food, Clothing and Medical Attendance; the sick, only until they are convalescent, and orphans, until capable of earning their own living.
3. Medical Attendance and Medicine will be provided Free of Cost, to all labourers and their families, and others on the station, when needing it.
4. All children will be Educated free and those capable of receiving instruction, will be required to attend school at the hours fixed. Youths, and others engaged in farm work, will be afforded the opportunity of learning at night school, or such other times that might be agreed upon.[16]

The document goes on to specify the house rules and the responsibilities of the super-intendent, farm overseer, medical officer and school master. 'Inmates' must rise (not later than 6.45 a.m. from 30 September to 31 March, and not later than 7.15 a.m. from

Adults and children, Poonindie, *c.* 1885.
(Courtesy of Mortlock Library of South Australiana.)

31 March to 30 September), attend prayers and start work. School hours and sanitary laws were prescribed. Liquor, drunkenness, swearing, obscene language, insubordination and impertinence were forbidden. Corporal punishment was banned except in extreme cases. Good conduct was to be rewarded with prizes.

Despite the hierarchical nature of the institution, Poonindie was in many ways a socialist experiment. It was financially independent, although, unfortunately not free from outside interference. The funds raised from its farming enterprise paid the wages of white and Aboriginal staff, paid for food (other than government rations) consumed on the mission, housed the families of staff and workers as well as the sick and unproductive and the orphaned and deserted children, who were also clothed and fed. It supported a school and free medical service. The institution did not only maintain its own invalids, deserted or orphaned children, but any Aboriginal person whom the Protector of Aborigines chose to send to it, including many children unable to support themselves and the sick and dying who had nowhere else to go.

Most of the farm work was done by the Aborigines: shepherding, droving, shearing, fencing, boundary riding, ploughing, reaping and sowing, breaking in of horses, training bullocks for ploughing. They did some of the maintenance work including carpentry, thatching and painting. Because no one was ever trained to do blacksmithing or mechanical repairs, white men were always employed to do these tasks. A white man was also generally employed to do the baking, cooking and butchering of meat. Aboriginal women did all the domestic work in their own houses as well as cleaning, cooking and sewing for the orphan children, cleaning of the communal areas including the church, and worked as servants for the white staff. They were paid wages for work apart from their own domestic tasks. In addition to the superintendent, overseer and teacher, white staff were employed from time to time to do cooking, maintenance work and occasionally farm work. The dismissal rate for drunkenness among white staff was higher than among inmates.

'Wurley natives' (that is Aborigines living in the Port Lincoln district who were not part of the institution) were employed to do labouring work at Poonindie, mainly grubbing and clearing of land.[17] In 1873 there were forty Aborigines employed in this way but by the 1880s very few were visiting Poonindie.[18] The Poonindie authorities assumed many of them had died, although it is possible their movement patterns changed and they no longer came to that part of Eyre Peninsula, despite Poonindie's attraction as a ration station.

In the mid-1860s Poonindie was still a relatively isolated community, but by the 1870s Port Lincoln was a thriving town and the mission land was surrounded by other farms and pastoral stations. In 1869 a ford was built across the Tod River making access to Port Lincoln much easier. Although the Tod seldom flows strongly, and often not at all, in times of heavy rain it can become a torrent. Before 1869 people had to wade through it or wait if they wanted to go to Port Lincoln. In 1873 a number of mines were operating in the district including one very close by at Louth Bay, on which Poonindie was located. Miners could earn much higher wages than the men were paid at Poonindie and the missionary was concerned that the men, particularly the young, single men might go there to work.[19] A hotel was operating nearby at North Shields in the 1870s not far from Poonindie and in 1878 a jetty was built at Louth Bay increasing the amount of shipping and traffic near Poonindie's boundary. Hale's early dream of a totally isolated community was well and truly buried by the 1870s.

This was not only due to the proximity of industry, farming and traffic. Poonindie men were always in demand as labourers on properties in the area. They had excellent reputations as ploughmen and shearers and this became a problem for the farm overseer. When he needed men to shear they were likely to be away working on properties around Eyre Peninsula. At one time the overseer made the men sign contracts to ensure Poonindie sheep were shorn.

Poonindie men also competed in local sports competitions. They played cricket regularly against the Port Lincoln team and played several matches against a prestigious Adelaide Anglican boys' school, St Peter's College, both in Adelaide and at Poonindie. They were also good athletes, winning most of the competitions against local whites. In the late 1870s and early 1880s they competed in ploughing and shearing competitions, generally taking out most of the prizes.

Many white people who visited Poonindie, particularly those who supported its missionary enterprise, were full of praise for its pretty whitewashed cottages and its neat and orderly appearance. Some claimed it was superior to English villages on which it had been modelled. Yet, despite the orderly, quaint appearance, living conditions were basic to the point of being depressed. The cottages were all uniform, consisting of one or two small rooms, which may have been adequate in the early days of childless couples, but were quite inadequate when children were born and survived. By the mid-1870s, Tom Adams and John Newchurch had five or six children each and their cottages were severely cramped. Tom Adams was given permission to add a room on to his cottage in 1878.[20]

No one went hungry at Poonindie: those who were not capable of working and earning a wage because they were too young or too sick were given rations. Apart from flour, tea and sugar, these might include mustard, pepper, pipes, treacle, vinegar, soda, and kerosene.[21] Generally there was enough work to keep all the able-bodied employed. Occasionally there was a shortage of workers, particularly at times of sickness or at shearing time when men went elsewhere in search of higher wages. From time to time Aborigines complained about wages particularly while Newland was overseer. Much more could be earned on pastoral stations. For much of this period the men earned 10 shillings a week plus rations on the mission, while they might earn 15 shillings or even £1 elsewhere. They could also earn higher wages at the mines in the area, particularly at times when labour was scarce. White men who worked at Poonindie in manual jobs were paid more than the Aborigines.

At one time when it appeared there would be a large exodus of men from the mission in search of higher wages, the authorities insisted that if men left Poonindie they would have to take their wives and children with them. That is, they were given the option of staying at Poonindie with its free accommodation, education and medical services, or maintaining themselves and their families on whatever wage they could earn somewhere else. Confronted with this choice most of the men opted for the security offered by Poonindie. On other occasions men did leave for a few months or years to work else-where. John Solomon and Andrew Hamilton left in June 1874 because Newland would not give them the wages they felt they deserved for cutting thatch. They wanted rates equal to those a white man would earn for the same work.[22] The men were paid accord-ing to the task they undertook—more highly skilled work such as shearing and plough-ing was paid at a higher rate than unskilled work such as clearing land.

Women were paid at a much lower rate than men for their work of cleaning, cooking and sewing. Complaints were occasionally made by the superintendent that some of the women took on paid employment, such as sewing for the orphans, to supplement family incomes rather than concentrating on their unpaid domestic duties.

Notwithstanding the vicissitudes of administration during the 1860s and 1870s, Poonindie became a stable, long-lived community. The forces holding it together were stronger than the disruptive ones and Poonindie became home to many families and young children. There are very few documented cases of people retreating to their places of origin, although there are occasional glimpses which suggest that many were probably not happy when they first arrived. Nellie Williams from Kingston wrote to Mrs Stuart, the missionary at her old home, after she came to Poonindie with two others from Kingston:

> Mr Holden said Dondle could go home. He was very sorry to hear his father died Dondle says when he once gets there he would not come back in a hurry he says he don't like Poonindie I wish I was going home with Dondle I don't like Poonindie a bit Bradley wants to know if you would be kind enef to tell is mother that he is coming home as soon as he can get enef money he is coming home.[23]

Matthew Mortlock, a long-time resident of Poonindie, wanted to go back to his coun-try of origin for a short visit. He appears to have had no wish to stay there but merely to renew acquaintance with the land and see the people. A few others also made brief visits 'home' at various times. There are no records of people not returning from these trips. Poonindie offered them security and a chance to marry and bring up a family in the knowledge that they would not be attacked or displaced by whites or find themselves in conflict with other Aborigines.

Disintegration and demise

By the 1880s the role of the institution had changed, but no one acknowledged it. When Hale established Poonindie he took teenagers who had spent their childhood in traditional Aboriginal society, followed by a few years in a European school, and trained them in European farming and domestic skills. By the 1880s Poonindie had a stable population of people who had learned these skills as a matter of course, either growing up at Poonindie, in other institutions or in the employ of white people. Poonindie was, therefore, no longer a training centre, but merely an institution where Aboriginal people lived and maintained themselves through their own labour under the supervision of white authorities. By this time a number of Poonindie Aborigines had acquired enough skills to run the institution without white supervision. Alternatively, with encouragement and financial assistance they could have established their own independent farms. These options were never considered by white authorities, and although many of the Aborigines considered alternatives at different times they never had the support or resources to carry them out.

The role of J. D. Bruce who was appointed farm overseer in 1878 and superintendent in 1882 is pivotal to the history of the latter years of the Poonindie mission. Bruce demanded complete subservience. Those who had previously held a privileged status at the mission because of their competence and experience, such as Tom Adams, clashed with Bruce who insisted 'The women are not permitted to go away from the Station without first asking Mrs Bruce permission and they have cheerfully complied with our wish and I think with kindness and firmness they will try to do what is right . . .'[24]

Bruce's attitude put him on a collision course with many of the Aboriginal people at Poonindie. Those who accepted his authority and kowtowed to him got on best. Those who stood up to him or insisted on independent action were locked in continual conflict with him. His reports to the trustees rarely have a positive word to say about the people's work and behaviour unless they won a competition or a cricket match. They are full of complaints and accusations. In 1884 typical reports from Bruce included such comments as: 'Ben Varco won £30 at the races and spent it all, he is a useless fellow'; '[Tom Adams] said he felt faint, I know what that means, but it won't go down just now, I mean to keep him going as long as I can get a . . . out of him'; '[Emma Donnelly] had to be sent away for bad conduct'; 'I do not want him [Tim Adams] back again, I would like to get his brother Tom to join him there it would be a good thing for Poonindie if he was gone'; 'I came across Todbrook in the dark armed with waddys, he threatened me'; 'Wetra and Todbrook stole a blanket last night out of the Boys Room. I will have to give them in charge of the police if they dont clear out'.[25]

When the previous superintendent, Shaw, left Poonindie, Bruce complained that he had spoiled some of the men. He claimed John Milera had got ideas above his position because Shaw had wanted to make a parson of him (he did eventually become a lay preacher); and that Tom Adams had been paid 15 shillings per week (instead of the usual

10 shillings) for doing next to no work.[26] Those who pleased Bruce were those who offered no threat to his authority and made a point of keeping on side. Tom Harbour wrote to one of the trustees in Adelaide,

> ... Fanny and I want to give both Mr and Mrs Bruce a birthday present [a box of ladys white handkerchiefs and a gentleman's watch guard] as we do like them so very much indeed Mr Bruce is very kind to us all more and more every day you don't know how kind he is to us all I for one have nothing against Mr Bruce.[27]

This letter does not sound convincing and contradicts the strong feelings expressed by a number of Poonindie men in a petition they sent to the Protector of Aborigines in 1887:

> Our grievance is that Mr Bruce is to us a like a tyrant master. We the undersigned do make it our business to tell you how Mr Bruce is treating us here he just does as he likes with us and when we tell the trustees about our grievances on Poonindie they don't take no notice of us . . .[28]

The Protector sent the complaint to Bruce and no further official action was taken. Bruce made strenuous efforts to find out who had signed it; he assumed Tim Adams was the instigator.[29] Despite Bruce's attempts to contain and control Poonindie completely, the conditions of the leasehold enabled free movement of Aborigines through Poonindie lands. Since 1852 Poonindie had been a ration depot for Aborigines of lower Eyre Peninsula. Local (non-institutionalised) Aborigines and those who had been dismissed or voluntarily left the institution had a right to remain on Poonindie lands. Bruce also tried to curtail the charitable functions of the institution. In 1883 he asked the trustees to have the ration depot moved to Port Lincoln, but the application was refused. In 1890 he tried again to limit entry so he could prevent Aborigines who did not belong to the institution camping there, but again without success.[30]

The lives of the Adams and Solomon brothers illustrate some of the effects Bruce had on lives of Poonindie residents. Tom and Tim Adams and the Solomon brothers were among the earliest children of mixed descent sent to the institution. They survived the early years of epidemic disease, did well at school and (apart from George Solomon who was handicapped and died young) became first-class farm workers with expert skills in shearing, ploughing, horse-breaking or thatching. After Bruce came to Poonindie, the fortunes of the Adams brothers, who did not get on with him, took a very different turn from the Solomon brothers, who did.

Tom and Tim Adams

An unskilled, uneducated labourer, Thomas Adams, married an Aboriginal woman Kudnarto (a name meaning third-born child in the Kaurna language)[31] from Crystal Brook in January 1848. This was the first legal marriage between an Aboriginal woman and white man in the colony of South Australia. After his marriage Thomas Adams applied to the Colonial Secretary to occupy some Aboriginal reserve land near Clare on Skylogolee (current spelling Skillogalee) Creek. In May 1848 Kudnarto (now Mary Ann Adams) acquired a licence to occupy Section 346 Skylogolee Creek during her lifetime.[32] This action set a precedent, and thereafter a number of white men, who were married to Aboriginal women applied to the Colonial Secretary to occupy Aboriginal reserve land (one of these men was George Solomon, father of John, Emanuel and George).

Kudnarto and Thomas produced two sons: Thomas (junior) was born in 1849 and Timothy in 1852.[33] After Kudnarto died in 1855 their father sent the two boys to Poonindie. Apart from a brief period Tom spent with his father, the two Adams boys grew up at the mission and became stalwarts of the institution. Tom was regarded as the top shearer in the Port Lincoln district for many years and did the maintenance work on the mission. Both men were good sportsmen, Tom excelling both at cricket and running. In the 1860s and 1870s Tom Adams was regarded as the most dependable and capable man at Poonindie: hard-working, productive, helping with church services in the absence of the superintendent.

Despite regarding Poonindie as his home and working hard for the success of the institution, Tom Adams (who was possibly speaking for his brother as well) applied many times for land in his own right where he might work as an independent farmer. When he was still a minor, his father, Thomas Adams, applied unsuccessfully on his behalf to regain the family's lost rights over section 346 on Skylogolee Creek. As early as the mid-1860s Tom Adams (junior) was making his own applications. After several fruitless applications for the lost land, Tom began making applications for land near Poonindie which continued sporadically over the next forty years.

He married Louisa Milera (née Roberts) in 1867.[34] She was of mixed descent and the widow of Frederick Milera by whom she had two children, Jessie and John. Tom and Louisa (known as Louie) had nine children, seven of whom were born at Poonindie. As the largest family on Poonindie they had accommodation problems in their small two-roomed house. In 1878 Tom received permission to build an additional bedroom and did all the work himself, including the thatching. The Adams had financial problems despite both Louisa and Tom working for wages at Poonindie. While William Holden was superintendent Tom's hard work and abilities were acknowledged and rewarded, but after Holden left Tom's slightly privileged position at Poonindie declined. Louisa did not get on with Mrs Randall when she was matron, and Tom clashed with Bruce from the moment of his arrival. Tom was somewhat protected from Bruce so long as Shaw remained superintendent, but thereafter his life became nearly unbearable. He had drinking and domestic problems in the 1880s. He fought with his wife and she fought with their daughter, Maria, who ran away several times. Eventually, in 1887 Tom and Louisa decided to move away from Poonindie and settle at Point Pearce, a mission to the east on Yorke Peninsula.

Tom's position at Poonindie had been completely reversed over a period of ten years. In 1878 the trustees were greatly concerned that he and his brother, two of the bastions of the Poonindie community, might leave; by 1887 Tom Adams and his family faced great pressure from Bruce to go.

Tom continued to think of Poonindie as his home and applied for land in the area on several occasions after he went to Point Pearce. In 1888 he wrote to the Protector of Aborigines:

> I am waiting for your reply about lease of land. There are only 80 acres in the section, but I prefer it to 160 acres anywhere else. I believe Mr Bruce has been trying to prevent me from having land, he makes out it is too close to Poonindie and has been talking to Mr Blackmore. Mr Bruce has been treating me very wrong and unjustly, it is not too close to the mission. I have seen natives down at

Point McLeay with land within 2 miles of the station. Thomas Playford offered me land by the harbour, but I didn't take it, I wanted it nearer my neighbourhood.[35]

In 1907 he finally gained his grant, but by this time his family was ensconced at Point Pearce, all, but one of his daughters were married there and Louisa did not want to leave.[36] Tom and Louisa both died at Point Pearce.

Fewer details are known of Tim Adams' life. Despite his early promise and a good report from Hammond in 1858, Tim was overshadowed by his brother in later life. He also suffered the tragedies of his first three wives' deaths. In 1871 he was recorded as married to Fanny from Franklin Harbour. By 1877 he was married to Bessie and they had four children, the eldest of whom, Lewis, was five. In 1878 Bessie died during an epidemic. In 1880 Tim married for the third time to Esther, who came from Kingston.[37]

By 1884 Tim was no longer registered as a resident at Poonindie. Probably accompanied by Esther, he moved restlessly around, mainly on upper Yorke Peninsula, leaving his four children to be looked after with the orphan children at Poonindie. He returned from time to time, much to the annoyance of Bruce. Tim left Poonindie in the late 1880s and settled at Point Pearce, where he married for a fourth time. He died on 5 March 1908.[38] Tom and Tim Adams' descendants stayed at Point Pearce and became mainstays of that community.

George, John and Emanuel Solomon

George Solomon married Rathoola, an Aboriginal woman, in January 1851. He and his wife obtained a licence to occupy section 1512 at the southern end of Fleurieu Peninsula on the same terms that Thomas Adams and Kudnarto had obtained reserve land. George had four children with Rathoola, who died on 20 August 1858 while the youngest was still a baby.[39] He then faced many of the same problems that plagued Thomas Adams. He eventually sent three of his sons to Poonindie, although Emanuel Solomon did not go to Poonindie until 1870.

John and Emanuel survived into old age. The Solomon brothers, like the Adams brothers, were highly respected at Poonindie. John married Lucy, one of the women sent to Poonindie from Western Australia. Mrs Holden, the superintendent's wife, held Lucy in high regard as the only woman she could depend on to do her washing and other domestic work. The couple left Poonindie in 1874 because John was dissatisfied with the wages the overseer was paying him for cutting thatch. He wanted the equivalent of European wages (which he was paid for thatching but not for cutting thatch). John and Lucy moved to Port Lincoln where they intended to stay until John earned enough money for a passage to Adelaide.[40] But Lucy was lonely away from her West Australian friends and within a few weeks they were back.

Not only was John a top ploughman, he also did shearing, horse-breaking and other farm work. When Newland was sacked as overseer in 1878 he succeeded in getting John to work for him for the high wage of 25 shillings per week at Moonabie, the northern run he bought from Poonindie.[41] In 1880 John won two prizes in the Port Lincoln district ploughing match. In 1883 he paid his own way to the national ploughing championships in Ballarat, where he performed very well, although not gaining a place.[42] His reputation made it easy for him to get work on other properties. Unlike the Adams brothers, John did not have his position at Poonindie undermined by Superintendent Bruce. To the great benefit of the family, relations between Bruce and all the Solomons, on the whole, ran smoothly.

John and Lucy had no children. Their marriage seems to have survived a period when John conducted an affair with Charlotte Yates, Robert Yates' wife. This created tensions between the Yates brothers and Solomon brothers resulting in physical clashes and temporary dismissal from Poonindie. In 1887 the Solomon brothers again were dismissed for a misdemeanour, but Bruce took them back in March as there was a State election pending and he did not want their presence in Port Lincoln stirring up feeling against Poonindie amongst the white community.[43]

John Solomon applied for, but did not obtain land when Poonindie was subdivided. In August 1896 he wrote a letter to the Surveyor-General asking if he could rent some of the Aboriginal reserve land as he was living in a tent adjacent to it and had no land of his own. He undertook to clear the land of rabbits and allow Aborigines to camp on the section not under cultivation. Although his application was supported by Mortlock, the local member of parliament, it was refused as the land had been dedicated as a reserve. In 1897 he applied again and was granted a permit to farm 160 acres of section 121 west. He owned a 4-ton boat and supplemented his farming with fishing and collecting guano.[44]

Emanuel Solomon arrived nine years after his older brother; presumably he lived with his father prior to being sent to Poonindie in 1870. Two years later he had a conversation with one of the trustees, whom he believed had promised him a place in a private school in Adelaide. When Emanuel realised he had been misled, he lost interest in education. As he could read and write well, he left school to work briefly for Newland, the overseer, then left Poonindie to work for higher wages (15 shillings per week) at a nearby farm.[45] After accumulating some money he moved to Adelaide. He later returned to Poonindie and married Jessie Milera (the daughter of Louie Adams and her first husband, Frederick Milera) on 24 November 1879. Jessie died of consumption in 1881.[46] In 1884 Emanuel married Amelia Stubbs (Milly) with whom he had four children. Like his brother, Emanuel lived sporadically at Poonindie, moving away from time to time to take up work on other farms. When the institution was closed in 1895 Emanuel was the only Aborigine to acquire any Poonindie land. Until he died in 1922 aged 66, he leased section 122 in the hundred of Louth which his brother, John, inherited. John, in turn, farmed it for a number of years, then sold it in 1936 for £1254. Emanuel's two daughters, Myrtle and Daisy, also stayed at Poonindie farming the land, first with Myrtle's husband, Walter Hirschausen, and after he deserted her, battling on alone with some financial support from their uncle.

Lucy, John's wife, died of cancer in 1924, but John survived until 1946. He continued to live at Poonindie and was caretaker of the church until he died. He was well known and respected in the district, as an Aboriginal man who had adopted the lifestyle and values of the dominant culture.

The long-term effects of Bruce's calculated use of favouritism to bolster his authority were that the Solomons were able to move away from institutionalised life, farm their own land and maintain an independent existence. The Adams, in contrast, who possessed the skills and desire to maintain themselves independently, were hounded from Poonindie to another institution. Many of their descendants now lead independent lives, but identify with Point Pearce, the institution where their parents grew up or with the Kaurna area where their ancestor Kudnarto originated, rather than Poonindie with which their ancestors Tom and Tim Adams identified.

Outside pressures to close Poonindie

Ultimately Bruce demonstrated that he was less concerned with the welfare of Poonindie people than with his own personal authority and welfare. As early as 1859 there had been resentment among the Europeans that the Aborigines were allocated so much land in their district. In 1881 it was rumoured that three out of four candidates for the State Lower House elections campaigned in Port Lincoln to have Poonindie land subdivided and sold.[47] In 1886 a petition was circulated among Europeans in Port Lincoln asking for Poonindie to be divided into working men's blocks and attempts were made to get some of the Poonindie Aborigines to sign it too by offering them alcohol as a bribe.[48]

There were suggestions in the 1880s and early 1890s that Poonindie should be moved from Port Lincoln to the interior so that the fertile land could be made available to Europeans. This, like all the other suggestions, showed total disregard for the Aborigines. They were considered usurpers of the land and fit only for the desert that no European wanted. In fact very few, if any, Poonindie people came from arid or semi-arid regions: they came largely from the coastal areas and many had grown up at Poonindie and only knew the lower Eyre Peninsula. They would have felt as alienated in arid areas as the Europeans did.

This continual agitation by local whites affected the Aboriginal residents as much as it did the administrators of the institution. The men worked on farms in the district and the Poonindie people did their shopping in Port Lincoln. They read local newspapers so they were aware of the whites' attitude to their home. The morale of the community slumped. Bruce noticed it in terms of increasing insubordination, but surprisingly the agricultural productivity of the institution was unaffected. Poonindie continued to produce top quality wool and cereals.

The economic depression of the 1890s, accompanied by high unemployment in rural areas, increased the pressures to make Poonindie land available to unemployed whites. An article in *The Register* in 1893 pointed out the plight of unemployed white men in the Port Lincoln district and how the breakup of their homes could be prevented if Poonindie land were made available to them.[49] In 1892 a question was put in parliament: 'Is it the intention of the Government to communicate with the trustees of the Poonindie Mission Station with a view of ascertaining on what terms they will give up their present holdings?'[50]

This mildly-worded question proved to be the death knell of Poonindie. The trustees wrote to the Minister of Education saying they assumed the government felt the time had come when the Poonindie Institution should cease to exist and submitted the terms under which they would hand over the lease. By 1896 all the Poonindie land had been subdivided and sold. The Anglican Church and the Poonindie trustees had abandoned the people without a fight.

The people were, of course, deeply concerned at the prospect of being thrown out of their home, but they had no control over disposal of their land and institution and obtained no support from the general community in their attempts to retain at least some of the Poonindie land. No one showed the least concern about the fate of up to eighty Aborigines. In 1895 several Poonindie men signed a petition to parliament in an attempt to retain some land for themselves:

> We the undersigned have been living on Poonindie for a number of years. We are very sorry to hear that the place is to be taken from us. It is very hard to be turned away from what has been our home. We would ask that the whole of the land on the south side of the Tod River, comprising we believe about 3,000 acres more or less of the poorest land on the whole run should be given to us. If this is given we propose to live on it and cultivate and work the land among ourselves. With this and what we can earn by shearing, fishing and getting guano, we can support ourselves and our families. We will do our best to work it and maintain ourselves which we shall be sorry to be turned away from.[51]

The majority of the population treated them with nonchalant disregard. The Aborigines were told that because most were of mixed descent they would get no special consideration in the apportioning of land at Poonindie, but they could apply and would be considered along with other applicants. When the land was allocated only two people from Poonindie obtained land (Emanuel Solomon and J. D. Bruce). The Aboriginal applicants queried why they had not been successful. They were told others had stronger claims. It is hard to imagine non-Aboriginal people could have a stronger claim on the land than those people who had lived on it for the past forty-four years and 'improved' it from scrubland to agricultural and pastoral land. One can only conclude that it was considered that white people had a prior claim over non-white. Unemployment among Aboriginal people posed no political problem.

In contrast, J. D. Bruce did very well out of the closure. He applied and was allotted land in 1894 in preference to John Milera and Fred Wowinda who had applied for the same block. In 1896 Bruce claimed that Fred Wowinda, Charles Power, Richard Newchurch and John Milera also lodged applications which they later withdrew.[52] This view does not accord with the reports from 1894 and suggests Bruce was interpreting the past to suit his own ends. He not only obtained land through dispersal of Poonindie lands, but through his association with the institution he bought land and stock at half-price from the trustees.

In 1896 he made a further application to lease the Aboriginal Reserve adjoining section 121, next to his property, and proved unsuccessful only because it had already been officially dedicated as reserve land. Only this section 121 and land to the east were saved for Aboriginal people from among all the thousands of acres which once constituted the Poonindie station. Aboriginal people could camp on this land, but they could not at first farm it. This was the same block John Solomon applied to farm, but it was not until 1897 when it was infested with rabbits that he was finally granted permission to farm and then only on the condition that the government retain the right to cancel his permit at any time.[53]

This photograph from the Public Record Office, South Australia, is labelled 'Port Lincoln, the last tribe'. It was probably taken about the time Poonindie closed in the 1890s.

Dispersal of the people

The dispersal of the Poonindie people was a much simpler and less controversial task than the disposal of the land. The trustees had insisted that they would not be responsible for anyone once the institution closed, yet they demanded compensation so they could continue work among Aboriginal people elsewhere. This new missionary work never eventuated. The trustees' attitude towards the Poonindie people after the closure reinforces the impression that their commitment to those people who had already been Christianised and 'civilised' was minimal. They had quite forgotten the ideals of Archdeacon Hale. Attempts by the Aboriginal people to retain some of the land for themselves were not supported by the trustees, and the trustees never made it a condition of the transfer of land that the Aborigines be given consideration. The superintendent's interests were in direct conflict with those of the Aborigines. In fact he was in direct competition with them for land. Long after Bruce had relinquished his position as superintendent he maintained influence over the lives of Poonindie people. His opinion was always sought over Aboriginal applicants for land in the Port Lincoln district; his recommendations continued to determine whether their applications were successful.[54]

Most of the Aborigines had been moved from Poonindie by mid-1894, a matter of satisfaction to the trustees who had to support them as long as they stayed at Poonindie. Sale of the land left the trust with no income. Most of the people chose to go to two other missions, Point Pearce on Yorke Peninsula, and Point McLeay south-east of Adelaide, but some stayed in the hope of being allocated land. At least one, Tom Harbour, went back to his people in the bush.[55]

The demise of Poonindie and the resulting disintegration of the community it housed is a gross example of greed and inhumanity. The original name of the institution, the Native Training Institution, had been lost along with its original function long before it was closed down. Mathew Hale had established a home and educational facility for Aborigines. One might criticise the reasons for which he established this facility, but once it was established he believed the Aborigines had a stake in it and when he left Poonindie he made it clear to them that it had been established for them. Nevertheless his words were not followed up by actions and he could not ensure the Aborigines would have any control over their own lives. By 1894 the Anglican trustees had abandoned any idea that the Aborigines had a stake in the institution. The trustees did not see themselves as having a continuing responsibility to Christianise, 'civilise', educate, feed and house the Aborigines. Nor did they retain any lingering vision of a holy village peopled by self-sufficient farmers. Their negotiations related only to the land. The government would have to dispose of the people and the easiest means the government had of disposing of them was to send them to other Aboriginal institutions.

At no point were the people treated as though they had real choices. They could go to another Aboriginal institution or remain at Poonindie, surviving on rations distributed by Bruce, as many did, and wait for the allocation of land they had little chance of obtaining. If they had obtained land, they would have had to go into debt to establish themselves on their blocks and few would have survived that experience. If the Poonindie trustees had underwritten the Poonindie farmers with financial guarantees, or distributed the £1000 the government paid them for Poonindie, a number of the Aborigines would have survived on the land as John and Emanuel Solomon did. Instead the money was put 'in trust' and ultimately disappeared.

Unlike the white authorities, the Aborigines did see options. A number were probably resigned to going to another institution. They had grown up and lived in a ghetto-like situation and would have found it difficult to adjust to another lifestyle, others saw the demise of Poonindie as an opportunity to lead independent lives and get away from their rural ghetto. Some had previously made attempts to leave by applying for land to farm. The only land they could apply for without financial resources was Aboriginal reserve land, which could only be leased and could be resumed with any improvements, at any time. The breakup of the Poonindie lands presented an opportunity for some to farm in their own right. Others believed they could continue to live collectively on part of the Poonindie lands and maintain themselves through farming, fishing and collecting guano from the off-shore islands. They petitioned parliament in the hope that they might obtain some land, keeping their sights low by asking only for the poorest sections. When this failed a number of men applied for working-men's blocks to farm as family units. This did not succeed either, so a few clubbed together and bought three sailing boats to collect guano which they sold as a fertiliser to farmers.[56]

Some of the Poonindie people decided to apply for residence on the rump of Aboriginal reserve land, despite the insecurity of title and tenure it offered. Some did obtain temporary leases which could be withdrawn at any time with no compensation for their improvements.

The meaning of the Poonindie experience

For all their tragic losses in 1894 the people survived, but without their treasured communal identity as Poonindie people. Most became Point Pearce or Point McLeay people. Yet Poonindie had played a vital role in their survival. Today descendants of Poonindie people claim Kaurna descent through their ancestors the Adams. Others could, if they chose, claim descent from the Pangkala/Nauo, the Meintangk in the south-east, the people from the upper Murray and possibly the Nukunu from the mid-north of South Australia.

In its early days Poonindie had an important function in sustaining Aboriginal people, giving them a new collective identity and kinship network replacing the traditional one they had discarded or had had stripped from them. By the 1880s this process was complete. Many of the people who had come as children (such as the Adams and Solomons) or had been born there (such as John and Jessie Milera) were adults with a confidence in themselves and their abilities which continued institutionalisation could only partially undermine. Some like Daniel and Mary Limberry left the institution and survived independently in the white community, but they did not go into the community with the support of the institution. As a result, many of the descendants of Poonindie people waited another two generations for a different political and social climate, to break away. Although the twentieth-century political economy of South Australia marginalised their descendants as paid workers, the memory of the skills, the wages, the joys of self-supporting agricultural labour at Poonindie lingered on in oral traditions of many families.

The other group of people who were affected by the closure of Poonindie were the local Aborigines, who did not belong to the institution but collected rations from Poonindie, camped on its lands and obtained casual, unskilled work there. Their welfare was not mentioned in the terms negotiated for the closure. The last population returns for Poonindie are from 1887 in which seventeen Aborigines are listed as camped at Poonindie cutting scrub and catching wallabies.[57] It is not known how many were still visiting Poonindie in the 1890s and what happened to them after it closed. They would have had to go to Port Lincoln for rations and to camp on the reserve land which was retained after Poonindie closed. The history of these people was very different from that of the Poonindie people and few of their descendants are known to survive today.

Bishop Hale heard about the closure of Poonindie not long before he died and wrote a letter of condolence to the people who had been moved from Poonindie:

> I little thought I should receive the sad news that you had been torn from your homes, where you and your fathers and mothers before you dwelt more than forty years, and that you had been scattered some here and some there over the Colony of South Australia and separated from one another.[58]

Tom Adams wrote back in response (although Hale died before receiving the letter).

Point Pierce

March 29th 1895

My dear father
I with the rest of your sons and daughters who are still alive received one of your printed letters . . .
It pained us very much to learn that the news concerning the fate of poonindie had reached you for
we know such news . . . have been but a blow to you in your letter you refer to us no doubt having
heard that in the early days of Poonindie we often had sorrowful times when it pleased God to take
from us some of our beloved one first one and then another causing us much grief—[illegible] yes not
as one who have heard but one who saw and experienced those times we indeed had much sorrow
and how at those times you used to talk to us about the bible and taught us to remember how God
said we must through much trial and tribulation enter the kingdom of Heaven some of us now are
here on the Point Pierce Mission and some at Point McLeay mission separated from one another and
feel as if we are strangers in a strange land and now dear father Poonindie is taken from us but not
without leaving good results I am sure it would please you very much to see some of the young
people who have grown up to be young men and women and who are a credit not only to themselves
but to the place where they have been brought up and who are now living monuments of the good
work Poonindie has done and of Christ Jesus . . . but we can't help feeling that we are amongst
strangers and the times is indeed hard with us but we know that here we have no continuing city but
we seek one to come.

And in a covering letter to Mr Hawkes Tom wrote: 'it is very hard for us to think of our
dear old homes and white people living there and we've got to pass by like strangers . . .
Although I did not belong to Poonindie when it was taken away, still we all love our dear
old home.'[59]

Notes

1 SRG 94/W83 Poonindie resident lists 1/4/1871, 30/9/1877, 13/12/1877, 31/12/1878,
   31/12/1880, Mortlock Library of South Australiana.
2 SRG 94/W83 correspondence 7/3/1870; 15/9/1873.
3 Fred Wowinda came from Victoria.
4 Children from this school were also sent to other missions, for example, Ramahyuck in Victoria: see
   Bain Attwood, *The Making of the Aborigines*, Sydney, 1989.
5 Holden also did not want to recruit from this area because it was within walking distance of
   Poonindie and he thought they would not stay at the mission: SRG 94/W83 correspondence, n.d.
6 SRG 94/W83 correspondence 3/8/1869.
7 SRG 94/W83 correspondence 14/9/1874, 28/9/1874, 16/1/1878, 23/2/1878, SRG 94 1049,
   13/10/1880.
8 SRG 94/W83 correspondence 30/10/1869, 26/12/1870; SRG 94 1062, 11/7/1870.
9 SRG 94/W83 correspondence 16/8/1869, 8/11/1869, 1/8/1873, 13/6/1877.
10 SRG 94/W83 correspondence 29/6/1877, 6/11/1877, 11/10/1877, 20/9/1877, 30/8/1877.
11 SRG 94/W83 correspondence 6/7/1877. Reproduced as written.
12 SRG 94/W83 correspondence 2/5/1879; 7/1/1881, 29/4/1881.
13 PRG 275 130/206, 18/3/1895, letter from G. W. Hawkes to Mathew Hale, Mortlock Library of
   South Australiana, GRG 52/1/376/1888, 239/1895, SAPRO.
14 GRG 52/1/239/1895.
15 SRG 94/W83 correspondence 23/2/1878.
16 Poonindie Native Institution, signed A. Adelaide in SRG 94/W83.

17 Wurley is an Aboriginal habitation. Before European contact wurleys were made from tree boughs over which were draped twigs, leaves or bark to give shade and shelter. After European contact materials such as old bags, canvas and tin were used.

18 SRG 94/W83 correspondence, 16/4/1873.

19 1874 Yearbook of Synod and Church of England Diocese of Adelaide, in J. D. Somerville, vol. 3, p. 228, Mortlock Library of South Australiana.

20 SRG 94/W83 correspondence 6/12/1878.

21 SRG 94/W83 correspondence 2/5/1879.

22 SRG 94/W83 correspondence 16/2/1874.

23 SRG 94/W83 correspondence 12/3/1874.

24 SRG 94/W83 correspondence 10/2/1882.

25 SRG 94/W83 correspondence 8/1/1884, 10/2/1882, 4/4/1884, 3/5/1884, 18/7/1884, 15/2/1884, 22/8/1884.

26 SRG 94/W83 correspondence 8/1/1884, 10/2/1882.

27 SRG 94/W83 correspondence 24/1/1886.

28 SRG 94/W83 correspondence 8/1/1887.

29 Part of the petition, including the signatories is missing, so this cannot be verified.

30 SRG 94/W83 correspondence 13/6/1883; Somerville, vol. 3, 1/11/1890.

31 Meredith Edwards, *Tracing Kaurna descendants: The saga of a family dispossessed*, Adelaide, 1986, p. 1.

32 GRG 24/6/15/2/1848, 4/A/1855/1633.

33 Thomas Adams (senior) signed a declaration on 11 January 1869 that Tom was born 19 June 1849 and Tim 11 October 1852 (GRG 52/1), but Poonindie records show Tom as being ten years older than Tim, that is, in 1877 Tom Adams was 36 years old, Tim 26 years (SRG 94/W83, 30/9/1877) which suggests Tom was born in 1841 in which case Kudnarto was not his mother (she was 9 years old in 1841). It is possible Adams senior falsified his son's birthdate in his efforts to regain the land at Skylogolee.

34 GRG 52/7 Protector of Aborigines Letterbook, vol. 3, 7/2/1867.

35 GRG 52/1/129/1888.

36 Somerville, vol. 5, 164 Aborigines Office 72/1907.

37 SRG 94/W83.

38 P. Brock and D. Kartinyeri, *Poonindie: the rise and destruction of an Aboriginal agricultural community*, Adelaide, 1989, p. 94 genealogies.

39 GRG 52/7/13/1/1851; Somerville, vol. 2, 149; CL & I Office no. 649/1858, 11/10/1858.

40 SRG 94/W83 correspondence 20/6/1874.

41 SRG 94/W83 correspondence 6/9/1878.

42 SRG 94/W83 correspondence 22/8/1880; SRG 94/W83 correspondence –/6/1883.

43 SRG 94/W83 correspondence 18/7/1878, 2/9/1881, 11/3/1887.

44 Somerville, vol. 4, 373, Surveyor-General's Office, 8/2/1896; GRG 52/1/1897/32; GRG 52/1/1895/236/21/1895.

45 SRG 94/W83 19/3/1872, 21/4/1881.

46 SRG 94/W83 21/4/1881.

47 SRG 94/W83 correspondence 16/3/1881.

48 Somerville, vol. 3, *The Review* 1/11/1890.

49 9 May 1893. Similar attitudes prevailed in Western Australia, where Aborigines in the south-west were forced off the land at the turn of the century: see Anna Haebich, *For their own good. Aborigines and government in the southwest of Western Australia 1900–1940*, Perth, 1988, pp. 28–35.

50 Somerville, vol. 3, 524, CSO 199/1892.

51 SA Legislative Council 5/9/1895, pp. 291–2.

52 Somerville, vol. 4, 431, Church of England, 99; J. W. Davis, 'Poonindie Aboriginal Station 1850–95. A study in race relations', unpublished BA (Hons) thesis, University of Adelaide, 1971, p. 37.
53 Somerville, vol. 4, 334, Surveyor-General's Office 3242/96 30/3/1896; Somerville, vol. 4, 331, Crown Lands Office 542/1896; GRG 52/1/1897/32.
54 GRG 52/1/1897/32.
55 Somerville, vol. 4, 429, Church of England Poonindie Papers, 87a; GRG 52/1/1895/284.
56 PRG 275 130/206.
57 SRG 94/W83 correspondence 13/3/1887.
58 PRG 275/130/205. Hale does not acknowledge that he created similar upheavals for the recruits he took to Poonindie forty-five years earlier.
59 PRG 275/130/207.

5

Koonibba, a Refuge for West Coast People

The west coast of South Australia extending from Eyre Peninsula to the Australian Bight was inhabited by the Wirangu, Kokatha and Mining peoples. At this historic distance it is not known with certainty how these different language and cultural groups were disposed at European contact, although it is generally accepted that the Mining occupied the territory at the head of the Bight and Eucla at what is now the Western Australian/South Australian border. The Wirangu (also referred to as Julburra speakers) extended further east along the coast and as far north as Ooldea.[1] But territorial definitions cannot be precisely described as the populations were not static in the nineteenth and twentieth centuries and perhaps never had been. The Kokatha, of the Western Desert cultural bloc, were moving south creating a disruptive effect among the Wirangu, Nauo (southern Eyre Peninsula) and Pangkala (eastern Eyre Peninsula) as well as introducing new cultural influences to these peoples. European incursion and, later, the 1914–15 drought, caused further shifts in Aboriginal populations.[2] By the late nineteenth century the Wirangu, Kokatha and possibly the Ngalia (north of Nullarbor Plain) were holding joint ceremonies on the west coast, in the Gawler Ranges and to the north.[3] This suggests that the Wirangu under pressure had adapted their cultural and ceremonial life to that of the Kokatha.

The Lutherans were told there were 500–600 Aborigines on the west coast in 1898.[4] The Wirangu, Kokatha and Mining moved throughout the district. The west coast area was able to support very large gatherings of Aborigines at this time. It was not unusual for 200–300 people to meet together for ceremonies. In the first few years of the mission, groups of between 150–250 would gather there preparatory to moving on to ceremonial grounds. This is evidence of a very vigorous religious and cultural life.

This impression of cultural fluidity among these peoples is reinforced by what is known of linguistic changes in the area. The first missionary at Koonibba ascertained

Koonibba and its region

that there were three or four languages spoken by visitors to the mission, but he identified Wirangu as the primary one and attempted to learn it.[5] By the 1920s Kokatha had
become the predominant Aboriginal language; the missionary at that time considered
Wirangu almost extinct.[6] During the twentieth century people from the north, who used
Ooldea as a staging post, moved south. The Kokatha, who had at one time predominated
at Ooldea, were displaced by Antikarinja and later Pitjantjatjara. These people began
visiting Koonibba from the 1930s.[7]

Australia's colonial economy stretched out to the west coast of South Australia and its
peoples when W. R. Swan established a pastoral station at Yalata between 1858 and
1860. Other pastoral leases followed. The first ration depot for Aborigines on the west
coast was established at Fowlers Bay in 1862, indicating that the disruptive effects of pastoralism on their movement patterns and economic activities were immediate.[8] By the

1880s a new industry had made a major impact on Aboriginal life, as kangaroo hunters set up camps on and around the Nullarbor Plain.

Both pastoralists and kangaroo hunters employed Aborigines, utilising their hunting and tracking skills and knowledge of the country. But while the pastoralists had a long-term stake in the far west, the kangaroo hunters were temporary intruders, present only so long as they had a sufficient supply of kangaroos. Aborigines were attracted to their camps by the ready supply of food and goods, but there were reports of women being badly treated and sexually exploited by the white kangaroo hunters. By 1894 most of the kangaroo hunters had left the area because of lack of water and game. It was also reported that the Aborigines were starving because they wanted to maintain their communal existence and would not split up to work for farmers, who refused to pay them wages.[9]

This report indicates two important factors in the process of acculturation of the west coast people in the 1890s. First, they had been in contact with Europeans long enough to realise when they were being exploited by unscrupulous farmers who refused to pay them wages for their labour. They were prepared to work for a return on their labour, but otherwise would not be enticed into employment by empty promises. Second, they participated in the rural economy as long as it did not threaten their communal existence, but individuals were not prepared to leave the group to seek work.

Aborigines also made periodic visits to the small towns in the region, including Fowlers Bay and Penong, where there were pubs and police stations. The towns introduced them to the degrading effects of alcohol and British law and penal detention. The police also distributed rations to Aborigines who were starving and unemployed, enabling them to maintain contact with Aborigines and keep track of their movements.

While pastoralism and kangaroo hunting disrupted Aboriginal life, they were not totally destructive. Aborigines showed they could adapt to changing circumstances. Those who were attracted to towns and homesteads for periods of time could always retreat to their own people, maintaining their ritual and ceremonial life and accustomed diet. Had these conditions prevailed, a balance between new and old elements of their lives might also have been achieved.

But change followed change. The pastoral leases granted from 1860 expired in 1888, and there was strong pressure on the government to divide up the land into smaller agricultural units. The government responded by sending surveyors out to subdivide the Hundreds of Horn, Bartlett, Moule and Catt and the County of Way into blocks suitable for agriculture. These became available under Right to Purchase Leases or Perpetual Leases and through the 1890s and into the twentieth century land subdivision extended to the edges of the Nullarbor Plain.[10]

Agriculture used land far more intrusively than pastoralism and represented a formidable attack on Aboriginal ritual and economic activities. From the late 1890s there were reports of Aborigines near starvation. In 1898, 100 starving Aborigines were in the Penong district and another 350 were expected from Streaky Bay and the Gawler Ranges. They accused the whites of killing all their game. Again, in 1902 large numbers of Aborigines were in desperate straits around Bookabie.[11]

It was at this time of change from pastoralism to agriculture that the Lutheran Church decided to establish a mission on the west coast. This mission station, later to be called

Koonibba, thrust a double-edged presence into the region. It offered a refuge to Aborigines increasingly displaced by the new land use, but it also operated to accelerate alterations in the lifestyle and values of the Aborigines who came to depend on it.

In addition, Aborigines of mixed descent were present on the west coast who had had extensive contact with Europeans and had acquired their work skills and understood their modes of behaviour. Some were keen to establish themselves independently on farms. There are records of at least three people of mixed descent leasing blocks, and the police at Fowlers Bay believed there were several who would work the land if given the chance.[12] But most did not have the opportunity to establish themselves independently, and those who did attempt it did not have the financial resources to sustain their independence. These men were to be a major influence at Koonibba in its early days.

A farm overseer, J. Pannach, launched the mission in June 1898 as no missionary had yet been found. To an outside observer Koonibba must have looked like any other farm in the area, a few white men battling against the elements, not an Aborigine in sight. Then in October, while Pannach was in Adelaide collecting his wife and family, an acting manager reported the first Aboriginal visit to the station, five men and five women. The men were asked to work for rations clearing land. They were already accustomed to such demands, for on the first day they each cleared half an acre, greatly impressing the acting manager. A family group followed and it was rumoured that others were on their way from Fowlers Bay.[13]

By the end of 1898 Koonibba mission had taken over the function of distributing government rations to the old, sick and children from the neighbouring farmer, W. McKenzie. A supply of potential converts was thus assured. Numbers of Aborigines on the station varied from week to week and even from day to day.

As many as a hundred people might gather for ceremonies and then suddenly move off to the ceremonial grounds, leaving only the old and sick and a few people of mixed descent who did not want to participate.[14] Sudden drops in numbers also occurred when the station ran out of rations (for example, May 1900, September 1901). It is difficult to identify precisely who these people were. There were reports of Gawler Ranges and Wilgena people in the district and also unspecified 'wild blackfellows' frightening the local people. Early in 1899 Pannach counted seventy-four Aborigines at the station, two-thirds of whom he had not seen before. Not long after this, he received a letter from an Aborigine at Yardea in the Gawler Ranges (a previous visitor to the station whose letter was written for him by a white), who said they were waiting for 'a mob' from Port Augusta and would then all proceed to Koonibba.[15]

Pannach also helped Aborigines at Koonibba to write to people all over the west coast and Wilgena inviting them to meet at the mission. Each letter included the observation that a 'mob of wild Blackfellows is coming'. Pannach did not realise the implication of this warning until one morning pandemonium broke out at the station when some of the women said they had seen wild Aborigines spying at their camp. The women ran in all directions screaming, the workers abandoned their work, leaving plough and horses in the field while they ran to borrow Pannach's rifle and arm themselves. But it turned out to be a false alarm.[16] (Who might these 'wild' people might have been? Were they Kokatha, and if so from where? It is obvious that the Wirangu and Kokatha from the

Gawler Ranges were in frequent contact; perhaps the Wirangu were expecting a pay back [revenge attack] for some real or perceived injury done to a member of another Aboriginal group.)

These west coast people learned quickly that letters were a powerful means of communication even though they themselves were illiterate. They used letters written by intermediaries to make contact over long distances and when the opportunity presented itself at Koonibba to learn to read and write, many enthusiastically jumped at the chance—an indication of Aboriginal agency and adaptation, using European innovations for their own purposes.

Most Aborigines only stayed for short periods on the station, helping with land clearing or other farm work, but others stayed for extended periods. Two who later became permanent and valued members of the mission were Jimmy Richards and Willoughby. Jimmy Richards was of mixed descent and is first mentioned as visiting the station in May 1899. Willoughby is also first mentioned in 1899 as a reliable worker who even at this early period was encouraging other Aborigines to come to Koonibba.[17]

In these early years the Aborigines used Koonibba as they would any other camp. There were no European houses. They arranged themselves according to their own strict social forms. The first missionary noted:

> They have the custom that strangers must not enter the camp after sunset and see to it that they are not admitted. They arrange their camp in a certain order. Those who belong to the same tribe also camp together. When they greet each other they do not shake hands.[18]

As the mission settlement became established, the camp remained physically and ideologically separate. It experienced minimal interference from the mission staff. It was a refuge where people were able to maintain their own social and cultural forms.

Reports from these early years suggest three overriding motives for people to visit the mission station. First, there was curiosity. What did this new phenomenon offer? They found it resembled other ration depots; the sick and infirm were issued with rations, while the able-bodied were expected to work for rations provided by the Church. Some expected the mission to be benevolent and insisted that a mission should maintain them without expecting work in return.[19] Second, people came to get water during periods of drought. Pannach was continually carting water from distant tanks because the tanks he built had not filled during the drought and his well produced salt water, which had to be distilled. Third, Koonibba rockhole was a ceremonial ground and traditional meeting place. It was convenient for people to collect rations while they assembled for ceremonies. As long as there was no missionary at the station they faced no undue pressure to abandon their religious and cultural activities. Pannach showed them pictures and told them stories from the Bible, but he was not in a position to try to convert them.

Koonibba depended as much on the Aborigines as the Aborigines depended on it. The mission could not exist without Aboriginal labour to clear land, build and farm. Pannach reminded the mission board that although it was paying for rations of the able-bodied workers, it was getting very cheap labour in return. While it would have cost £91 to pay white labour to clear 280 acres, Aborigines did it for rations costing only £30.[20] This cheap route to land improvements made good business sense. In 1900 Pannach had the highest return from scrubland of any farmer in the district. By the end of 1900, 600 acres of land had been cleared and 300 of them fired, a four-roomed stone house had been built, as well as a smithy, an iron hut, a stable, a hayloft and a wagon shed roofed with pepper bush and three tanks capable of holding 32,000 gallons.[21]

The first missionary period 1902–16

C. A. Wiebusch arrived at Koonibba with his wife in December 1901 to take up the post of missionary to the Aborigines. Though born and raised in Germany he had studied at the Lutheran seminary in St Louis in the USA and spoke English well. He immediately set about instructing adults, youth and children in the basic precepts of Christianity. He faced a very different task from Mathew Hale's pioneering work at Poonindie. Few of the Aborigines spoke English, and only one or two had had any previous schooling. Wiebusch spoke no Aboriginal language. His task was formidable: no common language, no common cultural norms, totally different lifestyles. He was a literate teacher with a non-literate pool of potential converts. Wiebusch found that the best way to communicate was through music and pictures. Visual cues and music are both essential aspects of Aboriginal life and culture and the Aborigines were very happy to add new songs to their musical repertoire.

Unlike Hale at Poonindie, the Lutherans had no articulated set of principles or aims for their missionary work on the west coast. There is no recorded discussion on how the mission should relate to its regional environment, or on the ultimate fate of the Aborigines. It was noted that the Aborigines wandered in all directions and that if the Church wanted to evangelise them, they must be encouraged to stay in one place through provision of food and clothing.[22] The missionaries also believed in the principle of no work, no bread; all Aborigines who joined the mission were expected to be productive members of the community. The assimilationist aims of the mid-nineteenth century were no longer evident. Education, an important aspect of the mission process, was related to Christianising, rather than preparing Aborigines for a role in the general community (this expectation changed later in the second era of assimilation). Nevertheless, the mission was run on very strict principles whereby willingness to conform to missionary expectations was strongly rewarded.

Wiebusch set himself the task of learning the names of all the people who came to the mission. He would gather the Aborigines together at their camp site in the bush at 6 o'clock in the evening for a roll call. In the first few weeks he compiled a list of fifty-four names including children. Men were too tired for religious instruction after work so he started classes in the morning. A flag was raised at 7.45 a.m. to indicate the beginning of school. The flag also signalled mealtimes; if people did not get their food while the flag was up, they missed out. In the evenings Wiebusch would take his violin to the camp and teach the Aborigines to sing hymns, in the hope that these songs would replace their 'bad' singing, that is, their ceremonial songs, but he concluded that it had the opposite effect, because after an evening of singing hymns they would then move on to their own traditional songs and continue dancing and singing right through the night. Occasionally these ceremonies continued on for days until the Aborigines were exhausted and little farm work was done. Much as he disliked these 'corroborees', Wiebusch realised he could not ban them or all the Aborigines would leave the station. By 1907 ceremonies were no longer held on the station but nearby so that people living at Koonibba could attend—another indication of the adaptability of the west coast people, who maintained their ceremonial life, while taking advantage of services offered by the mission.[23]

Koonibba's first clients lived in a richer cultural milieu than the first recruits to Poonindie. Hale had run his missionary programme as if his converts had emerged from a cultural vacuum. He never acknowledged having to work against a competing set of beliefs and cultural forms, but these were a major obstacle for Wiebusch. He ran classes for the men in the morning before work, for the young adults in the evening in his study—where he taught them reading and writing which some were very keen to learn—and during the day he ran a school for nine children. He taught them English and, while complaining of their restlessness, praised their rapid progress. He also related biblical stories to them and taught them the words of hymns. He found the children taught the words to the older people (who knew no English) back in camp. The children were most receptive to learning and he made much faster progress with them than with the younger and older adults.[24]

Wiebusch discovered that as well as music and pictures his students loved ceremony or special celebratory occasions. At the end of his first year at Koonibba he organised a 'Schulfest'. This was, in fact, an exam or test, but was accompanied by games and gifts of fruit and sweets. It was such a success that those who missed out on the 'Schulfest' because they were at Tarcoola for initiation ceremonies, vowed they would not miss the next one. Sure enough, the following year 175 Aborigines assembled at the mission for the 'Schulfest'. They camped about 3 miles south of Koonibba to conduct initiation cer-emonies, but put them off so they would not miss the ceremony at Koonibba. There were seventy children at the 'Fest' including German and English children. In the morning the Aboriginal children were given their tests: 15 minutes reciting the catechism, 30 minutes writing and reading; and 20 minutes arithmetic. This was followed by geography, nature studies and singing. After the tests the children were given presents. Children resident on the mission received books, toys and sweets, while new arrivals received only sweets. Many of the Europeans had come specifically to hear the Aboriginal children sing, so in the evening they performed for an hour.[25] The parents were then allowed to take their children away for three weeks holiday, but were asked to return them in time for Christmas. Wiebusch said some of the children did not want to leave and begged their parents to let them stay. In the event eleven did stay rather than go with their people, indicating that both children and adults appreciated Koonibba as a secure haven.[26]

Christmas was another ceremonial time which the Aboriginal people loved, and it remained a major ceremonial and social event for both Christian and non-Christian throughout the years of the mission. The first Christmas celebration Wiebusch organised in 1902 was marred by a measles epidemic, which killed many west coast Aborigines. Nevertheless, he put up a sandalwood Christmas tree in the schoolroom decorated with lights. There was also a nativity scene. At 8 o'clock in the evening, after some had been waiting excitedly outside for two hours, the people were allowed in. They were amazed and delighted by what they saw, saying 'Minja gidja! minja Messeia' (the child,

Christmas at Koonibba in the first years of the mission.
(Courtesy of the E. W. Wiebusch Collection, Aboriginal Photographic Project, Aboriginal Heritage Branch, Department of Environment and Planning, South Australia.)

the little Messiah) when they saw the nativity scene. Their Christmas present was a football.[27]

Wiebusch claimed the rate of conversion at Koonibba was high compared to many other missions in southern South Australia. The first adult baptism occurred in November 1903 and by 1909, 45 people had been baptised, 28 of them on 21 February 1909. When Wiebusch visited Point McLeay mission in 1909 he was impressed by its physical achievements but shocked by the small number of people (41 out of a total of 300 at Point McLeay) he believed had been converted over fifty years.[28]

Wiebusch saw a need for careful teaching and explanation to the first generation of converts for whom everything was new. This put both the missionary and potential converts under pressure in their instruction. The converts learned the Ten Commandments, the short catechism, prayers and hymns and were publicly tested on both knowledge and understanding before being baptised. The first convert, Jimmy Richards, who could already speak English and had had some schooling, was under baptismal instruction for twenty-one months before he and Wiebusch felt confident about his knowledge and commitment.[29] Others continued under instruction for many years before they were baptised, either because they left the mission periodically, or because they could not speak English or because they were slow learning to read or write.

But the main problem seems to have been their uncertainty about giving up their own beliefs and way of life, making a commitment to Christian ethics and adopting the ethic of regular work, little leisure and a sedentary existence. The evidence suggests that the mission fulfilled very different roles for the Aborigines to those envisaged by the missionary. For many west coast people Koonibba was a refuge from the increasing pressures of agriculture and other changes in the region and a safe haven for their children. Their religious life was vigorous and had not as yet become seriously undermined by European colonialism. The majority of people were not seeking out an alternative set of beliefs. Conversion could result in loss of adult status in Aboriginal society, which is conferred through initiation and other life experiences, and the acceptance of the status of novice and eternal child. This dilemma did not face Hale's converts, who were uninitiated youth. Most of the earliest Koonibba converts were, therefore, drawn from people of mixed descent who had grown up in contact with Europeans, immigrants, or uninitiated minors. But the elders of the community apparently wanted to maintain cohesion among their own people and put pressure on all those associated with Koonibba to participate in the ceremonial life. A Ngalia man, Yendinna Jack, and other elders would visit Koonibba to take children away for initiations, returning them after the ceremonies.[30]

Wiebusch linked conversion to material rewards of food and shelter and the routine of mission life. He believed that these were valued by the Aborigines, when it is evident that they were not their only concern. As a result, Koonibba developed a special kind of landscape which reflected the peculiar nature of this struggle. Both Aborigines and missionary were united in a desire to maintain Koonibba as a refuge, but they divided the land into the two poles of mission and camp. Camp people received rations for work but were not constrained by the mission, coming and going as they pleased. Those in the mission settlement were hedged about with obligations and were punished if these were not fulfilled. If a person decided to be baptised—and for many it was a joyful and important event—there were the benefits of better food and clothes, better presents at Christmas, increased wages and eligibility for a cottage.[31] On the mission, they advanced from second-class to first-class citizens.

Baptism was not the final goal for the missionary. He faced continual 'backsliding' and many converts left the mission temporarily (some permanently) or reverted to what the missionary regarded as sinful ways, particularly related to sex, drinking and gambling. The lives of some of the early converts are quite well documented and, although we can only view them through the eyes of the missionary (they have not left any first-hand accounts), it is possible to understand the great turmoil they went through trying to decide which direction their lives should take. Jimmy Richards was the first adult convert and Wiebusch recorded his conversion in detail.[32]

Jimmy (Thomas) Richards

It is not known from where Jimmy Richards came when he arrived at Koonibba in 1899. He was of mixed descent, born about 1873, had been to primary school in Port Lincoln for three years and could read and write. He was also a skilled workman, although it is not known where he learnt blacksmithing, carpentry and other skills. Richards was a great boon to the farm manager, who was short of skilled labour. Richards proved to have skills and discipline equal to any white worker.[33] Although he left the station at some stage he returned in 1900 with his family and worked with two other men of mixed descent for food, clothing and tobacco. When Wiebusch arrived at Koonibba, Richards, who had been working on another farm in the district, came back to meet him and was persuaded to undergo instruction for baptism, the first Aboriginal person at Koonibba to do so.

He started instruction on 19 February, a momentous milestone for Wiebusch who recorded the struggle in great detail. By mid-April Richards had already learnt some prayers, the Ten Commandments and the Three Articles of Faith. He understood them and could explain them in his own words. But Richards' decision to stay on the mission and take instruction was not easily taken and he went through terrible traumas over whether to carry on or not. He had initially come to the mission to work. He was the only Aborigine to be paid in these early days for it was recognised he could earn a £1 a week anywhere else in the neighbourhood. He set up a smithy and did all the blacksmithing for the station.

He was less fortunate outside the workplace. He and his wife fought. He accused her of going with other men and not maintaining European standards of dress and cleanliness. He wanted to fight two other men whom he suspected had relations with his wife. After Wiebusch persuaded him not to do so, he left his wife and the station. When he returned he refused to have anything more to do with his wife, although he showed deep concern about his children's welfare.[34] He agreed to take religious instruction but was more interested in his blacksmithing work, until he was moved by a dramatic event at the mission. One very hot summer's day 130 acres of dry wood was being burnt after having been cleared of scrub. The heat and smoke were intense and for a few minutes the sun was blocked out making the scene quite unearthly. At this point Wiebusch brought out a picture of Christ wearing the crown of thorns kneeling and praying in the garden of Gethsemane. He explained to the gathered Aborigines how Christ could shield them from punishment for their sins. Wiebusch believed this event made a great impression on Jimmy Richards and cemented his commitment to religious instruction. He went to the missionary's house most evenings and was taken through the small catechism. The first evening after the fire he came to Wiebusch in tears believing he was too sinful to be saved. He stayed for two hours hearing how the love of the Saviour could save sinners. His enthusiasm for instruction continued for some time; he wrote himself songs in a small book which he took to the smithy with him each day. Wiebusch was deeply satisfied with his success.

Then Richards stayed away for four days having taken offence at something Wiebusch did or said. The proud missionary stood his ground refusing to go to Richards, waiting for Jimmy to repent of his anger and self-conceit. Then the lessons continued. Wiebusch dwelt on the sufferings of Christ (Leidengeschichte) hoping to worry Jimmy about his own earlier sins.

But there were counter pressures from Richards' family and other Aborigines, who disapproved of his conversion and tried to draw him away. This made him very volatile and moody as he tried to work out for himself what he should do. He rarely left the station when the others moved on for ceremonies or a change of scene; on the other hand he was not in a hurry to be baptised even when Wiebusch thought he was ready. He was determined to understand fully the religion he was planning to adopt, and was perhaps giving himself time to change his mind. Richards was as conscientious in his work as he was in religious instruction. During the day he worked in his smithy and found time to do most of the building work on the mission, a skill he seems to have taught himself. He built two rooms for himself on to the smithy. He also built a cottage for a white worker and two cottages for Aboriginal families and the first mission church.[35]

In August 1902 Wiebusch left the station for eight weeks and when he came back he found many adults, including Jimmy Richards, had left because of a death on the mission. Richards returned to the mission in time for Christmas, a celebration that greatly impressed him. That festival and the many deaths from measles on the west coast at this time reawakened his interest in Christianity which had waned in his absence from the mission, but doubts continued. When feeling low he would flare up at small things, would stop going to instruction, avoid Wiebusch and be rude to everyone. He would stir up feelings against the mission among the others. Then he would express shame at his behaviour, start his instruction again and delight Wiebusch with his questioning mind and enthusiasm.

In mid-1903 Richards seems finally to have come to a decision and Wiebusch claimed that everyone on the mission noticed his change in mood. He was much happier and even-tempered. He also remarried about this time. His young wife, Nellie Gray, an Aboriginal woman of full descent from Fowlers Bay was not interested in Christianity and tried to discourage him. He, in turn, tried to prevent her from mixing with the Aborigines who lived in the camp. Jimmy Richards was finally baptised on 18 October 1903 on the same day that the church he had built was dedicated. The night before his baptismal day he was very nervous, worried that he would not be able to answer the questions put to him and people would make fun of him, but then decided: 'With the help of God I'll face the people'. He began his examination very nervously, but gained confidence over the 50 minutes of questioning. He emerged the first Koonibba adult convert and took on the name Thomas Richards.[36]

His interest in religion continued, but so too did his doubts. He often discussed religious questions with Wiebusch and when George Saunders and Joe Miller started baptismal instruction, he would often attend and help them with the harder questions. He took prayers and Bible readings at the farm manager's house and divine service when Wiebusch was unavailable. But at other times his moodiness would return and he would refuse to pray or talk about religion. One such occasion was after he took a trip to Fowlers Bay and Penong where he met old friends who encouraged him to give up his new beliefs. He wanted to leave the mission and was in a black mood for many days. Eventually Wiebusch sent a letter across to the smithy:

> My Dear Friend Thomas! How long are you going to remain under the dark cloud of anger? Should you strive to get rid of it through sincere contrition and repentance, mindful of the word of your Lord: Let not the sun go down upon your wrath, and of the Fifth Petition: 'Forgive us our trespasses as we forgive those who trespass against us?' (signed) Your pastor and true friend . . .

Thomas responded a few hours later:

> Dear Teacher and Friend, I am very sorry that I have cursed and sinned against God and you. I will take back all my saying. Please lay not this charge against me. I will heartily repent. Please forgive me. Yours truly Thomas Richards[37]

What the missionary perceived as a purely spiritual struggle had secular aspects. Richards had other problems eating away at him relating to his work. He was the most skilled worker at Koonibba and knew it. He knew the mission would find it difficult to replace him if he left. He also knew he could earn much more working off the mission, as he was known as a good worker over much of the Peninsula. At times when he was at peace with himself and the mission he was happy to work there for a reduced wage. At one juncture the mission offered him 18 shillings per week (less than he could get elsewhere) but he would only take 14 shillings because he said the mission had given him so much.[38] At other times he expressed a strong urge to leave. The missionary and farm manager considered various ways of dealing with their prize pupil and worker.

Early in 1903 Richards indicated he would like more independence and asked for 40 acres of land to work in lieu of wages, plus board. This was agreed to as it would commit him to staying on the mission, but the authorities were equally happy to pay him a higher wage than the other Aboriginal workers. Their main concern was that they not set a precedent which would be demanded by the other workers, particularly Joe Miller. Unfortunately the experiment of giving Richards his own land to work failed when his crop, along with most of the Koonibba crop was destroyed by redrust. He was, nevertheless, compensated and also given a suit. He was allowed to do blacksmithing for neighbouring farmers to earn extra money: 1/6 per hour plus the cost of the metal. At one time after all the white workers left Koonibba, Richards, Joe Miller and George Saunders were given higher wages to take over their work, but Richards complained that he was expected to buy his own and his family's clothes, while others did not.[39]

And so his moods continued to seesaw. The mission authorities would periodically panic at the prospect of his departure while striving to conceal their realisation that he was indispensable (which he obviously must have known). On one of his trips away from the mission he became very sick and nearly died but he went to hospital in Adelaide and recovered. He worried that if he died his wife and children would leave the mission and return to the Aboriginal camps.[40] Thus, four years after his conversion the countervailing pressures on him even from his close family remained very strong.

In 1915 he was again very sick, but recovered and for many years he continued to be based at Koonibba, although moving away from time to time. He did more building on the mission, but still hankered after independence on his own farm. In 1908 he secured a share-cropping arrangement with the mission that allowed him to clear land and then remit half the harvest in payment for his work. This too must have failed for by 1909 he was back on a wage of 14 shillings per week.[41]

In 1925 Thomas Richards and his family were camped at Wirrulla when his wife, Nellie, caught pneumonia. Richards rang the mission for help, but could not summon a doctor before his wife died.[42] Nellie was under baptismal instruction at the time (over twenty years after her husband's conversion), but was never baptised. Even though Thomas Richards did not leave his own account of early days at Koonibba mission, the records convey the impression of a strong-willed, intelligent and sensitive man put through great intellectual and emotional turmoil, as he grappled with different cultures, while simultaneously striving to raise himself to the status of an independent farmer He worked hard all his life and taught himself useful skills as he went along. He was

Koonibba workers, c. 1901.
(Courtesy of the E. W. Wiebusch Collection, Aboriginal Photographic Project, Aboriginal Heritage Branch, Department of Environment and Planning, South Australia.)

obviously a remarkable man and Koonibba history would have been quite different without his early presence. He eventually moved to Point Pearce where he died as an old man.[43]

His decision for baptism was probably the hardest because he was the first, but many others went through similar traumas.

Ada and Arthur Richards

Ada Beadle was born about 1884 in Western Australia. She was of mixed descent and was brought up at the Fowlers Bay hotel where she did domestic work to earn her keep. She spoke good English, but despite some schooling could neither read nor write when she came to Koonibba. She had been promised in marriage to Arthur Richards (no relation to Jimmy Richards) who presumably also came from the Fowlers Bay area. Influenced by the white people with whom she was living, she at first refused to go with Arthur. Then she reconsidered and went with him back to the bush.[44]

Arthur and Ada came to Koonibba in 1901 or 1902 and stayed permanently in residence for more than a year. Both were able students at the school but did not undertake baptismal instruction. One evening in 1903 Ada and Arthur approached Wiebusch and asked if he would baptise their baby daughter. The missionary was taken by surprise. Ada and Arthur had made the decision entirely on their own while he was concentrating on Jimmy Richards. Wiebusch agreed to baptise the baby provided that they took a few weeks to think more carefully about it, and that they promised to keep the child on the mission to be brought up as a Christian.[45] They agreed to these conditions in writing. Wiebusch believed the contract would bind them to the mission they had previously contemplated leaving. Bertha Florence Richards (known as Florence, born 10 May 1902) was baptised on 3 March 1903. That evening Wiebusch assured Arthur and Ada that Florence was washed clean of all sins through the holy water and would be saved from future sins by the Saviour.[46]

Wiebusch's hopes of tieing the Richards to the mission through his paper contract were disappointed. Late in 1903 a large number of Aborigines gathered for initiation ceremonies nearby. All the adults were affected by so many of their people gathering in the neighbourhood, and most of them left the mission to join in. The few who remained on the station were torn between their commitment to the mission and their desire to join their people. They lost interest in their work and were rude and insubordinate, Arthur Richards among them. He got upset over small incidents, swore and was reprimanded. He was obviously looking for an excuse to leave. He requested a fortnight's holiday but was refused, so he left without permission. Wiebusch went to the Richards' camp and reminded them of their promises and asked that at least Ada and Florence remain at the mission. But Ada refused, was hit by Arthur with his spear and she, then enraged, attacked Wiebusch, biting him on the arm when those watching would not give her a weapon. Wiebusch had obviously pushed them too far and they both left, but promised to return soon. They were punished by losing their cottage and the wheat Arthur had earned as a bonus to his wages. That evening Wiebusch rode out to the camp where the Aborigines had gathered with the intention of reporting Arthur's bad behaviour, thereby shaming him before his own people.

The Richards returned to the mission eight days later repentant and depressed. Wiebusch decided to give them their cottage back, not only out of Christian charity, but also because he needed Ada's help in the kitchen. They got their board but not their wheat back. As with Jimmy Richards, the missionary's motives for wanting to keep Ada and Arthur on the mission were more than purely spiritual; he needed their services. Ada was the only Aboriginal woman with any experience in domestic service and was wanted in the kitchen. Without her Wiebusch would have had to hire white domestic help. He valued her assistance to such an extent that previously he had applied to the mission board to change the religious instruction classes so that Ada would be able to attend and still help in the kitchen. But probably what upset him most was that the Richards and others like them, who appeared to be progressing towards a European lifestyle, could suddenly turn their backs on the material advantages of the mission— stone cottages, regular food—and take part in 'heathen' ceremonies.[47]

On another similar occasion the Richards again left the mission to attend ceremonies taking place a few miles away. This time on their return they were put on six months' probation before being given their cottage and board, but Ada refused to work, claiming other women did not have to work for their food.

Despite these early conflicts Arthur and Ada must have stayed on the mission, perhaps leaving from time to time for short intervals. In 1917 the missionary reported Arthur and Ada as candidates for baptism and Ada was baptised in 1918.[48] Their daughter Florence married Micky Free, another long-time resident of the mission.

Joseph Miller and George Saunders

Two other examples of early converts facing conflicting pressures are Joe Miller and George Saunders (also spelled Sanders), who took up baptismal instruction after the baptism of Jimmy Richards.

Joe Miller was of mixed descent born about 1875 in Brisbane. He moved all over the country finding work as he went and was therefore used to working with white people. He had been at Kopperamana mission, but he could not read or write nor had he had religious instruction.[49] He moved to the west coast in the 1890s, and in 1894 applied for 160 acres to farm between Pintumba and Bookabie to the west of Koonibba. In 1903 he brought a wife and family with him to Koonibba where he was welcomed by Jimmy Richards with whom he had previously worked.[50]

George Saunders was also of mixed descent. Norman Tindale records that his mother came from the Ngalia people (north-west of Ooldea) and his father was a white man. He was born about 1885 and was therefore more than ten years younger than Joe. Virtually nothing is known of his life before he came to Koonibba in 1902. When others went off to initiation ceremonies he remained at the mission and was described by the missionary as modest, good-hearted and keen to learn.[51] He joined the school children in lessons and went round happily singing both hymns and Aboriginal ceremonial songs. He enjoyed the first 'Schulfest' that Wiebusch organised and talked about it in such glowing terms that the boys who missed it vowed they would go to the next one.

Several attempts were made by Aboriginal elders to put George through the initiation ceremonies but each time he refused to go. In February 1906 after again resisting pressures to be initiated, George married Eve. This marriage was wrong on three counts: George was not initiated and therefore not qualified to marry; according to kinship rules, George and Eve did not stand in correct relationship to each other for marriage; and thirdly, Eve had been promised to George's uncle, Jack Nhindina (elsewhere referred to as Yendinna Jack).[52]

Both Miller and Saunders were good workers. Joe carried an established reputation as a worker with him to Koonibba, so the authorities were willing to pay him a wage to ensure that he would stay. Joe Miller, like Jimmy Richards, had a wife who opposed his candidacy for baptism. Wiebusch saw her as a bad influence, egging him on to ask for higher wages instead of encouraging him in his religious studies. Miller, like Richards, became very moody sometimes, working well, particularly with the horses, and then losing interest. He often threatened to leave the mission but each time was dissuaded from doing so by Wiebusch. When he finally gained approval to leave, he realised he did not have enough money to travel so he stayed on a few months to accumulate some. This left George Saunders the only person under baptismal instruction and he stayed until, in 1905, he left with John Highfold, his first departure since coming to the mission in 1902.[53]

Miller and Saunders later returned and were baptised on 25 February 1906.[54] This not only made them members of the Lutheran Church but also enabled them to earn full wages, as they no longer needed time off for religious instruction. In 1908 Saunders again left Koonibba apparently at the instigation of whites who were trying to undermine the mission. The workers of mixed descent had demanded wine to drink while they were harvesting. The missionary refused as it was against the law, whereupon the 'halfcastes' refused to take Holy Communion arguing that this too was forbidden wine.[55] Saunders subsequently returned to the mission and treated it as his home throughout his life. A chronic diabetic, he was treated at the Koonibba hospital after its establishment. In 1939 he was reported to be too sick to work.

Jack Highfold and Jack Jebydah

Other people who undertook baptismal instruction in the first eight years of the mission included: Jack Highfold; Jack Jebydah and his wife Nellie; Micky Free and his wife Rosie; Paddy Nandy (Lame Paddy); Abbot Molina; Alice Murna; and Lily Bilney.[56] Two of these are of particular interest because their conversion affected many others on the west coast. Jack Highfold was an enthusiastic convert. He came to Koonibba in 1905 and was baptised on 21 February 1909. He was happy to work for reduced wages because of his 'commitment to the Holy Ghost'. While others were refusing to work because they were denied wine, Jack Highfold vowed:

> Teacher I will work through the harvest for 15/- [he was offered 18/-]. I am not here to make money, I am here to learn to know my Saviour. I love my Saviour and I do not work for an earthly master only, but I like to please my Saviour even if you do not see me. Money cannot make me happy for we soon must die. I like going to school because there I can learn my Saviour's Word.[57]

Such was his dedication that the mission paid him for work even when he was sick, because of his faithfulness.[58] He would visit the camp where the majority of people lived, to preach about the Saviour. These were the people who used Koonibba as a refuge but did not have close contact with the mission settlement. They spoke little or no English persisting with their own cultural and religious forms. They could, therefore, stay at the mission but maintain a distance from its evangelical thrust. Highfold encountered initial resistance to his message. He recounted how one group of young men who were temporarily camped at the mission laughed at him at first, but when he said he believed Christ was the son of God and Saviour of the world, even if all his people said he was wrong, they took him seriously. He decided he wanted to be a missionary and the Koonibba congregation raised money for him to continue his studies, but he died of 'consumption of the throat' in 1912 before he could realise his ambition.[59]

Jack Jebydah was an Aboriginal elder and an influential man among his people.[60] Unlike others who agreed to undertake baptismal instruction he was not marginal to the Aboriginal community, but a fully initiated member. His influence was important in persuading others to give up their ceremonial life and come to the mission. Yet, like others undergoing conversion, his enthusiasm was punctuated by periods of doubt, when he would leave the mission. In 1906 he talked several men out of attending ceremonies with the Kokatha from the Gawler Ranges.[61] He and his wife, Nellie, had their marriage consecrated in the church in 1909, at the same time as Micky and Rose Free. While most of the Aborigines remained removed from Wiebusch's evangelical influence, some inroads were made into camp life, the bastion of the Aboriginal conservative forces, through the agency of people such as Jack Jebydah and Jack Highfold.

At the same time that Wiebusch was struggling with the adults, he was also instructing children. He achieved quicker results with the children as he did not have to overcome such strongly held existing beliefs. On 15 July 1906 he baptised eight children. Seventy-five whites and 125 Aborigines witnessed the ceremony.

Daily life

The farm was essential to the success of the mission in the early period and established the basis for the success of the mission as a base for west coast Aborigines up to the present day. Although Koonibba was marginal land for agriculture, the mission board decided to grow crops so as to create employment for the Aboriginal people. Water shortages and droughts were frequent. One of the worst seasons on the west coast came in 1914–15, devastating the area from Murat Bay to Fowler's Bay.[62] West of Penong the farmers could not harvest enough wheat for seed. One farm near Fowlers Bay lost 100 horses and 20,000 sheep. With no farm work or game available on the west coast the Aborigines congregated at Koonibba. By March 1914 there were 175 at the mission, which could not pay them all wages but did provide clothes and board.[63] By 1915 the station's horses had become so weak from lack of feed that they could not be used for heavy work. Both men and women were put to work making tanks and cutting mallee tree stumps, arduous and unpopular work, although the mission looked on it as a means to improve the value of their land.[64] At one stage the Aboriginal men refused to go on clearing stumps; they wanted to leave their families in the care of the station, while they took time off. They were told that if they left the station they would not be permitted to return until the next harvest. Realising they could not support their families in the drought-stricken district, they resumed clearing stumps. During this period forty men and their wives cleared 1000 acres.[65] Then, dramatically, the drought broke with a fall of 152 points of rain in a single week of May 1915.

The farm work was done by Aboriginal workers under the supervision of white overseers. When they were not available, the more reliable Aboriginal workers (mostly of mixed descent) acted as supervisors. While the Mission Board was interested in keeping down the wages bill, the missionary and farm manager knew that if they did not pay their workers a competitive wage, they could not keep them on the mission. Neighbouring farmers needed their labour and were willing to pay for it. Wages were also used as an incentive for baptism. In 1905 it was decided to reduce the wages of the unbaptised to encourage them to become baptised.[66]

Wages were supplemented by rations and clothing; some baptised Aborigines were also given housing. The whole business of work and rewards required a delicate balancing act. On the one hand the mission wanted to attract Aborigines and hold them on the station in order to convert them. But they dared not drop the labour requirement in order to win adherents. They needed Aboriginal workers to develop and run the farm and wanted to train them to be 'productive members' of European society, not a parasitic population dependent on mission charity. The twin objectives were to imbue the Aborigines with the 'Christian virtues of work' and to secure their spiritual godliness.

As the government depot for the region, Koonibba was responsible for distributing rations to all those not able to work, regardless of their attitude to the mission. The basic government ration comprised flour, sugar and tea, sometimes supplemented by other items. Aborigines supplied their own meat. If rations ran out as they sometimes did in the early days of the mission when communications with Adelaide were slow and unreliable, most of the Aborigines left the station. In those early years there was little to hold them to the area other than the ready food supply.

Many resented the work required from the able-bodied, preferring to go to Denial Bay or Penong where they could camp without labour demands and still obtain food. Wiebusch learned that one way to retain his Aboriginal labour—and his potential converts—was to include meat in the daily rations. This was not always easy. The lack of permanent water limited the number of stock the station could carry. In 1903 Wiebusch noted that 100 pounds of meat a week was being consumed and that the Aborigines were still not satisfied with the supply. Without meat the adults did not work effectively and the children did not want to go to school.[67] Schürmann had had similar experiences at his school in Port Lincoln as had the Adelaide school, which suggests that rations were one of the main incentives for Aborigines to visit any mission. If the food was not forthcoming they left to gather their own food. Wiebusch tried to enforce the rule that only the able-bodied who worked would be fed at the mission ('[w]er nicht will arbeiten, der soll auch nicht essen') but Aboriginal communal sharing constantly subverted this reward system. Workers took their rations back to camp to be shared among their kin whether they worked or not. The 'problem' was eventually overcome by building a dining room from which the 'lazy' could be excluded, as well as the dogs. A 'native kitchen' served meals cooked by a white cook with Aboriginal assistance for all the 'deserving' Aborigines on the station. Thus were the Victorian workhouse distinctions between the deserving and undeserving poor translated to the remote reaches of South Australia.

Once the local Aboriginal people had become accustomed to camping at Koonibba, at least temporarily, the missionary's next concern was to get them to accept religious instruction. A two-tiered system evolved which gave more privileges to those who accepted instruction than to those who did not. Wages, as we have seen, were higher for baptised than unbaptised workers. Baptised people received better food and more of it. In 1906 a canvas wall was installed in the dining room to separate the baptised from the unbaptised.[68] Those who were baptised or under religious instruction and in regular employment at the station were also eligible for a cottage if one became available. But this system of privilege carried its own problems for the missionaries. They complained that the 'halfcastes', to whom they had given privileged treatment were becoming 'conceited' and 'spoilt'. They demanded wages equal to those of white workers and were dissatisfied when they did not get them. Authorities who, in the early days, had been pleased that the people of mixed descent worked so well had, by 1912, become concerned that these same people were insubordinate and argued with their white superiors.[69] They were described in mission reports as helpless and unreliable, eternal adult children who did not appreciate what was done for them and left the mission at a whim.

The majority of people, who camped in wurleys on the high ground above the mission settlement, were physically and symbolically removed from these pressures. They worked for their food but otherwise had no stake in the missionary system of rewards and punishments. Their movements to and from the mission were unimpeded. They maintained their own social and cultural controls.[70]

Early missionary efforts were primarily directed toward men. The first converts were men and it was the men who had the opportunity to adjust to the work ethic and the cash economy. The male-dominated mission administration did not, at first, have strategies for training and educating women. Both Jimmy Richards' and Joe Miller's wives were viewed by Wiebusch as bad influences on his potential converts. It is difficult to ascertain from the limited data available whether the women were initially a more conservative force than the men, or whether they merely lacked the opportunities to become acculturated to the mission ethos. From the missionary viewpoint the only proper place for the women in the workforce of the future was as domestic servants. Virtually no other work was available for white country women at that time. But for Aboriginal women living in wurleys there was no recognised domestic work immediately available to them. One report in 1905 complained that the women went hunting, set the camp fire, baked the bread (presumably damper) and did nothing![71] Their traditional activities of hunting and gathering were of secondary importance once rations were available, and

Six young women on the verandah of the Children's Home, *c.* 1914.

(Courtesy of the E. W. Wiebusch Collection, Aboriginal Photographic Project, Aboriginal Heritage Branch, Department of Environment and Planning, South Australia.)

the training and socialising of young children was being undermined by the mission school. In short, the women, who had not fallen readily into the full range of domestic duties imposed on white women, found that many of their traditional activities were no longer valued or relevant to their lives on the mission.

By 1908 a number of the women were living in cottages where it was possible to teach European concepts of domesticity. The woman appointed to train them, Miss Baumann, inspected the cottages each morning to check that they were clean. She also supervised the cleaning of the dining room and taught the women and girls sewing. But the women continued to be less willing to conform than the men. Wiebusch noted in 1915 that the men's side of the church was usually full on Sundays, while the women, although present at the beginning of the service, gradually drifted out with their small children and sat outside smoking their pipes.[72]

While various strategies were being devised to encourage, 'civilise and Christianise', the mission's main hope was the children. Initially the most effective way of reaching them was through the school. Soon after Wiebusch arrived at Koonibba he had nine children attending school each morning. By June 1902 he had thirteen children attending school at a time when most Aborigines had been forced to leave the station because of water shortages.[73] The parents had agreed to leave them at the school, no doubt believing that they would be better cared for at the mission than moving through the drought-stricken country looking for water. The parents returned to Koonibba after the drought had broken, only to depart soon after for Tarcoola to attend initiation ceremonies. This time four boys went off with their parents, while nine others remained.

While the local people soon became accustomed to their children attending school, those from farther afield at first would not allow their children near the mission, and even when they did bring them to the mission they would not let them near the buildings. They feared that once the children were under the control of the missionary they would not get them back.[74] Gradually Wiebusch won their trust. First he took two girls—and their mothers visiting from Fowlers Bay—to his house to give the girls clothes. They were washed and combed after much initial resistance. He then took them to the schoolroom where they looked around fearfully but eventually agreed to attend. In this manner five Kokatha children were persuaded to come to the school in 1903.

Like Poonindie, and in strong contrast to the United Aborigines Mission mission at Nepabunna, the school was pivotal to the work of the mission. The education, training and control of the children was seen by the missionaries as a central responsibility. In 1905 a full-time teacher was appointed to release Wiebusch for other work.[75]

In the separate settlements of the station landscape—mission and camp—education was defined as something that happened in the missionary quarter. Wiebusch worried that things taught at night in the camp would undo most of the good work carried on by day in the mission school. He therefore encouraged the children to sleep in a cottage in the mission settlement. As the numbers increased the accommodation had to be expanded. In 1912 the mission was warned by the Protector of Aborigines that under the new *Aborigines Act* 'neglected' children of mixed descent would be taken from their parents and that if these children were to remain at Koonibba the accommodation would

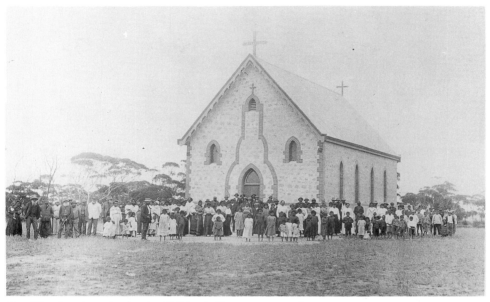

Koonibba church on the day the Children's Home was opened.
(Courtesy of the E. W. Wiebusch Collection, Aboriginal Photographic Project, Aboriginal Heritage Branch, Department of Environment and Planning, South Australia.)

need to be upgraded. It was decided to build a children's home to house the growing number of children at the standards required by the government. This grave threat from the government swung the balance of Aboriginal opinion at the camp. They supported the project as insurance against losing their children. The fourteen-room home opened on 7 March 1914. Its building imposed a large financial drain both on Koonibba and the Church and the debt that was incurred would haunt the mission board for many years.[76]

Although parents put their children in the home voluntarily, once they were there it was difficult to get them out again. Parents were allowed to visit their children for half-an-hour twice a day. By August 1914 of seventy children at the mission, forty were living in the Children's Home. Its building solved many problems for missionaries intent on educating and 'civilising' the children. The next worry was what to do with them as they grew up. The boys could stay in single men's quarters and work on the farm, but the girls were more difficult to deal with. The first generation of girls finished school in 1909 and work was found for all of them on the station.[77] But girls who finished later had no jobs waiting for them. This would be a continuing problem for the mission.

Two other welfare services provided by the mission were distribution of clothing (second-hand) and medical care. Clothing was considered part of the 'civilising' process. Aborigines could not stay on the mission naked, nor could the missionary allow them to leave without clothing as he believed it would reflect badly on the mission to have them wandering around semi-clad. Lutheran congregations throughout the country were continually being asked to donate clothing to the missionaries who complained that as

Koonibba mission buildings, *c.* 1914.
(Courtesy of the E. W. Wiebusch Collection, Aboriginal Photographic Project, Aboriginal Heritage Branch, Department of Environment and Planning, South Australia.)

quickly as it was distributed to the Aborigines it became unwearable. The clothing was given to people who had no idea about how it should be managed. It tore and soiled as they walked through the bush. They had no other means of transport and no facilities for looking after their clothing even had they had the inclination to do so.

To summarise the first period of mission experience, Koonibba developed a special kind of landscape which reflected the peculiar nature of the relationship between Aborigines and the missionaries. Both groups were united in a desire to maintain Koonibba as a refuge, but they divided the land into the two poles of mission and camp. The mission was a version of the holy village attempted by Hale at Poonindie, while the camp sprawled unsymmetrically across the sandhills. Camp people were not institutionalised, came and went according to the fluctuations of the seasons, the game and, increasingly, opportunities for work. On occasion the population swelled as people gathered for important ceremonies. In the early days the missionaries won most of their stalwarts from among the floating population of mixed descent who had come into the area seeking economic opportunity. But through the school, the Children's Home, and the novelty of their religious doctrines, the missionaries made continual inroads into the camp.

In 1914 a commission from the Aboriginal Mission Board visited Koonibba. Its report describes the mission landscape and its divisions.[78] The settlement itself was on 10 acres of land with buildings on three sides. On the west side stood the church,[79] the missionary's house, the school and Children's Home. On the north were the teacher's house, an Aboriginal worker's house,[80] and the manager's house. Behind these buildings were the stables and barns. On the eastern side were the white workers' quarters, the kitchen, bakehouse, manager's office, the store and a collection of other buildings (which had formerly served as the missionary's home, manager's house, school children's bedrooms, stables, and the smithy). One two-roomed cottage for an Aboriginal worker's family was inside the square. The south side was reserved for future housing for Aborigines. In addition the station had fourteen water tanks. The missionary's house appropriately commanded a clear view of the entire settlement.[81] Symbolically and physically isolated, the Aboriginal camp comprised thirty-seven structures straggling across the side of a neighbouring hill.

Notes

1 Koonibba missionary, C. A. Wiebusch, initially referred to them as Julburra speakers: Koonibba records, box 4, Lutheran archives, Adelaide. Norman Tindale claimed Julburra was the Kokatha name for the Wirangu. N. B. Tindale, *Aboriginal Tribes of Australia. Their terrain, environmental controls, distribution, limits and proper names*, Canberra, 1974, p. 219.

2 R. M. Berndt, 'Traditional Aborigines' in C. R. Twidale, M. Tyler and M. Davies, *Natural history of Eyre Peninsula*, Adelaide, 1986, p. 128; Tindale, *Aboriginal Tribes of Australia*, p. 69.

3 For example, GRG 52/1/1896/55, 1897/402, 1906/75.

4 *Der Lutherische Kirchenbote für Australien* (LKA) 1898, p. 203.

5 C. A. Wiebusch diary, translated typescript, 17 and 18 December 1901, held by E. Wiebusch; Koonibba records Box 4, Lutheran Archives, Adelaide.

6 Nevertheless Koonibba never became the home of all Kokatha people. Their country covered a very large area and many remained on it along the east-west railway line, on stations, or as periodic visitors to missions at Ooldea, Port Augusta and Koonibba: Jane Jacobs, 'Land rights in Port Augusta', unpublished MA thesis, University of Adelaide, p. 215.

7 Hans Gaden claimed that in 1952 when the Ooldea people were moved permanently south to Yalata, 70 were Kokatha, the rest (about 300) were Pitjantjatjara: pers. com. C. Hoff, who had learnt Kokatha at Koonibba in the 1920s, found when he visited Yalata in 1952 that he could not communicate because most were Pitjantjatjara speakers: *Australian Lutheran (AL)* 19 November 1952.

8 GRG 52/1/1894/262, SAPRO.

9 GRG 52/1/1890/331, 349, 1903/414; GRG 52/1/1894/73.

10 D. W. Meinig, *On the margins of the good earth. The South Australian wheat frontier 1869–1884*, Adelaide, 1970; J. Faull, *Life on the Edge. The far west coast of South Australia*, Adelaide, 1988, pp. 57, 61.

11 GRG 52/1/1898/42,43,45; GRG 52/1/1902/365, 433.

12 John Coppering cleared and cropped 50 acres: GRG 52/1/1988/258; Joe Miller was granted 160 acres for four years: GRG 52/1/1894/73; Micky Free leased a block in 1896: SGO 2487/1905, Lands Department, Adelaide.

13 *LKA* 3/12/1898.

14 For example, *LKA* 2/8/1902, 20/10/1902, 4/1/1904.

15 *LKA* 20/5/1899, 'Mit letzter Post erhielt ich einen Brief von einem unsrer früheren Schwarzen ... Er schrieb, oder besser, er liess schreiben (denn sie lassen ihre Briefe von dem Weissen schreiben), dass sie auf eine Mob warteten, welche von Port Augusta nach Jardea unterwegs wären'.

16 *LKA* 20/5/1899.

17 *LKA* 21/3/1899, Aboriginal Mission Board (AMB) Minutes, meeting 4/3/1901, 15/5/1899, Lutheran Archives, Adelaide.

18 C. A. Wiebusch diary, 4/3/1902.

19   AMB Minutes, meeting 22/6/1899.

20   AMB Minutes, meeting 1/3/1899.

21   *LKA* 3/11/1898, 15/3/1900.

22   This view that Aborigines could only be evangelised if they settled permanently was commonly held among mission societies, for example, see Bain Attwood, *The making of the Aborigines*, Sydney, 1989, p. 2.

23   *LKA* 18/2/1902, 18/4/1902, 1/8/1907.

24   *LKA* 18/4/1902.

25   *LKA* 8/11/1902, 3/12/1903.

26   *LKA* 3/12/1903. But in July and September 1903 the children wanted to leave with their parents and Wiebusch had to argue persuasively to keep them. In September they hid from Wiebusch so they would be able to leave: C. A. Wiebusch diary, 31/7/1903 and 2/9/1903.

27   *LKA* 2/2/1903. This sport was to become a major focus of community activity and pride at Koonibba.

28   *Koonibba Jubilee Booklet 1901–1926*, Adelaide, 1926, 23 AMB Minutes, meeting 21/4/1909, *LKA* 12/8/1909. Graham Jenkin suggests that the majority of people were converted to Christianity in the first twenty years at Point McLeay, but does not give any figures. He appears to contradict himself elsewhere by suggesting Taplin had many failures and few successes in his missionary work: Graham Jenkin, *Conquest of the Ngarrindjeri*, 1979, pp. 108, 142.

29   *LKA* 2/8/1902: 'Jimmy could have been baptised long ago, but wants to wait until he has grasped the main precepts of Christianity' ('*Er selbst wünscht auch nicht eher getauft zu werden, als bis er wenigstens die Hauptstücke der christlichen Lehre ziemlich gut inne hat*').

30   GRG 52/1/1906/75, 1899/254; *LKA* 4/1/1904.

31   In the early days some were allocated a cottage before they converted, for example, Jack Jebydah and Willoughby in 1903: *LKA* 4/1/1904.

32   Wiebusch reported on Richards' progress to the mission board and in published reports to *LKA*, as well as in notes in his personal diary.

33   AMB minutes, meeting 22/6/1899; *LKA* 18/2/1902. Norman Tindale said he was Wirangu and came from Fowlers Bay: Field Notes 1939 SA Museum.

34   *LKA* 18/4/1902.

35   *LKA* 2/8/1902; AMB minutes, meeting 22/9/1904.

36   *LKA* 17/11/1903.

37   C. A. Wiebusch diary, 8/2/1904; *LKA* 2/4/1904.

38   *LKA* 1/9/1905.

39   AMB minutes, meetings 19/2/1903, 26/5/1903, 9/12/1903, 4/5/1904, *LKA* 17/6/1904.

40   *LKA* 14/2/1907.

41   AMB minutes, meetings 8/4/1908, 15/7/1908, 21/4/1909.

42   Koonibba records box 4 11/1924–25.

43   C. V. Eckermann, pers. com.

44   GRG 52 1/2/1910; *LKA* 16/5/1903.

45   It is normal Lutheran practice only to baptise infants of Christian parents, so such an assurance was necessary from Arthur and Ada before Wiebusch felt able to undertake the baptism: C. V. Eckermann letter to the author 15/2/1990.

46   *LKA* 16/6/1903.

47   AMB minutes, meeting 3/12/1902; *LKA* 4/1/1904: '*Beide* [Arthur and Jack Jebydah] *zeigten auch mehr Lust, mit den Schwarzen zu gehen und ihre heidnische Sitte mitmachen zu dürfen, als eine schöne Stube und gutes Essen zu haben.*'

48   Quarterly report 1917, Koonibba records box 5, AL 14/11/1918.

49 Royal Commission on the Aborigines, Final Report, Adelaide, 1917, p. 11; GRG 52/1/1910/2. Kopperamana mission was established by the Moravians in the salt lakes district in the north of South Australia in 1866.

50 *LKA* 17/3/1903; Royal Commission on The Aborigines, Final report 1916, p. 11; GRG 52/1/1894/73.

51 Norman Tindale Fieldnotes 1939 SA Museum; *LKA* 2/8/1902.

52 C. A. Wiebusch diary, Addendum 1906, translated typescript. See also GRG 52/1/1906/75.

53 *LKA* 1/9/1904; AMB minutes, meeting 27/7/1905.

54 AMB minutes 25/4/1906.

55 *LKA* 13/2/1908: the Protector confirmed that it was unlawful to give Aborigines sacramental wine, GRG 52/1/1907/397. It was illegal for Aborigines to drink in South Australia until the 1960s, see chapter 2.

56 *LKA* 7/5/1908.

57 *LKA* 13/2/1908.

58 'Er ist ein tapferer Streiter Christi', *LKA* 5/11/1908.

59 *LKA* 5/11/1908, 10/2/1910, 8/8/1912.

60 *LKA* 2/11/1906.

61 *LKA* 2/2/1906, 2/11/1906.

62 This drought affected most of South Australia. Tindale believed it was responsible for major movements of Aborigines in the far north-west of the State: Tindale, *Aboriginal Tribes of Australia*, p. 69.

63 *LKA* 19/3/1914.

64 *LKA* 18/2/1915.

65 *LKA* 8/7/1915.

66 AMB minutes, meeting 27/7/1902. When Joe Miller and George Saunders were baptised Wiebusch recommended they get 12 shillings per week compared with 7 shillings for the unbaptised Jack Highfold: AMB minutes, meeting 15/4/1906.

67 GRG 52/1/1906/320; *LKA* 17/3/1903 and 17/9/1903.

68 AMB minutes, meeting 24/6/1906.

69 *LKA* 11/1/1912.

70 For example, in 1904 a Wirangu man was killed by two (or more) Ngalia men, Steve Hart and Yendinna Jack (who were arrested, imprisoned and later released to Koonibba mission). Nevertheless, the Aborigines continued to impose their own system of payback and revenge. Two coastal men, Yarrie Tchuna and Spider, travelled inland to avenge attacks on Spider's family and the Ngalia then tracked them to the coast: GRG 52/1/1905/281.

71 *LKA* 1/9/1905.

72 *LKA* 8/7/1915.

73 *LKA* 18/2/1902, 2/8/1902.

74 One child from this area, an offspring of Lucy Washington and Robert Ware, may have been taken away by the government under its policy of removing children of mixed descent from Aboriginal camps, making the the people very fearful that others might also be taken: C. V. Eckermann letter to the author 15/2/1990.

75 There were 16 children at the school in 1905, which had risen to 47 by 1912: *LKA* 1/5/1905, 11/1/1912, AMB minutes, meeting 27/7/1905.

76 *LKA* 11/1/1912, 28/5/1914; *Koonibba Jubilee Booklet 1901–1926*, p. 26.

77 *LKA* 20/8/1914, 18/11/1909.

78 *LKA* 5/3/1914.

79 This church was built in 1910 to replace the one built by Jimmy Richards which had become too small for the expanding congregation. The old church became the schoolroom: *AL* 14/9/1914.

80 There were four cottages for Aboriginal families at this time: *AL* 14/9/1914.

81   There is no documentation to suggest that this landscape was carefully pre-planned as in some other missions, for example, Ramahyuck in Attwood, *The making of the Aborigines*, p. 8. In fact, the impression is of a rather haphazard building programme at Koonibba, nevertheless the outcome is similar to that of Ramahyuck and other Moravian missions.

6

INSTITUTIONAL UPHEAVAL
AND ADJUSTMENT

By the time of the First World War Koonibba was well established. It had a stable population; the great fluctuations in numbers which characterised the early years no longer occurred. When Wiebusch left the mission in 1916, 113 people had been baptised, 50 children attended school and 48 lived in the Children's Home. While the older people still left the mission to attend to ceremonial and other business, the children and younger people stayed on, only leaving to find work elsewhere.[1]

The war in Europe perilously impinged on a mission run by Lutherans who originated from Germany. The strong anti-German attitudes in Australia filtered through to the west coast of South Australia, affecting both white attitudes to the mission as well as the Aborigines themselves. The government was also influenced by anti-German views and appeared likely to take over the mission in accordance with the recommendation of the Royal Commission of 1913–16.[2] The drought was another factor making the early war years difficult for the mission. The drought broke at last in mid-1916 with the heaviest rains for twenty-five years, producing Koonibba's best-ever harvest.[3]

From this point the war proved a boon to Aboriginal employment as there was a great labour shortage. Five men of mixed descent entered military service in 1917; the rest had work where and when they wanted it. This created a temporary labour shortage on the mission. By January 1917 only fifteen men were employed there and the rest were working in the neighbourhood.[4] They came back once a fortnight to Koonibba to see their children in the home and to attend church services. Despite working away from Koonibba, they maintained their close ties with the mission, which by now was regarded as home.

By 1919 white labour was back on the west coast and the Aboriginal people were back on the mission. There were 100 listed as living permanently at Koonibba plus an average floating population of forty-five.[5] But days of full employment on the mission and supervision of the Aborigines from morning until evening were numbered. In 1921 the mission board decided that a radical change of policy was required to deal with the financial crisis which continued to haunt Koonibba. The board had exceeded its bank overdraft and was unable to pay wages in full; the missionary had stopped his own salary.[6] It was decided to drop the policy of full employment. Paying so many men on a property little more than 12,000 acres did not make good financial sense. It had been done to ensure a pool of potential converts and supervision for those already converted. By the 1920s this policy had brought forth a generation of Koonibba people who could operate effectively in European society. Many of the women were first-class house-keepers, while the men were capable teamsters, shearers, wheat lumpers, stevedores, stone masons, carpenters and blacksmiths.[7]

The change in employment policy led to a reorganisation of farming, involving less labour-intensive agriculture and more reliance on stock. The 1920s became a period of upheaval and readjustment both for the Aboriginal people and the mission authorities. It took a few years for the new policy to be fully implemented, but it caused a volatile reaction in the workforce. A large number of Koonibba people responded to the changes in the early 1920s by leaving the mission periodically in large numbers. A major exodus occurred in 1924 when virtually all adults left for five months. This reaction upset the mission authorities, who interpreted it as evidence of the unreliability of Aborigines, not considering that the Aborigines might view *them* as unreliable. Withdrawal of labour was one of the few means Aborigines had of demonstrating their concerns. The farm manager lamented on one occasion:

> We simply cannot rely on the natives I put up with as much as I think human nature will stand, for at least 3 weeks, but had to overflow at last, the result, however I have only Dick Davey and Percy Cox left doing farm work and one of the boys.[8]

Another factor affecting the attitude of the Aboriginal workers was growing self-reliance. They could earn good wages off the mission and owned cars which gave them greater mobility. If they did not like conditions at Koonibba they could leave and get work elsewhere. A shearer on the west coast could earn £2 per 100 sheep shorn and some Koonibba men could shear 100 sheep a day. At Koonibba they earned £4 a week for farm work.[9]

Yet despite these difficulties and the change in policy, many Aboriginal people continued to work at Koonibba during the 1920s and early 1930s. All the fences had to be sheep-proofed when it was decided to run sheep instead of cattle, scrub continued to be cleared and there was still agricultural work—ploughing, seeding, harvesting. Some of this work was undertaken on a contract basis rather than on a weekly wage.

In 1931, following another bad drought, the Board decided that mission work could proceed without the farm, and it was put up for sale. As with all the other decisions taken by the Church in relation to Koonibba, the Aborigines were not consulted or given any prior warning. It was a body-blow to the dreams of those converts who thought Koonibba could be a route to independence on their own farms. Here was a clear demonstration that when the Koonibba Board spoke of self-sufficiency they referred to their own solvency, not Aboriginal self-sufficiency.

Community leaders sent a letter to the mission board, signed on their behalf by Robert Betts, Secretary Koonibba Native Congregation:

> An appeal by the Native Congregation at Koonibba to the Mission Board, and the Laymen, and all members of the Evangelical Lutheran Synod in Australia
>
> —the mission property has been a great asset to us and home for us and our children. But alas! What do we see staring in our eyes? Printed in letters, which no human eye can miss to see? Koonibba property up for sale, 10,000 acres of which we have trod, 10,000 acres which have been dear and familiar to us natives. It makes us sigh and think that now the land which has been our castle is to be sold—. Why sell the land when we have got first class labourers who would make excellent farmers in the district. Let it out in shares to them; give them a start in life—[10]

The appeal was ignored, but in the midst of the world depression no buyers came forward, so in 1933 the Board decided to share-farm the land, not with Aboriginal partners, but two white Lutherans. The sharefarmers were responsible for all the work, employing their own labour, supplying their own seed and super phosphate, paying the mission board a quarter of the harvest. The mission sold its plant and horses but retained the sheep for meat, the share farmers tended the sheep, taking half the proceeds from sale of the wool.[11]

In 1934 when the mission was finally free of debt, the decision to sell the land was revoked. But apart from one or two Aboriginal men employed by the sharefarmers, there was no longer any farm work for Aboriginal people at Koonibba. Not surprisingly, the movement away from the mission which had started in the mid-1920s accelerated as the people adjusted their personal and group survival strategies.

This marked the end of the experiment to make Koonibba a self-sufficient Aboriginal Christian community with full employment, similar to that envisaged by Mathew Hale in the early years of Poonindie. But unlike Poonindie, financial self-sufficiency was never achieved. Aboriginal missions had tried to establish similar villages elsewhere in Australia but with equal lack of success.[12] The change from ghetto or total institution and employer to a training centre which encouraged adults to seek work away from the mission required many readjustments from the Aborigines. For years they had been encouraged to think of Koonibba as their permanent home. A range of inducements had been offered to make them stay and penalties imposed on baptised people if they left without permission. The staff also found it difficult to adjust. Paternalism rather than trust continued to inform their relations with their 'charges'. Their ultimate aim had never been Aboriginal independence. Even if they had encouraged Aborigines to cut loose from the mission, the wider Australian community was not willing to accept Aboriginal workers as their equals in an era when 'protective' policies and legislation were, in fact, implemented to control Aborigines and keep them separate from the general community. So from the 1920s the Lutheran Church maintained a compromise between the self-supporting Christian village and abandonment of the mission altogether.

At the same time as these policy changes were being implemented, technological and industrial changes were coming to the isolated west coast. In 1924 the railway line between Wandana and Penong was completed. The line ran through a property adjacent to Koonibba, known as Gersch's farm which the mission board leased for five years so as to secure direct access to the line for transportation of their supplies. Communications improved through installation of a telephone line. The mission now had instant contact with the outside world. Cars became a common sight on the west coast. The mission bought its first car in 1925 which enabled the missionary to visit people who had moved away. By this time some Aboriginal people had already acquired their own cars with wages they had earned, not only on farms but on the railways and at the new deep sea port at Cape Thevenard. Cars gave them increased mobility and independence at a time when they might have to travel long distances in search of work.

Despite the movement of people away, Koonibba continued to be permanent home to over 200 people. This apparent anomaly is explained by the large increase in population during this period and by continual movements on and off the mission. Other changes also occurred. The population figures for 1937 show that of a total population of 195 there were 57 adults of full Aboriginal descent (18 of whom were old or sick) and 38 adults of mixed descent. However the statistics for children show the proportions were rapidly being reversed. There were 15 children of full Aboriginal descent and 85 children of mixed descent in 1937. In 1957 the proportion of children had greatly increased. Of 244 people 97 were adults and 147 were children. During the period of high employment in the 1950s many men were travelling 50 miles to work and only returning to Koonibba for the weekends, so the population fluctuated from day to day and week to week.[13]

Life on the mission settlement

The basic routine of life at Koonibba did not change when Wiebusch left and was replaced by Ernest Appelt in 1916. The practice of rewarding conversion with better living conditions continued, although there was a shortage of accommodation due to the halt in building work that had occurred when the mission was under threat of government takeover. Appelt reported that during that period two couples had to postpone their marriages because there were no cottages available and he discouraged them from returning to camp life. On the other hand, he worried about the evils of a long engagement and the temptations this provided for sinful behaviour. In desperation he decided to put up temporary huts of iron and sacking.[14] The great divide between mission and camp still informed most aspects of mission life.

The Children's Home and school were largely unaffected by the war years.[15] In 1917 there were sixty-three children in the home plus seven older girls to help with the work. Three of the girls had been taken out of school to help alleviate staff shortages in the home. By 1920 there were seventy-six children and the home had to be extended to accommodate them. The school was also well attended, growing from fifty-two children in 1918 to sixty in 1923.[16] But while the rest of the mission adjusted to new policies, the Children's Home continued as a total institution. Strict supervision of the children and the young women retained to work in the home was maintained. It faced many difficulties as a result.

The home had been conceived in an era when it was accepted that Aborigines should be segregated and given an education in the culture of the white society. It had the advantage for Aboriginal people, compared to similar institutions established elsewhere in South Australia, that they did not lose sight of or touch with their children. It did, however, remove the children from the camp life of their parents. As the girls grew up, they looked after the younger ones and helped with the house work. An important motive for keeping them was to protect them against early or Aboriginal marriage as well as illegitimate births.[17]

A few girls—or, more accurately, women who did not marry—were being kept, virtual prisoners, in the Children's Home well into their twenties, never allowed out for holidays, never allowed to associate with men. In 1940 the sister of one 'inmate' applied for her to be let out of the Children's Home to visit at Yantanaby for a month. She was 29 years old and still in a home for children. She feared she would spend the rest of her days in the home as she had no prospects of marriage. W. R. Penhall, Secretary of the Aborigines Protection Board, was told by Hoff, Secretary of the Mission Board, that although he had no objections, it was Lutheran Board policy to 'keep complete control over inmates of the Children's Home. Anyone understanding the native will realize that discipline is necessary. Nevertheless I feel it would be an injustice to deprive natives of their freedom especially when they are of age.' After her holiday, the woman was less than keen to return to the Children's Home and applied to work for a woman in Minnipa. The missionary still did not think she was capable of looking after herself and pointed out that her brother-in-law was a notorious gambler who would take all her savings if she lived near him.[18]

Another woman of 22 who left the Children's Home to visit her sick mother at Yardea in the Gawler Ranges, decided to stay and look after the invalid. When the matron of the home refused to send her bank book with her savings in it, she wrote a letter of complaint to Penhall. She was told that her mother was not sick enough to need her and that she would not get her bank book until she returned to Koonibba or found work as a domestic. She eventually found a job in Streaky Bay where, presumably, her life savings were sent on to her.[19]

Many other women applied to leave the Children's Home. Some, in desperation, ran away. Penhall instructed the Lutheran Mission Board that people could not be confined to an institution simply because they were unemployed. He pointed out that when Aborigines reached the age of 21 the Aborigines Protection Board was no longer their legal guardian and suggested the Children's Home should be a training institution, not a place for disciplining adults.[20]

The Children's Home had always worked on the principle that children were brought to the home voluntarily, but once there they must stay until released by the authorities. Parents continually applied to the mission to have their children released either because they wanted them to help at home, or because they had moved away from Koonibba. Few children were released on application. One family of full Aboriginal descent from Ooldea was refused on the grounds that they could never live like Europeans and children would only be released to their families if they had reached a certain level of Europeanisation. The Cox family, who went to live in Fowlers Bay, were allowed to take their children only because they were highly respected by the missionary.[21]

Children were generally allowed to join their families for a holiday at the end of the year and were returned to the home for the new school year. A number of families took

A group of children on the verandah of the Children's Home, *c.* 1914.
(Courtesy of the E. W. Wiebusch Collection, Aboriginal Photographic Project, Aboriginal Heritage Branch, Department of Environment and Planning, South Australia.)

this opportunity to remove their children. The mission authorities responded by refusing to release children whose families might not return them. Parents became so hesitant to put their children in the home, particularly their daughters, that eventually some girls were released on application from their parents in the hope it would encourage others to come.

The education the children received at Koonibba school was of a high standard and top pupils were encouraged to continue their studies in Adelaide, either at the Lutheran Concordia College or at one of the technical high schools. This encouragement contrasts starkly with most other Aboriginal schools at the time.[22] Koonibba produced some of the best-educated Aboriginal people in South Australia. In the 1950s and 1960s many went on to successful careers in Aboriginal affairs, nursing and the public service.

Health services were also provided at Koonibba. In 1938 a hospital opened which continued to function throughout the mission's existence, only closing temporarily in 1950 because of lack of staff. It had no resident doctor and was reliant on the doctor in Ceduna, but it was the only hospital in the area to treat Aborigines.

In the 1940s Koonibba continued to fulfil a function as an outback Aboriginal ghetto. It was a permanent home for some families and a place of refuge for others who found the pressures of the outside world too overwhelming, were temporarily unemployed, needed medical attention or nursing, wanted to be with their children while they attended Koonibba school, or were women whose husbands were not supporting them. But living conditions at Koonibba were overcrowded and substandard by general community standards. A number of families shared two-roomed cottages with no running water and very basic effluent systems. Water had to be carried up to half a kilometre to the cottages until 1948 when pipes were laid from the tanks.[23]

In 1955 a welfare officer from the Aborigines Department reported that there were only sixteen two-room cottages at Koonibba housing 100 permanent inhabitants, whose number doubled on weekends when the men returned from work. Up to four families lived in each cottage. Most houses were built of stone but there were a few tin ones. The cooking stoves were old, some were burnt out. Doors and windows did not fit properly and ceilings were unlined. As a result the cottages were cold and damp in winter. The welfare worker thought the conditions were well below that of the government reserves at Point Pearce and Point McLeay.[24] In 1957 the Aborigines Department supplied some tents as a temporary measure to alleviate the overcrowding.

Koonibba communal pride was strongly expressed through their sporting activities, especially football. Since its earliest days the Koonibba team had dominated west coast football. In the 1920s it was led by Dick Dolling and supported by Dick Davey and Dudley (the three 'Ds'), but the game declined during the depression years. By the late 1930s Koonibba were competing well again and by 1947 they had won seven premierships in a row. In 1949 they were playing so well that they challenged the rest of the Murat Bay League and later the Streaky Bay Association and won both matches.[25] This run was spoilt in 1955 when the whole team was reported by the umpire, but this did not dent enthusiasm at Koonibba which had enough good players to form a second team, the Rovers, based at Denial Bay oval.[26] The Koonibba team continued to play excellent, winning football until the early 1960s. Many of the players from the late 1940s still played and there were younger first-class players. Koonibba players won many medals for 'best and fairest'. The white racist society of the west coast appreciated their football prowess but, as will be seen in the following chapter, rejected them as neighbours and schoolmates for their children. Football and other sports were the only avenue Koonibba people had to express their communal pride publicly. They involved the whole community and the outcome of the weekly matches was a major preoccupation of the people.

While dramatic changes occurred in the secular life of the mission, the religious work continued. By the time Wiebusch left Koonibba over half the people residing at the mission were baptised and baptisms of young and old continued. In 1920 missionary Appelt reported (just before he was replaced by C. Hoff) that a total of 153 people had been baptised at the mission in nineteen years, of whom 19 had died and 4 had left the Church. In 1930 there was a congregation of 204.[27]

In 1930 the new missionary, Albert Mueller, decided to finish the work begun by his predecessors and baptise all those people still outside the Church. In 1931 he baptised 38 people—19 from the Children's Home, 10 from the cottages and 9 camp people, some of whom had started their instruction with Wiebusch. Later that same year Colona Tom, who had been described in an Adelaide paper, the *Observer*, as an agnostic in 1914, was brought very ill to Koonibba from Fowlers Bay.[28] Mueller baptised him before he died. Colona Tom had grown up on White Well station, where he had worked for G. W. Murray. He had a reputation as a good tracker and was an influential man among the west coast people. As a result of his baptism other Wirangu people who had not previously stayed at Koonibba came to the mission and agreed to take baptismal instruction.[29]

There is very little documentation to indicate how many west coast Aborigines still carried on the old ceremonial life in the 1930s. Hans Gaden, who was a sharefarmer and later station manager at Koonibba, recalled that the last ceremony held at Koonibba was in 1934 and that 300–400 people attended.[30] Even if this figure is grossly exaggerated it suggests that the event attracted large numbers, but there is no indication what the purpose of the ceremony was, or who attended. For the majority of Koonibba people, and certainly for the generation that had grown up on the mission or was closely associated with it, Christianity had supplanted earlier beliefs and religious forms as the dominant religious influence.

The dichotomy between camp and village continued, however. As the older generation died or moved from the camp to the settlement, new people came to Koonibba from Ooldea and the country to the north. A census of married couples at Koonibba in 1960 classified 30 people out of a total of 104 as having spent at least their pre-school years living a camp life.[31] As long as movement of people on to the mission continued, there was a pool of potential converts for the missionaries to evangelise. In the late 1940s missionary Eckermann still had five to ten people per year requesting baptism.[32] Some had been at Koonibba in the early days but had left at the time of the 'flu epidemic in 1919 and only now were returning. Eckermann was helped in the task of evangelising among people in the camp by Lame Paddy (Paddy Nandy, baptised in 1909).[33] But the missionaries' main effort was put into maintaining an active commitment to Christianity among those already in the Church. This required much travelling as Koonibba people were spread all over Eyre Peninsula and far to the west.

Dispersal

Many families left Koonibba temporarily, and some permanently, in response to the mission policies of the 1920s and 1930s. They set up camps in neighbourhoods where they could get employment or at least have access to water. They found that while the mission and government encouraged them to move into the community, they were given no assistance to establish themselves and were still under the surveillance of the Aborigines Protection Board, the mission, the police, the local district health authorities and their non-Aboriginal neighbours. They found that their labour was in demand, but they were not welcomed as neighbours and, although they paid taxes, government and community services were not available to them.[34] They were also open to exploitation by unscrupulous employers. The Aborigines Protection Board had no authority to monitor the wages of Aboriginal people and they were often underpaid or occasionally not paid at all for their work. Most of the work available was casual, so people were forced to move frequently to remain in employment. Only domestic work was available to women. Many lived with the families who employed them and were easy targets for sexual exploitation. Koonibba people spread themselves throughout Eyre Peninsula and the west coast, so wherever they went in search of employment they were sure to find relatives and friends.

Mr F. M. Linke with confirmation class, Koonibba (between 1905–15).
(Courtesy of the E. W. Wiebusch Collection, Aboriginal Photographic Project, Aboriginal Heritage Branch, Department of Environment and Planning, South Australia.)

In the 1920s the largest camps away from the mission were at Bookabie, where the Millers lived (white men married to Aboriginal women), and Ceduna/Thevenard deep sea port, where employment could be obtained loading wheat and wool. The lives of some Koonibba people illustrate the conflicting pressures that assailed these people in the twentieth century.

Micky Free (also known as Willis Michael Lawrie) and family

Born on 5 November 1868 at Eucla across the Western Australian border, Micky Free spent his childhood around Fowlers Bay. Although he had no formal schooling, he taught himself to read to fill in the time while patrolling the dog fence.[35] He was a noted athlete at both local and interstate competitions. In 1896 he leased a block of land in the Hundred of Catt just south of what became Koonibba land.[36] Lacking the resources to establish a farm he became indebted to the store-keeper and farmer A. B. C. Murray of Penong. He bought a buggy in the same year but was unable to pay for it. Free held on to the lease but went off kangaroo hunting to supplement his income. He may have been on his own land hunting kangaroos in 1897 when the Lutherans came looking for land suitable for an Aboriginal mission. It was he who showed them the country around Koonibba waterhole.

Free's kangaroo hunting took him all over the west coast area. In 1903 he was hunting with people from Ooldea, who then went on to attend ceremonies at Denial Bay. Later that year he hunted with Yarrie Tchuna, who put in a complaint to the Protector of Aborigines that white men were killing all the Aborigines' kangaroos.[37] During this period Free had hung on to his block of land, despite his £300 debt to Murray. Murray claimed that Micky Free had sold him the land several years before to pay off his debt but had then gone to the Nullarbor Plain kangarooing so no papers of transfer had been signed. He then applied for right of purchase of the lease and Free officially transferred it to him in 1906.[38] Murray promised Free could go on farming the land or other land he owned but there is no record to show whether this promise was fulfilled. Murray claimed that Micky would never be able to farm in his own right because he shared ('squandered') all his money with other Aborigines. (This view does not accord with later reports which described Free as being a good financial manager; perhaps he learned from experience.)[39]

In 1902, while working in the Fowlers Bay area, Free inquired about sending his children to school at Koonibba. Wiebusch was keen to have the whole family as no Aborigines from Fowlers Bay had so far associated themselves with the mission. It appears, however, that Free did not bring his children to Koonibba school until 1906 and did not decide to settle at the mission himself until 1907. Wiebusch was pleased to have him because of his reputation as a good worker. Free brought his wife, Rose, and four children. For the first year he earned 6 shillings a week plus clothing for his wife and children. In 1908 while Micky and Rose were under baptismal instruction they suddenly decided to leave the station. Wiebusch tried to dissuade them, but they insisted. A few days later they returned, Micky, with tears in his eyes saying he could not bear to be away from the Word of God, or be responsible for taking his children away from school.[40] The following year he and Rose were baptised with twenty-six others and had their marriage consecrated in church.

Rose died in 1919. In 1922 Micky proposed to Flora Richards, Arthur and Ada's daughter, and they married in 1923 and had five children. In the 1920s Free, like so many of his friends, moved between the mission and employment off the mission. At one time he acted as guide to an exploring party to the Warburton Ranges.[41] He was an elder of the Koonibba congregation. In the 1940s, although still a loyal and active member of the Koonibba community, he expressed dissatisfaction with aspects of life on the mission. He did not like the missionary and wrote a warning to the mission board: 'the things are not going so good on the natives or else where. I have resection [direction] from the native congregation to put this matter to remove Pastor Traeger regantly [recently] if you board want [won't] take any notice my reports there will be no native on Koonibba mission now look out.'[42]

In 1946 he wrote to the Aborigines Department complaining about the failure of the children's education to prepare them for a better future. People remember him rounding up the children to make sure they went to church and school. Apart from being concerned about the future of Aboriginal children and the administration of the mission (although this latter concern was rectified when a new pastor was appointed in 1946), Free had his own family problems, particularly with one of his son-in-laws who was not supporting his wife and nine children. Free was drawing an old age pension by this time, so he was financially secure. Nevertheless, he continued to work on the mission until 29 March 1947, when he collapsed and died climbing down from his buggy after a morning spent cutting wood in the scrub.[43]

Robert Betts and family

Betts was born about 1904 and came to Koonibba when he was 4 or 5 years old. His mother, Jabadee or Nellie, was from the Ooldea/Gawler Ranges region. Gifted in music and sport, he grew up at the mission and later lived with a Lutheran family. He played the organ, guitar and piano and was choirmaster.[44] His daughter, Doris, maintains that he could have gone to the Conservatorium but was not accepted because of his colour.

In 1924 Betts and another young man, Willie Coleman were drinking on Christmas Eve and got into a fight. The missionary, Hoff, could not break it up, so called the police and the two men spent Christmas in gaol. This action on the missionary's part was not popular among the Aboriginal people; the antagonism and tension it caused continued throughout the Christmas period. On Christmas Day people were caught breaking the ban on playing cards and gambling in one of the cottages. Gambling on Christmas Day made the offence doubly reprehensible. One cannot help thinking the culprits set out deliberately to further antagonise the missionary by their game. Among the gamblers was William Carbine, who had previously been banned from the mission. Hoff sent him away blaming easier access to alcohol for the increasing problems he was having at Koonibba.

Robert Betts and William Coleman appeared in court after Christmas and were fined—Betts £6 and Coleman £6/10/-. The following Sunday Hoff had a meeting which forty men attended to discuss whether he should in certain circumstances take legal action as he had done on Christmas Eve. After two hours' discussion he took a vote and it was unanimously decided that he did have the right. He even claimed that Coleman and Betts bore him no grudge. The following week Robert Betts married Olga Free, Micky's daughter.[45]

Robert did not get on with the farm manager, and left the mission. He worked at Wirrulla and then instead of returning to the mission went on to the Gawler Ranges. He wrote to Hoff from Yardea:

> Well Pastor, as I've told you that I was coming through to the Koonibba Mission Station, in about a fortnight time I've altered my mind, now, and won't be coming till Christmas. I do not (sic.) that I've got anything against the officials of the Station or anything else. Its because I can't get away from here. I was brought up and taught by the Lutheran Pastors and officials to abide by the true faith unto death. And may the Lord Jesus Christ give me strength that I may overthrow the evil temptations of the world. And that Jesus Christ may strengthen my faith unto the end.[46]

Robert's wife, Ollie (Olga) may not have been moving around with him because in September 1926 she was at Pintaacla, where she had a child and was ill presumably as a result of the childbirth. By 1931 the Betts were back at the mission and Robert wrote a letter on behalf of the Aboriginal community to the Lutheran Church complaining about the proposed sale of Koonibba land. The family remained at Koonibba during the 1930s and five of their children, Cecil, Reg, Doris, Edward and Andrew, were born there. Robert worked as a shearer and lumped wheat on to ships at Thevenard.[47]

In the 1940s, by which time they had six children, Ollie expressed a wish to leave the mission. Robert was working on the construction of the Tod River pipeline for the Water Works Department. He earned £4/16/- a week of which £1/2/6 was deducted for meals and camp and £2/10/- was sent to his family. During the Second World War the work was regarded as an essential service; he had to get exemption from the pipeline work to go shearing in 1942. While Robert was away working his family lived at Koonibba. He applied to the missionary to have his children released from school so that the family could live near him. The missionary agreed, but tried to get the children back when he heard that the family was in an Aboriginal camp and not in a house as promised and that the children were not going to school. Betts refused, saying he wanted to get his children away from the debilitating environment at the mission and keep his family together. He had a job as yardman at the Wudinna hospital and was looking for a place to live; his children would be accepted at the Wudinna school once they were properly housed.[48] For the next few years the family moved from one country town to another as Robert chased work on Eyre Peninsula.

About this time Robert won exemption from the controls of the *Aborigines Act*, giving him the same rights as white Australians, including access to alcohol. However, in 1943 it was revoked when he was caught supplying alcohol to an unexempted Aborigine. He gave up his job as a packer on the railways and went looking for work, leaving his family behind. They moved in with another Aboriginal family, the Larkins, in Wudinna, destitute until Robert found work and started sending them money. In 1944 Robert was shearing again and the family, who had been living in Minnipa, again with the Larkins, moved to Lock, where they went to school. They moved again, this time to Port Lincoln but by 1947 the family were living in Cummins where they stayed for many years. Robert built a solid camp from railway sleepers on railway land opposite the Lutheran Church. When the pastor from Koonibba visited on his quarterly rounds Robert would book the church for a service so he could play his beloved organ.[49] Robert continued to pick up seasonal work. Toward the end of his working life he and Olga moved to Ceduna and lived on a property he had at Duck Ponds. The family produced some of the best sportsmen and women on the west coast including two outstanding footballers, Reg and Eddie and two netballers, Doris and Olive.

Dick Ware

Dick, born at Old Colona station near Coorabie about 1907, had no early associations with the mission. His parents were Mingia (Lucy Washington) and Robert. As a young man he worked as a stockman in Western Australia, Northern Territory, Queensland and New South Wales. After returning to South Australia he worked on Eyre Peninsula and farther west. As a young man he had married Jessie and had a daughter Daphne, but they separated. Later he lived with Molly Smith at Wudinna, but eventually settled down with Melvina Highfold, with whom he had a large family, and they established themselves at Koonibba.[50] Melvina had grown up in the Children's Home at Koonibba and then worked as a domestic at Streaky Bay. She and Dick had eight children. When they first moved to Koonibba they lived in one of the army tents which the Aborigines

Department had supplied and then in a two-roomed tin shack; by the early 1960s they had a two- to three-bedroom stone house.

Dick was respected at the mission and around the district as a man who could work hard at anything. At Koonibba he carted water from Charra, did farm work seeding and harvesting, and also took seasonal work off the mission lumping wheat at Thevenard. He drove the Koonibba truck and bus, taking people into Ceduna/Thevenard for which he was paid £12 per week in 1961, supplementing this wage with work on the wharves.[51] When the government took over the mission Dick worked as a sharefarmer along with Dickie Le Bois.

Dick's interests were work and sport. He took some interest in religion, but never involved himself in politics. He was a life member of the Koonibba Football Club and played football for Bookabie and the Rovers (the Aboriginal team established in the late 1940s with its home ground at Denial Bay). His brothers were also respected workers on the west coast. Edmund worked mainly as a stockman and overseer at Old Yalata station but moved to Koonibba when he married. He went to Bookabie in 1954 returning to Koonibba about 1960. Unlike many Koonibba people he was an experienced manager and was, therefore, given responsibility for supervising other workers. He was also put in charge of the stock on his return to the mission. He was a community representative during the attempts to negotiate with the Church and government at the time of the takeover of the mission. In the early 1960s Edmund returned to Colona Station where he remained as manager until his retirement.

Notes

1 *Der Lutherische Kirchenbote für Australien* (*LKA*) 14/9/1916.
2 See *LKA* 23/11/1916, Koonibba records, box 5, 2/11/1916, 8/11/1917, Lutheran Archives, Adelaide, for Lutheran reactions to the threatened takeover. See chapter 2 for discussion of the Royal Commission.
3 11,000 bags of wheat, 1,000 bags of oats and 320 tons of hay were harvested: *LKA* 15/3/1917, 27/9/1917. The figures from the later date are 11,500 bags wheat, 800 bags oats and 300 tons hay.
4 *LKA* 17/8/1917; *Australian Lutheran* (*AL*) January 1917.
5 Protector of Aborigines' Report, Adelaide, 1919.
6 *AL* 13/3/1921.
7 C. V. Eckermann letter to the author 26/3/1990.
8 Koonibba records, box 11, 21/5/1925.
9 *LKA* 14/11/1926, Koonibba records, box 4, 8/1/1925.
10 *LKA* 11/12/1931.
11 *LKA* 21/7/1933; *AL* 21/7/1933, 29/9/1933.
12 For example, New Norcia in Western Australia, established by Bishop Salvado, and Ramahyuck in Victoria.
13 GRG 52/1/1937/48, GRG 52/1/1957/154, GRG 52/1/1952/88.
14 Koonibba records, box 5, 19/1/1917.
15 The school was the only Lutheran school in Australia not closed down, perhaps because no German language was used in the school.
16 *AL* 20/9/1917, 11/7/1918, 18/12/1920, 11/4/1923.
17 Koonibba records, box 4, 15/1/1925 and box 7, 23/3/1923.

18 GRG 52/1/1940/16 and 16a.
19 GRG 52/1/1941/3.
20 GRG 52/1/1940/129; 1941/3.
21 GRG 52/1/1942/10 and 10a.
22 Colebrook Home was another institution which encouraged its children to go on to further training.
23 One family had an average of 29 people living in two rooms: Hans Gaden pers. com. 18/2/1988; *AL* 16/3/1948.
24 GRG 52/1/1955/35. These missions had been taken over by the government on the recommendation of the Royal Commission on The Aborigines.
25 J. Gascoyne, *Far West Football 1906–1986*, Ceduna, 1986, pp. 151, 152.
26 This team fielded a side from 1955 to 1959: Gascoyne, *Far West Football*, p. 153.
27 *LKA* 7/7/1920, 21/2/1930.
28 *Observer*, 25/7/1914, p. 43.
29 *LKA* 7/8/1931, 16/10/1931, 30/10/1931.
30 Hans Gaden, pers. com. 18/2/1988.
31 GRG 52/1/1960/20.
32 C. V. Eckermann, pers. com. 1988.
33 *AL* 7/3/1951; C. V. Eckermann, letter to the author 16/7/1990.
34 Some women were eligible for child endowment, otherwise there was no government assistance other than that offered at Aboriginal institutions.
35 A fence constructed across southern Australia to keep wild dingoes out of pastoral and agricultural areas.
36 Surveyor-General's Office 2487/1905, Lands Department, Adelaide. It was lease number 8660, section 3, Hundred of Catt, an area of 2825 acres.
37 GRG 52/1/1903/414.
38 Surveyor-General's Office 2487/1905. The policeman at Fowlers Bay, who had assisted Free in his inquiries, suspected that Murray might be taking advantage of him.
39 Aborigines in the south-west of Western Australia were experiencing similar problems in their battle to maintain themselves independently on the land: Anna Haebich, *For their own good. Aborigines and government in the southwest of Western Australia*, Perth, 1988, pp. 28-35.
40 AMB minutes, meetings 1/1/1907, 9/4/1907; *LKA* 30/7/1908.
41 *LKA* 18/6/1947.
42 Koonibba records, box 11, 3/8/1945.
43 GRG 52/1/1946/25, GRG 52/1/1944/33, *AL* 18/6/1947.
44 GRG 52/1/1910/2, Doris Keeler (née Betts), pers. com. 11/4/1990.
45 Koonibba records, box 4, 1/1/1926.
46 Koonibba records, box 4, 25/9/1925.
47 Doris Keeler, pers. com. 11/4/1990.
48 GRG 52/1/1941/38, GRG 52/1/1942/10 and 10a.
49 C. V. Eckermann, letter to the author 26/3/1990.
50 Most of the subsequent information on Dick Ware was, unless otherwise indicated, obtained from his son Bob Highfold at an interview on 18/4/1990.
51 Koonibba records, box 3, 12/3/1961.

7

DISPERSAL AND THE
END OF THE MISSION ERA

People who had been closely allied with Koonibba moved to towns and properties scattered over Eyre Peninsula, west to the Nullarbor Plain and as far east as Point Pearce and Adelaide. They lived in Ceduna and Thevenard, Port Lincoln, Cummins, Penong, Minnipa, Wudinna, Lock, Fowlers Bay, Wirrulla, the Gawler Ranges, at Bookabie and Penalumba and stations on the Nullarbor Plain and north and west of Penong. In almost all cases they moved from Koonibba in search of work. Having found employment, their next major problem was finding a place to live. There was no public housing for them unless they worked as fettlers with the railways. It was difficult and often impossible to get their children admitted to government schools. They were being set up to fail in the white community and many of them did. Amazingly, some struggled through against all the odds and achieved an independent existence. Conditions off the mission, not on it, explain why so many people lived at Koonibba, left their children there, or returned frequently between jobs. Like the urban ghettos, it was a haven from the hostile outside world.

The places where Aborigines could camp or build in towns were designated 'reserves' lacking services of any kind. They had to construct their own dwellings out of whatever materials came to hand. Often all they could manage was a simple wurley, although some built more substantial structures of scavenged wood, iron, sacking or flattened kerosene tins, but these structures could never come 'up to the standard' of white family homes, with their makeshift construction, no electricity, water or sewerage services; cooking was done on an open fire and there was no water for washing and cleaning. White families in towns such as Ceduna, Penong and Wudinna pointed to these conditions as an excuse for their racially motivated demands that Aborigines be moved out of their towns. Whites said they were a health hazard and excluded them from schools on the ground that Aboriginal children would contaminate their schoolmates.[1]

There were, therefore, good reasons for people to return to Koonibba, though few if any employment opportunities remained there. If they stayed on without work they were accused of laziness. Those who passed the time gambling and drinking were criticised for their low morals. It took great determination and strength of character to overcome these obstacles and the combined authority of the Aborigines Protection Board, the police, the mission authorities and the powerful white society in which they lived.

Most people left the mission voluntarily, but some were forced to leave because of alleged immoral or criminal behaviour. Included in this group were young, single girls who became pregnant. They were encouraged to stay with family members who had already left Koonibba, or made their own way in the world either by domestic service or prostitution. There were one or two who tried quite deliberately to escape their Aboriginal condition by associating with or marrying white men or encouraging their daughters to do so in the hope that 'white' offspring would not suffer the same fate they had.[2] To counteract the assertion commonly made that misplaced idealism led to 'welfare dependency' among Aboriginal people, it is instructive to examine more closely the problems which faced Koonibba people who moved away from the mission.

Ceduna/Thevenard

In the 1930s Koonibba's population was not much smaller than Ceduna's and larger than that of any other town on the west coast. Understandably, when numbers of Koonibba people moved to Ceduna in search of work local citizens became very uneasy, but they needed Aboriginal labour to bag and load wheat and gypsum at the port at Thevenard. Although the work was seasonal and erratic depending on harvests and the arrival of ships, it paid well. There was no housing available for the Aboriginal workers at the port or in the town, so the men with their wives and children camped on the designated reserve. As at other camps, their homes were makeshift with no services, no rubbish disposal, no latrines or ablution facilities. The children could not go to school and the women had little to occupy them.

Koonibba authorities constantly worried about the moral climate and living conditions at the Ceduna reserve. In 1926 the missionary reported:

> Thevenard is again the Mecca of our Natives . . . I went down there on Tuesday for the first time to see them. And it nearly broke my heart. There they lie about in their dirty scanty camps. The men work for a day or two and then retire till necessity forces them again into activity. And the women, some with little babies, lie about in the dirt, a temptation to the low white men. I will write to the the Protector to see whether their camping at such places cannot be stopped. If the men want to work there, let them leave their women folk behind. It is a blot on our civilisation to allow such a state of affairs. The low white men are full of venereal diseases and naturally communicate it to those with whom they come in contact . . . .In the interests not of our Mission only, but in the interests of the natives they should be banned from camping there.[3]

Apparently conditions were no better in 1941. Pastor R. H. Traeger complained about the conduct of the Aborigines on the reserve and the Ceduna policeman went to investigate. He found their conduct reasonable, but instructed them to send their children back to school at Koonibba and clean up the reserve. He pointed out that there was a scarcity of labour due to men being called up for the Second World War and the wheat could not have been loaded without Aboriginal labour. The Aboriginal people were, nevertheless, warned that they would have to move on when the work finished, as the Ceduna reserve was only suitable as a temporary camp for people passing through the town, not for families to set up semi-permanent homes. Hans Gaden, the sharefarmer at Koonibba, recalls helping to move the people at the Ceduna and other local reserves back to Koonibba on three separate occasions.[4]

In 1945 there were plans to move the reserve to Denial Bay about 8 miles west of Ceduna. People living at the reserve were very worried about the proposed move and wrote to Dr Charles Duguid, an activist in Aboriginal affairs, to voice their concerns and seek his support,

> . . . We see that it [the Denial Bay location] is not suitable. We will face many hard times, inconvenient for everything. And where we are, we can get our living here, work, here and there, but at Denial Bay we will starve and this is our free country. We want our reserve near town where we can work and earn our tucker. We dont get government rashion and nobody feed us. We battle ourselfs we dont want to be chased about from place to place . . . . The minister dont want us on the Mission Station & from there he hunt us away . . . . And when we are in Ceduna, they get the Policeman to hunt us away from here. We dont know where to go they chase us like wild dingoes . . . . They dont like to see us walking about the streets, but they want black people to do their dirty work. They want native people to live on the Mission Station, but no proper place and very hard for water and wood since the British won the War they seem to be get very nasty to us native people . . .[5]

Fortunately for the people who camped at the reserve and worked at Thevenard, the reserve was retained. In 1947 the Protector of Aborigines decided to improve the facilities by building lavatories, bringing the water supply closer to the reserve, providing garbage bins and supplying tents as temporary accommodation. Not until the late 1950s did the government begin to make houses available to Aboriginal people in Ceduna. Again individual life stories help illuminate the collective experience.

Yari (Harry Russel) and Lena Miller

Of the families who at one time or another were able to find houses in Ceduna in the 1930s and 1940s, one family, the Millers, managed to resist enormous pressures from the local white population who demanded their removal. They lived in the centre of Ceduna from 1942 until the mid-1950s, when they moved to a reserve away from the centre of town. They had originally come from Penalumba/Bookabie area. Yari, the son of the white Joe Miller and his Aboriginal wife, Maggie, had moved with his family to Koonibba in the late 1920s.[6]

In 1942 they moved to Ceduna where Yari Miller got a job carting night dirt with the Ceduna Council. There were continual complaints from the white population about this family living in the centre of town and only very occasional support.[7] The Ceduna primary school refused to accept the Miller children, or any Aboriginal children for that matter, arguing that a school was provided for Aboriginal children at Koonibba. (No white child was expected to go to a school 30 miles away.)[8] The Secretary of the Aborigines Protection Board wrote to the Director of Education pointing out that if the children were forced to go to Koonibba, their father would probably give up his job and go too, leaving the family without financial support. He added that it was government policy to allow Aboriginal children into the government school system as long as their home conditions measured up to the standard of the general community.[9] Despite the support of the Secretary of the Aborigines Protection Board (W. R. Penhall) Aboriginal children continued to be barred from the Ceduna school.

The family responded by arranging correspondence lessons supervised by the sister-in-law of the school-age children. In 1947 the head teacher of the Ceduna School argued that if the children from one Aboriginal family were admitted the school would be swamped by an influx of children from other families. Penhall promised to control the entry of other Aboriginal children, but as late as 1951 there were still no Aboriginal children at the school. This time the excuse given was that the Millers did not own their own home. Penhall wrote to the government minister responsible, pointing out that children could not be discriminated against because their parents did not own their house and that as long as the house and children were clean the school must accept them.[10]

Discrimination was not the only obstacle facing this family who had decided that they had a right to live among white people. As the only Aboriginal family living permanently in Ceduna, their house was the meeting place for Aboriginal people visiting Ceduna. As a result the house was sometimes reported to be overcrowded; people would bring alcohol to the house and drink. There were occasional brawls and fights. Whites blamed the Miller family for the behaviour of their guests and for attracting them to the main street of Ceduna. In 1945 Yari Miller lost his job with the Ceduna Council ostensibly because he was not working well, but the real reason was that the Council realised it would not be able to move the family out of town as long as he was gainfully employed.[11] After his sacking the District Clerk tried to get the Secretary of the Aborigines Protection Board to move the family out of Ceduna. However, the Millers obstinately remained, the men picking up casual work on the wharves and the women finding domestic work at the hospital or in the town. The pressures from the townspeople never abated. Visits from the police and the Aborigines Protection Board welfare officer must have been an upsetting part of their lives. Generally, the reports on the living conditions in the house were good but, despite Lena's high standards of housekeeping (every dirty cup had to be washed and put away as it was used, food was covered and everything was left spotless),[12] it was occasionally reported that the house was dirty or overcrowded. Yari pointed out to the authorities that there was nowhere else for Aboriginal people to meet or wait for transport if they were visiting Ceduna to shop or visit the doctor and he suggested a hall or some shelter could be provided as an alternative to the family house on Poynton Street.

The family was penalised in other ways for continuing to live in Ceduna. They were refused exemption from the controls of the *Aborigines Act*, not because fault could be found with their own behaviour but because other Aboriginal people used their house as a meeting place. Once exempted from the *Aborigines Act* an Aboriginal person could no longer associate with non-exempt Aboriginal people. They were allowed to drink alcohol but were not allowed to supply other Aboriginal people with drink. Although the Aborigines Protection Board claimed that the family would not be able to fulfil these requirements as long as they lived in the centre of Ceduna, they were finally exempted in 1947.

The frustrations of the family's position are expressed in a letter to Penhall on 12 October 1946:

as long as I have lived in Ceduna. You have always been well awake for any report like this [from the police] to have me shifted from the town back to the Mission. But Im afraid Ill have to disapoint you in saying that you or any one else will never shift me from where I am . . . I am paying my own way for the house Im occupying here. Did the Aboriginal Board find me this house Im occupying here . . . did they help to buy the belonging I now posses diffenately no. Then why try and control me and my family as you claim you can . . . .So in future I wont you to understand my house is run by me and me alone and not by the Police or the Board. I claim Im enderpentent [independent] from the Prodection board, and I wish to remain so, Ive lived at the Mission all told about 10 years, I found as a Aboriginal a man dont get enough assistance what so ever. And another thing I would like to impress on you and its this that Im not a aboriginal [under the Act] . . . .[13]

Penhall was not impressed by this show of independence and wrote back pointing out that under section 4 of the *Aborigines Act* anyone descended from the original inhabitants of Australia was an Aborigine, came under the control of the Board, and could be removed to an Aboriginal institution. 'From the foregoing you will see that the Board has power to remove you to Koonibba if it deems such course to be necessary but I sincerely hope you will so order your life and those of the members of your family that you will become a useful citizen.'[14]

In 1956 the family left the house in the centre of Ceduna and moved to 18 Tank on what was then the edge of town (where Yari Miller Hostel now stands). There Yari leased 4 acres of scrub land from the district council. The Millers lived in tents supplied by the Aborigines' Department and their kitchen was constructed of bags with painted bag walls. In 1959 after Yari suffered a stroke, the family moved to Duck Ponds (section 13 Hundred of Bonython), land he had bought in 1942. Two of his sons with their families had already moved there and built two shacks. They got their water from soaks, and their children, who by then had been admitted to the Ceduna school, were transported to school by the Education Department. They earned money by cutting wood in the adjoining scrub for the plaster works at £4/10/- per ton and shearing.[15]

In 1960 Yari died believing he had left his family secure on their own land. However, in 1965 the State Department of Aboriginal Affairs forced a new arrangement on them. In exchange for water being connected to the block an area was excised from their holdings so the Far West Aboriginal Association could establish an Aboriginal reserve known as Halfway Camp. This reserve (section 197) was gazetted on 20 September 1965. About the same time the Council objected to the reserve because it blocked access to the beach and shell and sand deposits it mined for road building.[16] In 1966 there were calls to have the Aboriginal reserve relinquished and made a nature reserve because the Aborigines were denuding the area of wood.[17] The Department of Aboriginal Affairs did not respond to this pressure. It remained a reserve, even though it was by now the department's stated policy not to set up fringe settlements on the outskirts of towns, but to encourage Aboriginal families to live in towns. Today the reserve area, Halfway Camp, is still used by Yalata and some Koonibba people and the Millers lease the remainder of the land from the Aboriginal Lands Trust.

Wudinna

Wudinna on the railway line in central Eyre Peninsula appears to have been a less overtly racist town than Ceduna. During the 1940s it attracted quite a large Aboriginal population. A few families settled permanently, while others went there for treatment at the hospital or to seek work either with the railways or the Engineering and Water Supply Department which was then constructing the Tod River pipeline. As with other towns in the area, there were no housing or other facilities for Aboriginal people. They camped on the reserve in the usual makeshift structures with no services. Occasionally a family found temporary accommodation in the town, but no family held on to a house on a long-term basis as the Millers had in Ceduna.

One family did, however, manage to lease private land next to the Aboriginal reserve on which they constructed their own home.[18] Prior to settling at Wudinna about 1942, this family had moved around Eyre Peninsula including the settlements of Wirrulla and Yantanaby where some of their children had briefly attended school. After the children had been dismissed from these schools, two daughters were then sent to Koonibba. Once the family settled in Wudinna they began a protracted fight to get their daughters released from the mission. Normally children in the Children's Home were allowed to return to their families for the Christmas holidays, but because this family had been adamant about having their daughters released the missionary refused to let them go, fearing they would not be returned at the end of the holidays. Penhall supported him by insisting that the police had to certify that the Wudinna house was 'up to standard' before the children would even be allowed home for holidays. These parents were labelled troublemakers because they fought to have their children returned to them.[19]

In February 1944 the mother wrote to the Secretary of the Aborigines Protection Board claiming the teacher at the Wudinna School had agreed to take her children. But when the teacher and policeman later went to inspect her house, the policeman described it as a two-room place made out of scrap iron on a block adjacent to the Aboriginal camp with the usual influx of dogs and fleas. He went on to say she would have to live in a reasonable building away from the camp before her children would be admitted to school.[20] She eventually got the authorities to agree to release one of her daughters from Koonibba and allow her to board with another family who had recently left Koonibba and moved to a house in Wudinna. The girl was allowed to attend Wudinna school while living in this house.[21] To this extent, the Wudinna community was more tolerant than Ceduna where no Aboriginal child was admitted, however clean, intelligent or 'assimilated' he or she might be.

Soon the newly arrived family from Koonibba were embroiled in other troubles. Another family had moved in with them and it was reported that the house was dirty. The children were sent home from school with head lice. At this point they considered returning to Koonibba. It was a never-ending struggle maintaining themselves in the general community, but they did not relish returning to the crowded conditions on the mission where, they said, twelve people had to share each two-room house. This family later moved on to Port Lincoln where they lived in a two-room shack in an Aboriginal camp and the father found work in nearby towns.[22]

The daughter of the Wudinna family who remained in the Children's Home at Koonibba became pregnant when she was 14 years old and, although a youth was charged with carnal knowledge, her family could justifiably claim that the mission had proved unable to control or protect her and she should be returned to them.[23]

As Wudinna hospital was subsidised by the Aborigines Protection Board, it was obliged to take Aboriginal patients (unlike the Ceduna hospital which refused to treat any Aborigines). Prior to the Second World War the police had been reimbursed for petrol used to transport Aborigines who needed medical attention. When this subsidy was dropped Aborigines had to make their own way to hospital. Admitting Aborigines and on the railway line, it became the favoured hospital for Aborigines from northern and western Eyre Peninsula. The families and friends of people attending the hospital camped on the reserve. In 1943 hospital authorities complained that the Aborigines who came for treatment took up the majority of the hospital's ten beds. Penhall pointed out that Ceduna was not a subsidised hospital and Streaky Bay, although subsidised, did not have a resident doctor. Wudinna would therefore have to continue to accept Aborigines in order to qualify for its £700 subsidy.[24] The hospital did not complain about behaviour or cleanliness of its patients, only of their predominance.

There was a large Engineering and Water Supply Department (E & WS) camp in Wudinna next to the Aboriginal reserve, housing men who worked on the Tod River pipeline. There were casual contacts between the Aborigines and the single men involving liaisons with the Aboriginal women and illegal supply of liquor to the reserve. There were reports of drunkenness and accompanying fights. The proximity of the reserve to the camp made it difficult for the police to supervise the Aborigines and their contacts with the men at the E & WS camp, many of whom had police records and unsavoury reputations. As a result, from 1945 there was talk of moving the Aboriginal reserve, even though it was a permanent fixture in the town and the E & WS camp was temporary accommodation associated with the building of the pipeline.[25] In 1946 the Aborigines Department's Superintendent of Reserves visited Wudinna and reported:

> The camp was in a shocking state, with rubbish and filth all round the camps. The living quarters comprise bag huts and wurlies of bushes, all in a dirty state. There are no sanitary arrangements of any description, with the result that flies are present in large numbers. The dogs also are in large numbers, and do not add to the cleanliness of the camp. I instructed the natives to clean up as much as possible, also to erect a lavatory out of bags, and I would inspect the camp the next day.[26]

The only water supply for the whole camp was located on the privately leased block next to the reserve.

The Wudinna council offered to give the Aborigines Protection Board 6 acres of land lying almost half a mile west of the town to establish a new reserve, close to the pipeline and easily supplied with water. Various members of the Wudinna white community pointed out that the state of the present Aboriginal camp precluded their children from being admitted to the Wudinna school. It was estimated that as long as there was work at Wudinna the Aboriginal reserve would have at least six families permanently camped there, with a fluctuating population of up to sixty.[27]

The policeman planned to build huts in military formation each with its own garden on the new reserve, but these grand plans were stymied by lack of building materials which were in very short supply during this postwar period. Living conditions on the new reserve soon replicated those on the old site:

> Rubbish is lying around in all directions, and, with the exception of Highfolds and MacNamara's huts, the rest are a disgrace. Most of the huts appear to be overcrowded, due to lack of material to extend premises. The sanitary conditions are very poor, some crude lavatories having been erected out of old tins or bags, these have a rough seat and a shallow hole only . . . Most of the men were away working on the Pipe line and Railways; the women state they try to keep the area clean, but the children go to the Council rubbish tip, which is very close to the camp, and bring in all sorts of rubbish from this dump.[28] . . . They seem to have some genuine grievances,
> 1. If material was available they could and would make more substantial dwellings.
> 2. If material was supplied, they would make a couple more lavatories.
> 3. That some arrangements be made to supply drinking water, as the Tod water is undrinkable. They suggested water from Poldina Tanks be laid on.
> 4. That facilities for bathing be erected.
> 5. That a couple of wheel barrows be supplied to wheel away rubbish.[29]

As in Ceduna, Aboriginal people were expected to emulate the lifestyle of the white community without having the means to do so. Exemptions from the *Aborigines Act* also became an issue. One family, who lived permanently in Wudinna, were exempted, only to find themselves almost immediately accused of supplying liquor to Aborigines living on the reserve. Their exemption also prohibited them from living on the reserve with the other Aboriginal people. In 1948 all but one of the exemptions was revoked.

In 1948 the E & WS camp at Wudinna was disbanded and moved to Port Neill, halfway between Port Lincoln and Cowell on the east coast of Eyre Peninsula. The E & WS wanted the Aboriginal men from Wudinna to move too as they were among their best workers. The Highfolds, Reids, Eyles, MacNamaras, Benbolts and Peels decided to go. The men moved with the rest of the workers leaving 14 women and 23 children at the reserve in Wudinna in November 1948. By March 1949 the reserve was deserted. However, a few Aboriginal people remained in the town of Wudinna including one family, the Larkins, who lived in a railway-owned cottage and a couple of families camping on private land. This experience underscores the point that neither laziness nor inertia sustained such settlements.

Port Lincoln

This town provides yet another example of the dismal living conditions Koonibba people found when they moved away from the mission in the hope of establishing themselves independently. Many initially moved to Port Lincoln in the 1940s to work at the freezing plant. Casual employment was also available on the wharves. Some men, who based their families in Port Lincoln, worked for the E & WS at Port Neill, the railways, the highways department or on farms on lower Eyre Peninsula. Two families, including the Daveys, who had enjoyed the reputation for being one of the most dependable at Koonibba in the 1920s, moved to Port Lincoln in the early 1940s where they found a house at Kirton Point. They did not face the same harassment from the local white community that the Millers met in Ceduna, and their children were admitted to the local primary school. In 1944 the Daveys were reported to be sharing their house with two other families. But Port Lincoln is a long way from Koonibba so there were not the same pressures on them to play host to a continual stream of visitors.

Most Koonibba people who gravitated to Port Lincoln in search of work camped near the large Cresco fertiliser plant, more than a kilometre from the centre of town. Living conditions there were very basic. There was the usual lack of services. However, because the area was not an official Aboriginal reserve and a number of families owned the blocks where they camped, the Aborigines Protection Board had no control over who lived there, nor could they prevent white men from going there as they could on proclaimed reserves. In 1950 a local policeman reported there were two camps near Cresco: one alongside the fertiliser works and the other one behind it:

> The condition of the camp alongside the works is of a higher class than that of the other. All Natives are living in wood and iron places, and none are camped in tents or the open. These Natives seem to conduct themselves better than those living in the lower camp. I noticed that the shacks in general were kept clean and tidy . . . I then made a visit to the rear of the Cresco. This is where all the trouble starts in respect of Natives in Port Lincoln. It is the general meeting place for all Natives passing through town. There are not any sanitary arrangements, the whole camp is filthy, even for Natives, and some are living in wood and iron shacks and some in bag humpies and tents.[30]

While this report was filed by an unsympathetic police constable who went on to describe some of the Aboriginal inhabitants of the camps in rather derogatory terms, his description of the living conditions gives an impression of the poverty-stricken and deprived circumstances in which many people lived. Illegal drinking, drunkenness and prostitution with sailors from the ships in port was common. In the sixteen months from July 1949, forty-four Aboriginal people were convicted in Port Lincoln for liquor-related offences and five white men charged for supplying liquor to Aborigines.[31]

In 1957 the government finally moved to improve living conditions by declaring a reserve at Mallee Park in Port Lincoln and building housing for Aboriginal people there.[32]

Station life

Not all Koonibba people gravitated to towns; some preferred to work on pastoral stations and farms and live on the land or in small rural communities. They found work in the Gawler Ranges to the east of Koonibba, and in the west from Penong to Fowlers Bay and the Nullarbor Plain as well as farms in central and southern Eyre Peninsula. These people were relatively free from outside interference as long as work was available and their children were in school. The major problem with leading an itinerant life in remote areas was the education of children. A number of families who chose this life were prepared to leave their children in the Children's Home so they could attend school; others were determined to retain control over their offspring. When these itinerant families lived in small, outback settlements which had a school, such as Coorabie and Kooringabie, the children were able to attend them, but their families never stayed in one place very long. Thus the children's schooling was erratic and far from satisfactory.

These rural families found casual work including shearing, woolpicking and boundary riding on pastoral stations or hunting kangaroos and trapping rabbits for their fur and carcases. In 1947 many Koonibba people went to the Nullarbor to trap rabbits. There were large camps on the Plain. Freezer trucks made regular trips to Melbourne taking rabbit carcases and returning with goods to sell to the trappers and their families. But in a normal season only a few families found work on the arid western lands. Many of the station managers are reported to have treated their Aboriginal workers fairly, but a few exploited them, paying low or no wages at all and miserly rations.[33]

One family who had kept their children with them as they moved from one job to another in the west eventually agreed to move to Koonibba so the children could attend school without being parted from their parents.[34] This decision meant the father had to travel long distances to work. In 1951 he was working at the salt works at Penong and spending $4 of his weekly earnings of $18 to get back to Koonibba at weekends.[35] Another family was persuaded to put their children in the Children's Home, which made their mother quite distraught. It is reported she cried for two days when her 6-year-old daughter was taken from her.[36]

Apart from the problems associated with schooling, families who chose to remain in the bush avoided the transitional problems confronting Koonibba people who looked for employment in towns. If housing was provided they used it, if not, they built their own camps without the pressure of local councils and health authorities checking on them and trying to move them on.

The relationship between white station staff and Aboriginal people was generally amicable as they worked together. Many townspeople, in contrast, had no direct personal contact with Aboriginal people. One rural white family, the Millers, had particularly close associations with Aboriginal people. Three brothers from this family, one of whom had a property at Penalumba near Bookabie, married Aboriginal women. Many west coast Aboriginal families are descended from them (including the Millers in Ceduna). There were often Aboriginal people camped on their land.

Women

Special issues and problems faced women in this period, some of which have already been alluded to. Strict traditional mores no longer governed people's behaviour; they had disappeared after decades of contact with white society and mission education. The first generation of Christian converts generally conformed to the morality that was preached to them at the mission, but the following generations lived in environments less hedged round with moral certainties. Factors which contributed to this situation may include the breakdown of the family and extended family unit as the main enforcer of social and cultural behaviour, and the double standards encountered in white society.

The mission, and particularly the Children's Home, took over the role of bringing up children, depriving parents and other traditional authority figures of much of the power and influence they had previously wielded in Aboriginal society. While the missionary and the institution were able to control the behaviour of children when they were young, their influence waned with the advent of adolescence. The children had been taught not to emulate their parents' lifestyle.[37] However, there were no substitute parents available as role models for the children.

The mission taught a Christian code of ethics and behaviour, but the encounter with the general community indicated that white people seldom applied these standards in their dealings with Aboriginal people. Women were particularly vulnerable to exploitation. The mission discouraged arranged marriages and adolescent girls from Ooldea being sent to their promised husbands.[38] But the institution of early sexual relations and marriage even among long-term Koonibba residents persisted despite the missionaries' influence.[39] The mission tried to protect/control adolescent girls and even women in their twenties by keeping them in the Children's Home, but this did not prevent pregnancies and illegitimate births.[40] Some of the women who had illegitimate children left the mission, although mission policy towards them varied, depending on the missionary in charge. Traeger felt he was condoning immoral behaviour by having them on the mission.[41] Eckermann, on the other hand, believed it was better if the mission continued to try to rehabilitate those who had misbehaved and not send them away.[42] Traeger banned men and women who lived in de facto relationships from the mission, some even after the relationship had broken up.[43]

The prospects for a single woman with a baby were not good. Her only form of income was child endowment unless she could find someone to look after her baby while she went out to work. Like other Aboriginal people she had nowhere decent to live once she left Koonibba. In 1944 it was reported that six women and three babies were sharing a house in Thevenard. One of the women was said to procure the others for the Greek workers at the port.[44] Another report in the same year claimed there were twelve women sharing one room in the house and loitering at the wharf when ships came in.[45] One of them, who was said to be responsible for running what amounted to a brothel, had been separated from her husband for many years and had lived in a de facto relationship. She was therefore banned from the mission. Another of the women was also separated from her husband and three of the women had illegitimate children, so none of them had a male wage earner to support them.

There were also single women living in the camps in Port Lincoln who picked up men from the wharves and would offer sex for money or grog. Women living on reserves in other towns were known to have liaisons with white men, which under the *Aborigines Act* were illegal. In some instances the authorities were able to prove the paternity by white men and arrange maintenance payments for the mother.[46]

Girls and women who found legitimate employment were not thereby protected from sexual exploitation and some became pregnant by their employers.[47] There were also said to be those who had absorbed the values of the white society who wanted to associate with white men and have white babies, as they were more acceptable in the wider community.[48] Some families had left Koonibba so that their light-coloured children would not associate with the darker children on the mission.[49] There were also reports of girls becoming pregnant by boys on the mission, and then failing to get permission to marry because their parents did not want their children marrying someone with a darker skin.

The rate of illegitimacy and marriage breakdown increased in this period and it was generally the women who suffered the worst consequences, although men and boys also suffered. (For instance, one youth was gaoled for carnal knowledge, others were banned from the mission as punishment for their sexual misdemeanours.) But the males were not as vulnerable as women to continuing exploitation, were not left with the responsibility of child care and had more avenues of employment open to them.

Movement on to the mission

At the same time as people were leaving Koonibba to try to establish themselves in the general community, a trickle of new residents joined the community. Most came from the 'spinifex country' in the far north via Ooldea. Ooldea Soak, located 6 kilometres north of the railway line, was an ancient trading and ceremonial ground, the only source of water for hundreds of kilometres. The novelty of the line and the opportunity to obtain food from construction workers and later travellers, attracted Aborigines from the north. In 1919 the ethnographer, Daisy Bates, moved to Ooldea Siding to distribute food and provisions, thereby giving the ancient site a modern context. In 1933 the United Aborigines Mission (UAM) established a settlement at the Soak. Twenty years later it was disbanded at which time the Aborigines were forced to move away.[50] Many moved south to a new site at Yalata, administered by the Lutherans.

There had been continual movement of people between Ooldea and Koonibba over the years. Some Ooldea people had brought their children to the Children's Home. Adults also visited kin at the mission or came in search of work. A large influx of children came to the home when the UAM mission was disbanded. Many of the converts at Koonibba in the 1940s–1950s were from Ooldea. The movement of Ooldea people to the west coast had another dramatic effect on Koonibba. It more than doubled the Aboriginal population of a region, which had previously been unable to support even the people at Koonibba. Scarce employment became scarcer as Ooldea people, with little experience of wage labour, willingly accepted lower pay and more basic working conditions. This put added pressure on Koonibba people to move away.

The end of the mission era

Through the 1950s Aboriginal people, government officials and some members of the Lutheran Church increasingly acknowledged the Church's inability to maintain a standard of living for Aboriginal people in line with contemporary expectations. Aboriginal people were also coming to realise that they could publicly articulate their own concerns both individually and as a community. In 1958 the whole population walked off the mission during a protest and camped at 18 Tank. The initial reason for leaving the mission was their support for one man, Cyril Coaby, who had been banned from Koonibba. The missionary had refused to let him back even on the compassionate grounds of visiting his sick daughter, and had called the police when he ignored the ban. Coaby was gaoled for three months but on his release the ban remained in place, so everyone walked off the mission. They sent the mission board a list of complaints including: the discontinuance of the distribution of rations at Koonibba; the lack of work; inadequate housing; unsatisfactory shopping hours; the lack of single men's quarters; and a request for Aboriginal representation on the Church Board of Aboriginal Missions.[51] Though the dispute was finally resolved by a representative from the Department of Aboriginal Affairs, it did indicate that Aboriginal people themselves were concerned about living standards and, more important, were asking for a say in running their own affairs.

By the late 1950s there was alarm at the poor physical fabric of the mission. In 1959 the Church established a Commission under the chairmanship of E. W. Wiebusch, a son of the first missionary at Koonibba, which was to investigate conditions and make recommendations as to the future of the mission. Even before the Commission was established, the government had indicated that it would consider taking over the mission if asked to do so by the Church.[52] After much discussion and deliberation the Commission recommended that the government take over the administration of Koonibba. Lengthy negotiations followed before the takeover became a reality in July 1963.

The Koonibba people protested at decisions being taken about their future and their homes without consultation. They petitioned the Executive Council of the Evangelical Lutheran Church of Australia and the Minister of Works and sent a delegation to the Board of Missions. They also wrote to the Minister of Works asking him to receive a deputation of Koonibba people. A copy of the petition was sent to the Church with a covering letter from Robert K. Miller and Albert J. Lawrie stating Koonibba people found the offer of the Church to the government unsatisfactory because:

—it set out as its declared aim 'the eventual disbandonment of the Koonibba Mission' and 'depopulation of the whole establishment' and Koonibba people would as a result lose their home, the centre of their spiritual training and the opportunity to continue in communal life with their own people;

—it would reduce the mission from 22,000 acres to only 2000 acres;

—it suggested a limited vocational programme instead of a full-scale one.

They expressed a fear that people would be forced out to stand on their own feet before they were ready. The petition covered similar ground but in more detail and outlined their own blueprint for the future of the mission. It pointed out that assimilation and dispersal should not go too fast and that there should be a right of self-determination. In the past good, self-respecting families had left the mission and had become degraded in white communities, where they often mixed with the worst elements and went to pieces under their influence. The petition went on to describe an alternative to that offered by the Church and government. There could be a native cooperative run by staff and a local Aboriginal management committee elected annually. The Church could donate the land, buildings, livestock and plant at Koonibba, while the government would contribute its proposed annual expenditure of around £36,000 a year. The aims and activities of the cooperative would be to provide employment and training at Koonibba. A trial period of three years for the experiment was suggested. The petition had seventy-one signatures on behalf of eighty-four people living at Koonibba.[53]

With its exaggerated deprecation of life off the mission, the petition shows the unmistakable influence of C. V. Eckermann who returned to Koonibba for a third term in 1960 and was inspired by the old ideal of a self-governing, self-respecting community at Koonibba.[54] He strongly opposed the government takeover. The Board of Aboriginal Mission's response to the proposals of the Koonibba people was to request the Minister of Aboriginal Affairs to stay proceedings while it considered the plan. There is no further evidence that it was considered. The government response was similarly unenthusiastic. When Robert Miller wrote on behalf of a Koonibba delegation to the Minister he received a reply saying the discussions with the Lutheran Church had not advanced enough to foretell the outcome, however the purpose of the discussions were to ensure the people were advanced. There was no acknowledgement that the Koonibba people might want to have a say in their future. A deputation of Edmund Ware, Cyril Coaby, Clem Chester and Robert Miller accompanied by Eckermann saw the Minister on 17 June 1962. They went over the same ground covered by the petition and the Minister made a predictably non-committal response.[55]

Soon after this, A. J. Copley from the Aborigines Protection Board visited Koonibba to report on conditions. His main purpose was to see how the government's assimilation policy could best be implemented by assessing the people's readiness to join the general population. He recommended that in the event of a government takeover the Children's Home be closed and those children who had no relatives be fostered or adopted by whites or people of mixed descent (there were fourteen children in the home at the time of his visit). He also recommended that the Education Department take control of the school where ninety-four children seemed happy and were receiving a satisfactory education. Copley was adamant that the Church should only retain responsibility for the spiritual well-being of the people and relinquish all other administrative functions. He criticised Eckermann for fostering the feeling among all the scattered people that Koonibba was their home to which they could return at any time. He blamed the missionary for the annual oscillations of people between outside jobs and Koonibba. He did not take into consideration the hostile conditions Aborigines encountered once they moved away from Koonibba, nor did he reflect that these might explain why people returned from time to time. He showed no appreciation of the decades of historical development that lay behind these movement patterns.

Copley claimed morale at Koonibba was low, that 34 out of 75 men were on unemployment benefits and housing conditions were poor and unhygienic. He believed that within twelve months of a government takeover people would respond to incentives and encouragement to stay in employment away from Koonibba. He listed all the families at Koonibba and ranked them according to his criteria of suitability for assimilation. He also noted whether they had spent any part of their childhood in Aboriginal camps rather than in European conditions. Based on this classification he believed that 28 out of 52 couples were suitable for training of which 12 to 16 would be able to move away from Koonibba in 12–18 months. That left 24 families who 'could not be assimilated'.

Copley concluded:

> I agree with the principle that Koonibba must be depopulated as quickly as prudence will allow, but we have still to work out a solution for the increasing semi-tribal population of Yalata. With the goal of assimilation the semi-tribal Aborigines at Yalata will need some training ground where small numbers can be gradually brought for training towards that eventual goal. For this reason alone as much of Koonibba should be retained as finance will permit . . .
>
> The Lutheran Church has endeavoured to solve the problem over a period of 60 years, but the

ultimate goal of assimilation into the general community has proved to be beyond the physical and financial capabilities of the Church.

The only practical solution which can and must succeed is for the Government, through the Aborigines Department, to take over the full control and management of the Koonibba Mission.

The irony of Copley's report was that it blamed the mission rather than the long years of hostile government action and white racism for making Koonibba a valued refuge and home.

Negotiations were finalised in 1963 and the official handover took place on 1 July. The government agreed to buy 2,000 acres of land known as the 'homestead area', of which 5.75 acres, on which the church and manse were situated, were excised and retained by the Church. The rest of the 17,908 acres were leased by the government; the Children's Home was closed and the school came under Education Department control.[56] On the day of the handover Copley accompanied the new superintendent, Dudley Brown, his wife, the storekeeper and welfare officer to Koonibba. The following evening a social was held at which Eckermann introduced the new staff. And so began a new era in Koonibba history.

It was unfortunate for Koonibba and its people that the Aborigines Department and its administrator interpreted their policy of assimilation in a very inflexible, doctrinaire way in the initial years of their control of the station. This, coupled with the State government decision to legalise the consumption of alcohol by Aborigines, made the period of adaptation from one system of administration to another difficult, if not catastrophic, for many Koonibba people.[57] What Koonibba people remember about this period are the access to liquor with its harmful social consequences, and their regret it was no longer a Christian community.[58]

Despite the upheavals caused by the government takeover and the disruptive effects of the assimilation policies in the 1960s, Koonibba survived as an Aboriginal community and is now self-governing. It controls its own land which was purchased from the Lutheran Church through the Aboriginal Development Commission in 1988. In January 1988 there were twenty-nine households at Koonibba consisting of 143 permanent residents and a long waiting list of people wanting to move to the settlement.[59]

The significance of the institutional experience

The role played by Koonibba for Aborigines of the west coast in their struggle to maintain a communal life is full of ambiguities. As circumstances changed through the last century so did the function of the mission. In the first years it was a convenient stopping place with access to food and work. Only a few people, who had had a long association with white society, considered it a permanent home. But government policies towards children of mixed descent influenced many more people to move to Koonibba. Institutionalisation of their children was preferable to living with the anxiety of having children taken away from their camps. The price paid for security was baptism and mission education, which inevitably affected Aboriginal ceremonial and religious life as the supply of initiates dwindled. Communal survival, it seems, was considered more important than maintenance of religious forms.

By the 1920s the mission had become a total institution. This role was underpinned by the general society's insistence on segregating Aborigines. Discipline was strict and infringements punished. The language and attitudes of institutional life predominated as residents came to be referred to as 'inmates'. The Children's Home epitomised paternalistic control. The inability of the mission to become financially self-supporting led to a change in policy and adults were faced with the prospect of searching for work off the mission. They found that their labour was welcomed in towns and agricultural areas, but segregationist attitudes prevailed in all other aspects of life. The search for work dominated the lives of the west coast Aborigines. They displayed none of the characteristics of 'intelligent parasitism', rather it was the white community who parasitically fed off their labour without providing conditions which would allow them to establish themselves independently.

In contrast, pastoral areas still offered some degree of independence, although no security. The white Miller brothers at Bookabie, who were incorporated in the Aboriginal network, offered a rare opportunity for some to live independently of the institution and white employers.

As people moved away from Koonibba in the 1930s and 1940s, it maintained its role as a refuge for those unable to enter the general community. The children continued to be a central focus of institutional life. Their education and control was now the primary function of the mission. Koonibba was also the centre of communal life. At Christmas people converged on the mission from all over Eyre Peninsula and the west coast for the annual celebration to sustain kin ties and swap news and gossip. The Christmas celebration replaced the Aboriginal ceremonies as the vehicle for maintaining community links and identity.

The increasing exodus of adults led to de facto reassessments of the mission role. One missionary, Traeger, tried to impose strict authoritarian control with the backing of the Aborigines Department. Eckermann, on the other hand, sought quixotically and idealistically to revive the impossible nineteenth-century dream of a holy village, uncontaminated by the disruptive forces of the outside world. The people responded to Eckermann's evident deep humanity, but voiced their own dissatisfactions both with institutional life and their fear of the dispersal of the community through revived assimilation policies. They wanted control over their own lives, but did not trust the government to give it to them.

Throughout the post-contact history of the west coast there is evidence that individuals and the community yearned for independence on their own land, but as this option was not available to them until the 1980s Koonibba remained the focus of communal cohesion.

Notes

1 Ceduna and Penong registered among the highest 'no' votes in Australia in the 1967 referendum on Aboriginal rights: GRG 52/1/1967/418, SAPRO. Sanitation was an excuse for segregation around the world, for example, Maynard W. Swanson, 'The sanitation syndrome: bubonic plague and the urban Native policy in the Cape 1900–1909', *Journal of African History*, 18, 1977, pp. 381–410.

2 GRG 52/1/1942/56, 1944/10, 33, 1947/53.

 3 Koonibba records, box 11, 5/3/1926, Lutheran Archives, Adelaide.
 4 Hans Gaden, pers. com. 18/2/1988, GRG 52/1/1941/38.
 5 GRG 52/1/1945/63.
 6 W. J. Miller, pers. com. April 1988.
 7 GRG 52/1/1941/38. A neighbour, W. Sedgley, praised the Millers and said that the Aborigines
    brought business to the town.
 8 With the exception of Hartley Clothier and his sister, who had a white father and Aboriginal
    mother, pers. com. 10/4/1990.
 9 GRG 52/1/1941/38.
10 GRG 52/1/1947/53. GRG 52/1/1951/12. The Miller children were finally admitted to the school
    soon after.
11 GRG 52/1/1945/63.
12 Lola Richards and Maurice Miller, pers. com. 9/4/1990.
13 GRG 52/1/1946/9.
14 GRG 52/1/1946/9.
15 W. J. Miller, Lola Richards and Maurice Miller, pers. com. 9/4/1990, GRG 52/1/1956/76, GRG
    52/1/1966/874.
16 GRG 52/1/1958/145 (letter dated 1/6/1965), GRG 52/1/1966/874.
17 Maurice Miller pointed out the land being cleared was farming land across the road from the
    reserve, pers. com. 10/9/1990.
18 The family has not been named to preserve its privacy.
19 GRG 52/1/1942/10, GRG 52/1/1943/10,10a.
20 GRG 52/1/1944/10.
21 GRG 52/1/1944/10.
22 GRG 52/1/1944/10a, GRG 52/1/1950/55.
23 GRG 52/1/1944/10a.
24 GRG 52/1/1943/27.
25 GRG 52/1/1945/53 and 54a.
26 GRG 52/1/1948/53, A. Bray 7/2/1946.
27 GRG 52/1/1948/53.
28 The proximity of the tip was not mentioned by the Wudinna Council at the time the site was chosen
    as a reserve area!
29 GRG 52/1/1948/53, A. Bray's report 5/3/1948. C. V. Eckermann remembers the camp as being in
    a reasonable condition on his visits and not as described in Bray's report: C. V. Eckermann letter to
    the author, 16/7/1990.
30 GRG 52/1/1950/55.
31 GRG 52/1/1950/55.
32 GRG 52/1/1957/75.
33 GRG 52/1/1944/45, 1940/95.
34 GRG 52/1/1948/28.
35 GRG 52/1/1951/33.
36 GRG 52/1/1948/58. The missionary suggested she could live on the mission in a cottage and have
    her daughter with her.
37 One woman complained that her daughter had been taken away from her, put in the Salvation
    Army Home in Adelaide, sent out to work for a German [that is, Lutheran] family, married and had
    a child and she, her mother had been told nothing of this. 'Because the German people brought her
    up not to have any respect to her mother . . . ': GRG 52/1/1939/71.
38 GRG 52/1/1947/28.
39 Cyril Coaby, pers. com. 23/3/1989.

40 GRG 52/1/1940/16a.

41 At Point Pearce and Point McLeay single mothers were confined to the mission and the father, if he were Aboriginal, was expelled: GRG 52/1/1944/10a, 1944/10a.

42 GRG 52/1/1948/9, 1949/32.

43 In one instance the Koonibba congregation expelled a woman who was living in an adulterous relationship: GRG 52/1/1944/10a, 1940/16, 1943/10, 1939/71.

44 GRG 52/1/1944/33.

45 GRG 52/1/1944/33.

46 GRG 52/1/1940/107, 1942/10a.

47 GRG 52/1/1947/53.

48 GRG 52/1/1947/53.

49 GRG 52/1/1944/45.

50 There were many factors which contributed to the demise of Ooldea mission: the soak was located in sandhills which became denuded through the heavy traffic caused by the permanent settlement, its goats and the need for firewood. The soak and settlement were gradually becoming buried by the drifting sands. By the 1950s the settlement was no longer viable. The Woomera Rocket Range and later the atomic tests at Maralinga restricted the movements of Aborigines in the area and forced many south into what was not previously their country.

51 Koonibba records, box 3, Lutheran Archives, Adelaide; Aboriginal Mission Board (AMB) minutes, meeting 18/2/1958, Lutheran Archives, Adelaide; Cyril Coaby, pers. com. 23/3/1989.

52 GRG 52/1/1958/171.

53 Koonibba records, box 4 and box 6.

54 C. V. Eckermann had previously been at Koonibba as a teacher in 1941–42 and as missionary from 1946–53.

55 Koonibba records, box 6, minutes of meeting 25/5/1962; GRG 52/1/1960/20.

56 The original Koonibba property was 12,762 acres and two farms (Moody's and Foggo's) were later added bringing the total acreage to nearly 20,000 acres: GRG 52/1/1960/20.

57 See chapter 2 for details of legislation controlling drinking alcohol.

58 Interviews undertaken by the author with Koonibba people between March 1988 and April 1990.

59 Danny Dollard, Koonibba community adviser, pers. com. 20/1/1988.

8

ADNYAMATHANHA, SURVIVAL WITHOUT INSTITUTIONALISATION

This third case study is an important contrast to the previous two. The Adnyamathanha survived without institutional support for many decades. During this period they did not disperse but consolidated a number of separate peoples into one communal identity with a common language, which has survived 120 years of contact. This trend resembles the movement that was apparently taking place on the west coast between Wirangu and Kokatha. Consolidation proved to be a very effective strategy. Apart from the Pitjantjatjara and Maralinga people (who were first thrown into direct and sustained contact with Europeans in the mid-twentieth century), only the Adnyamathanha among South Australian Aborigines have maintained a strong, communal identity which incorporates many elements from their pre-contact past. At the same time they have taken a lively interest in new technologies and knowledge.

In contrast to the previous two case studies, the Adnyamathanha welcomed missionaries into their settlement. The missionaries did not have to devise strategies to gather them together. Nor did they need to link Christianity to the 'civilising' process. The Adnyamathanha were already familiar with European expectations and behaviour. Another major difference was the mission experience. The United Aborigines Mission is not a denominational church like the Anglican and Lutheran, but an independent mission society. It does not have an established body of doctrine or strict rules governing conversion.[1] UAM missionaries were lay people, unsophisticated and often poorly educated. They did not have the financial resources or church support to establish total institutions. These factors, coupled with the Adnyamathanhas' own strongly established communal drive, meant they were never subjected to the discipline and control evident on the other two missions.

The history of the Adnyamathanha comprises three fairly distinct periods: the first extends from the earliest encounters with Europeans in the 1850s to the late 1920s, during which time they moved from violent confrontation to accommodation with the pastoral industry; the second is characterised by close interaction with missionaries over four decades from 1929–73; the last is the post-mission era.

E. H. Spicer and others have argued against seeing the post-contact experiences of Amerindian communities as an uninterrupted, inevitable progression from autonomy to cultural disintegration and dependence.[2] Citing the case of the Yacqui Indians of north-western Mexico, Spicer showed that long periods of cultural autonomy could be followed by periods of intense interaction with agents of colonisation, after which the Yacqui regained a considerable measure of self-sufficiency.[3] So it was with the Adnyamathanha. At certain times they were forced into fundamental reappraisals of their way of life, from which they emerged as a strong and coherent community, only to find themselves decades later once again having to make major readjustments to ensure their survival.

The Adnyamathanha of today are descended from many different groups of the North Flinders Ranges and surrounding plains. Adnyamathanha means hill or rock people. People living in the North Flinders Ranges at the time of the first white intrusion into the area were known to each other as Wailpi, Kuyani, Yadliyawara and Pirlatapa and it is thought by some that a group called the Adnyamathanha may also have existed on the western slopes of the Ranges.[4] The people of the North Flinders and the plains to the east and west spoke related languages.[5] Ceremonial and cultural life, which may previously have been divergent, coalesced in the early colonial period.[6] The different groups merged under the one group name, Adnyamathanha, through intermarrying and combining for ritual and ceremonial activities. In this way they maintained a communal identity which had been undermined by violent contact, disease and other destructive aspects of white contact. In the 1890s, in what appears to have been a cultural watershed, an initiation ceremony took place at Mount Lyndhurst in the north of the Ranges when 300–400 Diyari, Arabana, Wailpi, Jadliaura and even Wangka-Aranta (Arrernte speaking) attended. This large gathering was organised to enable an initiation to proceed despite the shortage of people in the various language groupings.[7] It testifies to the capacity of these peoples to remake themselves when circumstances demanded. The European invasion created many such demanding circumstances.

Arrival of Europeans in the North Flinders Ranges

E. J. Eyre was the first European to make his way through the Ranges. In 1840 he assessed the availability of pastoral land, although pastoralists did not move into the Flinders Ranges until the 1850s. J. F. Hayward stocked Aroona run in 1851 and by the mid-1850s pastoralists had moved to Angepena and beyond. As stock monopolised water supplies and grazing land, cutting off Aboriginal food supplies, the Adnyamathanha were attracted to European camps with their apparent ready supply of food. Owieandana, one of the earliest camps, attracted many Aborigines. It was here that rations were first distributed and they were shown how to cook with European flour.[8]

Hayward, the pastoralist at Aroona run, kept a diary which is one of the very few contemporary accounts of the early interactions between Aborigines and Europeans in the Flinders Ranges. He and his neighbours were not unusual in treating the Aborigines as

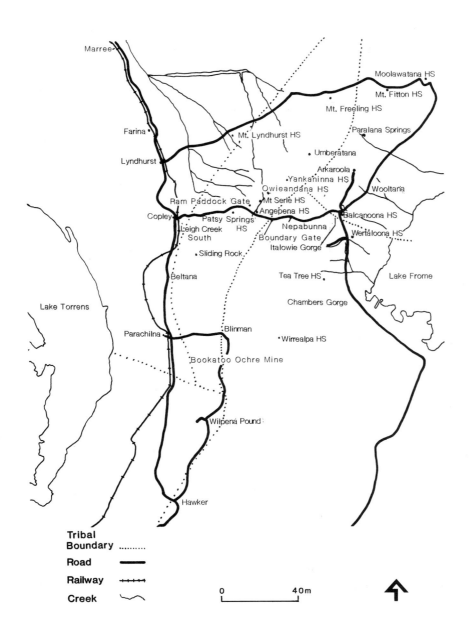

Marree

Moolawatana HS

Mt. Fitton HS

Mt. Freeling HS

Farina

Mt. Lyndhurst HS

Paralana Springs

Lyndhurst

Umberatana

Arkaroola

Yankaninna
Owieandana HS

Wooltana

Ram Paddock Gate

Mt Serle HS

Copley

Patsy Springs

Angepena HS

Balcanoona HS

Leigh Creek   HS
South

Nepabunna

Wertaloona HS

Boundary Gate
Italowie Gorge

Sliding Rock

Beltana

Tea Tree HS

Lake Frome

Lake Torrens

Chambers Gorge

Parachilna

Blinman

Wirrealpa HS

Bookatoo Ochre Mine

Wilpena Pound

Hawker

Tribal
Boundary ....
Road ▬▬▬
Railway ┼┼┼┼┼
Creek 〜〜〜

0   40m

Flinders Ranges

intruders with no rights. He recounts leading a party of men after a group of Aborigines, whom he believed had stolen some of his stock. He surprised the Aborigines, but the men escaped each carrying a child. Hayward claimed that they did this to protect themselves as he never shot women and children. Other evidence suggests that these niceties did not always prevail.[9] John Bowyer Bull, an adventurer who roamed over large areas of South Australia, claimed to have seen at Angepena station, a group of women and children who had been badly cut with stock whips. Two stockmen had found the group at a spring on Pernunna run and attacked them with whips to chase them away. Bull saw the women's breasts cut open, the babies and children bleeding. When, next day, the Aborigines killed a hutkeeper in revenge, the Europeans demanded protection from these marauders. The government sent an armed party to establish a police station on neighbouring Mount Serle leasehold.[10]

While droving sheep in the Ranges on another occasion Bull came across a group of Aboriginal women. He asked them where the men were and was told 'crackaback dead . . . all about white fellow shootam'. Bull commented that the Aborigines 'look upon the white man as their general enemy taking the water and hunting grounds from them and giving them no recompense for it, but shooting them down'.

Accommodation as well as resistance, accompanied the extension of the pastoral frontier. While the Adnyamathanha strove to maintain themselves by replacing native game with domesticated stock in their diet, they were learning to live with the invaders. They learned to ride horses and to use their own hunting skills in the management of stock. Even Hayward admitted that 'some of the black boys were quick to learn English and riding after stock and the men make capital trackers'.[11] Not all pastoralists showed Hayward's ferocity. John McTaggart, who employed Aboriginal labour on Wooltana 'got on well with the natives . . . he fought fair with the blacks with a waddy, not firearms'.[12]

Police from the Mount Serle station made regular patrols, but the rapid expansion of pastoralism meant they had to cover an increasingly vast territory through the Ranges and the plains to the east and west. The major part of their work was dealing with complaints of Aboriginal raids on stock. One reason that the Adnyamathanha survived, while their kin on the plains did not, is the ruggedness of the terrain. The cliffs and narrow gorges gave them easy escape routes from men on horses. They were more adept at climbing the rocky slopes, throwing rocks at their pursuers as they went. They hid stolen stock in the gorges, breaking the legs of sheep to prevent their escape. In October 1857 the police were called to Baker's station at Angepena after some cattle were taken. Two police troopers accompanied by three other men tracked the Aborigines to a gorge, down which they scrambled for about 2 miles. They came upon a group of twelve people with a large amount of meat, but when the police party was 20 yards away they 'made up the rocks like wallabi'. A police trooper fired hitting one man who turned and threw rocks almost killing the trooper. All the Aborigines escaped. It is said that the man shot was Wirrealpa Billy, and that he died of his wounds.[13]

The police and court system were not always arraigned against the Aborigines. Occasionally they did perform their function as protectors of Aborigines. The Mount Serle police sympathised with Aborigines on the plains who were 'annoyed' by hutkeepers and others 'playing with and making much of them one minute and ordering them around the next'. The police sided with an Aborigine who threw stones and a waddy at a pastoralist who tried to force him to do some work. In another incident several Adnyamathanha attacked and robbed a shepherd's hut. They turned on the police party, who tracked them down hurling stones at them. The police fired and shot two Aborigines for which they were later reprimanded and told they were not justified by law in shooting Aborigines, unless in self-defence. Two Aborigines were arrested. Pompey (Inabuthina) escaped and the other, Owieandana Billy, was released by the magistrate at Mount Remarkable when no witnesses appeared to testify.[14]

The Jacobs brothers, on whose 'property' this incident occurred, were themselves appalled at the violence against Aborigines:

> The Natives have great claim on our forbearance were it alone on the ground that we are as it were intruders on their country and the almost unavoidable consequences of the white man settling down there (to judge from previous experience) will be that in twenty years time, they will have become an almost extinct race, as where are now the fine tribes that were found in Adelaide as on the Murray in the early days.[15]

In the hope of averting other attacks motivated by hunger, the Jacobs applied for rations to distribute. Later after another incident on their property, in which a shepherd was killed, they requested that a Protector of Aborigines be appointed at the point at which Aborigines moved into the 'settled districts'.[16]

The Adnyamathanha gained respite from the invasion of their lands in the mid-1860s when the region was devastated by a drought which drove the police, the Jacobs and many other Europeans out of the Ranges. This was slight compensation for a people already weakened by over ten years of dispossession:

> In ordinary years aboriginal natives have ample supply of food in the numerous animals indigenous to this country. This year the terrible drought has been as fatal to those animals as it had been to the sheep and cattle of squatters.
>
>   The natural severity of the drought is greatly aggravated by the flocks and herds of the squatters which have utterly consumed or trodden out every vestige of grass or feed within miles of water. The aborigines have therefore but two resources—they are compelled to crowd around the dwellings of the squatters and beg for food or to follow tactics of Rob Roy and prey upon their flocks and herds. If they adopt the first course the settlers cannot supply them . . . if the natives adopt the alternative of helping themselves to food from the flocks and herds of the settlers they are hunted by the policemen, and if captured, are secured by a collar and chain rivetted around the neck and dragged away to stand trial under laws and customs they do not understand.[17]

The invasion of Adnyamathanha territory, had repercussions on other Aborigines, who valued the special resources of the Ranges, in particular, its high quality ochre. The ochre mines of Parachilna were valued by Aborigines as far north as south-western Queensland, east into New South Wales, west to Oodnadatta and south of the Ranges. Ochre was of high quality with a distinctive sheen and was traded for a variety of products including pituri from southern Queensland, green stone axes and flints, spears and decorated boomerangs. The ochre dust was collected and mixed with water or urine and formed into large cakes weighing around 30–40 kilograms with an indentation so they could be carried on the head on the return journey.[18] The journey to the mines, which might cover hundreds of miles, had many purposes. As well as a trading expedition, it was a major ceremonial and religious event. The Aborigines followed the Dreaming track of two mythical dogs *(Kintacawoola)* as they chased an emu *(Kurinii)* from near Innamincka, down Coopers Creek to Mount Freeling, along the western slopes of the Flinders Ranges and then east through the Ranges until they finally killed the emu at Parachilna. The emu's blood formed the highly valued ochre deposit.[19] Initiation ceremonies were also performed on the ochre collecting expeditions.

These expeditions were carefully negotiated ahead of time. As the expedition moved south, men from different communities joined it, but if all the negotiated conditions were not fulfilled, their path could be barred or other retribution sought. One such incident occurred in the late nineteenth century, which has been recounted by Adnyamathanha elders, when the traditional owners surrounded the mine and attacked the ochre gatherers as they came out.[20] The revenge party included Larrikin Tom, who died at Nepabunna in 1936 as a very old man.

The arrival of pastoralists added new hazards and benefits to the journey down the ochre trail. The northern Aborigines, referred to in contemporary accounts as 'Salt water' Aborigines, fed on sheep and cattle and raided shepherds' huts as they came south.[21] The Europeans regarded them as more aggressive than the local people, which is quite possible as they were only passing through and had a line of retreat to their own country if they were challenged. One such encounter was described by one of the police corporals stationed at Mount Serle police station.[22] A police party was searching for a party of Aborigines who had robbed huts and killed cattle at Mount Deception and on the plains. They eventually tracked down thirty-nine young men from the Lake Hope region, who were on an ochre expedition. When the Aborigines saw the police party they formed a camp and signalled to the police to stay on the track, but the police decided to accost them as they had stolen property with them. As the police approached the Aborigines threw waddies and boomerangs at them. The police responded with gunfire, but desisted when they realised they would have to kill most of them, if they were to make an arrest. The police surmised that only breech loading rifles would have intimidated the courageous young men.

In another incident involving Aborigines on the ochre trail, it was reported that eleven were killed outright for robbing a shepherd's hut on Beltana station and another forty to fifty of their companions died of wounds on their trip north to their own territory.[23] At other times Europeans attempted conciliation. In 1864 a hundred Aborigines were reported to have broken into huts at Leigh Creek, Mount Deception and Parachilna, but nothing was taken. Station owners along the Aborigines' route killed meat for them and offered them flour if they kept away from the huts. In 1869 the Sub-Protector of Aborigines tried to prevent attacks on stock by Lake Hope Aborigines who were starving as a result of the drought, by intercepting them on their route to the ochre caves with a wagon full of provisions. He tried again in November 1870, taking rations to Beltana run after there had been complaints of huts being robbed and sheep killed on the route through Beltana, Nilpena, Ercowie and Aroona runs. There were a reported 150 Aborigines camped on Beltana to whom rations were distributed and more were promised for the return journey.[24]

The Chief Inspector of Police, made a trip through the Ranges to assess the extent of the violence in 1863. He met a party of about 200 Aborigines at Tooncatchin on their way to Parachilna. They had stopped to perform an initiation ceremony. The police party later encountered about sixty more at Parachilna collecting ochre. The Chief Inspector found the reports of violence and intimidation had been exaggerated, that property and stock that was properly supervised was not attacked. The Mount Serle police did not agree. They believed that the forays of northern Aborigines into the Ranges had increased and many came to take advantage of the ready food supply, not for the traditional trading and ceremonial activities.[25]

Nevertheless, the Chief Commissioner of Police decided to investigate the possibility of supplying the red ochre to the Lake Hope and Coopers Creek Aborigines nearer their home. He erroneously believed that this would stop their forays south. Various alternative sources were considered. The Surveyor-General suggested a deposit on Lake Eyre; another suggestion was the Aroona Hills. Eventually tenders were called from contractors to mine the ochre from Parachilna and cart it north. No one tendered, so in 1874 ochre was mined in Adelaide and sent up to the Lutheran Mission at Kopperamana.[26] This experiment failed. The authorities did not understand the significance of the Parachilna ochre to those Aborigines who were prepared to travel long distances to procure it. They were not interested in inferior substitutes which did not match the quality at Parachilna. Furthermore the trip to the ochre mines was not made simply for the ochre or plunder; it was associated with other ceremonies such as initiation. The ochre deposits themselves were sacred sites associated with important myths. Interference by whites would desecrate them.

Aborigines from the north continued to collect ochre from the Parachilna mines well into the twentieth century. In 1904 Dr P. F. Shanahan from Hawker told Dr E. C. Stirling, Director of the South Australian Museum that local Aborigines threatened reprisals if the mines were taken over by whites.[27] He claimed that no more than 20 acres would need to be reserved to keep the precious mines in Aboriginal hands. A great gathering of Aborigines was planned in Brachina Gorge where the issue was to be discussed and it was suggested the Protector of Aborigines should go up and meet the 'King' of the tribe. The 'King' had warned that if the area was not reserved there were likely to be attacks against whites in the far North. In 1905 an area was reserved in the Hundred of Parachilna from the operation of the *Mining Act* 1893.[28]

Aboriginal attacks on stock and property were not haphazard forays but deliberate attacks to reap the benefits from the presence of the colonists and also to harass them.[29] This is illustrated by what is known of the life of Inabuthina or Pompey.[30] A. W. Howitt, an ethnographer, who was travelling in the region at the time, described Inabuthina as a leading man of his people, the Mardala (another name for Wailpi). He had taken refuge with the Diyari to the north because he was being hounded by pastoralists for attacking their stock and property. His dislike of Europeans extended to Aborigines who collaborated with them. His resistance to the invasion of his lands was prolonged and determined. After the attack on the Jacobs' property in 1858 Inabuthina and Owieandana Billy were arrested but Inabuthina escaped and fled north. In 1864 a group of 'Salt water' Aborigines led by Inabuthina came down from Lake Hope, robbed several huts on Umberatana station and demanded provisions from a woman who was alone at an outstation. Next morning the Aborigines on the station summoned the pastoralist, Stuckey, to their camp. They said Inabuthina had already killed one man and that his mob were going to kill them all. Stuckey subsequently claimed to have shot and killed Inabuthina, while he was attempting to escape. The Mount Serle police corporal expressed satisfaction saying that Inabuthina had led all the attacks carried out by Aborigines over the previous four years.[31]

The Adnyamathanha oral account of the death of Inabuthina differs strikingly from the documented one. Mount Serle Bob (also known as King Bob) badly wounded his brother in a fight. Inabuthina then moved in and killed the wounded man. The Adnyamathanha resented this interference and called the pastoralist, Noble, to aid them. It was he who shot Inabuthina.[32]

By the 1880s confrontations between the Aborigines and Europeans had grown infrequent. Those Aborigines who survived the early years of violence, disease and upheaval adapted to life in the pastoral economy, which now dominated the Flinders Ranges. They also involved themselves in the sporadic mining activities, which did not become permanently established in the Ranges until the Leigh Creek coalfields were opened by the Electricity Trust of South Australia in the 1940s. The physical environment of the Flinders Ranges had changed dramatically. Native animals had to compete with cattle, sheep and rabbits. The countryside was dotted with small mines, which, although they only affected local areas, often coincided with Aboriginal sites. The Adnyamathanha co-existed with the newcomers. Their main camps were located near the homesteads of the pastoral runs, the Blinman ration depot and the Yudnamatana mine.[33]

These sites were chosen because they were sources of employment, food and water. Some coincided with traditional sites, others did not. By the 1890s the main campsite was at Mount Serle, another government ration depot. Police from Beltana attempted periodically to take a census of the Aboriginal population, but their estimates were very approximate, as they only visited the large campsites at Mount Serle, Frome Well and Angepena, which did not encompass the whole population. Censuses from the 1890s indicate that the Adnyamathanha were still a mobile people: 1894—26 Aborigines at Mount Serle, 9 at Frome Well (some were away shearing); 1896—67 Aborigines at Mount Serle; 1897—11 Aborigines at Mount Serle; 1898—38 Aborigines at Mount Serle, Frome Well and Angepena.[34]

These figures represent a dramatic decline from figures presented to the 1860 Select Committee claiming that rations were distributed to 2,224 Aborigines at Mount Serle over a six-month period. This figure seems very high as a population figure for the north Flinders Ranges. There may have been a major ceremonial occasion which attracted people from outside the area. Nevertheless, the figure does suggest a huge depletion in the numbers of the Adnyamathanha in the ensuing forty years. Today's Adnyamathanha community trace their ancestry to just a few families, who are interrelated. This strongly suggests that large numbers of Adnyamathanha did not survive the early years of contact.[35]

The death rate among the Adnyamathanha from disease seems to have been lower than among the Diyari and other people to the north-east. Herbert Basedow, who made an investigative visit to the area in 1920, reported that the people in the north-east had been devastated, not only by 'ruthless slaughter and wanton massacre' but also by the effects of venereal disease (syphilis and gonorrhoea).[36] While these diseases were also found in the Ranges, they were not as virulent. The birth rate among the Adnyamathanha was maintained, some women having large numbers of children.[37] But there were other epidemics from time to time which killed many people. In 1902 measles at Mount Serle killed eight people (eight others had also died in the previous twelve months of unspecified causes). The measles epidemic was devastating for the community and left a number of men and women widowed with large families to care for. There were attempts by the Protector to have these children sent south to school at Point McLeay, but their parents refused to let them go and the authorities were unwilling to take them by force. The reason given for not allowing their children to be taken away, apart from the parental concern at losing their children, was a communal decision that after the measles epidemic they needed to keep the children to build up the 'tribe' again.[38] This is compelling evidence that the Adnyamathanha were concerned about maintaining their communal identity.

Ration depots were located near centres of Aboriginal population. As these fluctuated, old depots closed and new ones opened. In 1894 the official ration depots were at Blinman, where the police distributed the rations, and on the pastoral runs of Beltana, Mount Lyndhurst, Mount Serle and Parallana.[39] Dependence on rations was governed by the seasons. In a good season only the old and infirm were reliant on rations, the able-bodied were able to hunt game and collect fruits and seeds. There was also plenty of employment so they could buy European foods to which they had become habituated.

Station work was a vital source of employment but when station work was short in summer and in dry seasons the people collected gum (used as chewing gum), hunted dingoes and rabbits (they were paid per scalp for these vermin), kangaroos and euros (which they skinned). They also worked at the mines, or at the government camel depot when it was established at Mount Serle in the late 1890s. The Adnyamathanha were now very vulnerable in the dry seasons as they no longer had access to waterholes and springs which had been appropriated by Europeans. Also, the wild game, having to compete with stock for feed, had become very scarce in bad seasons. There are reports of Aborigines who were classified as able-bodied and therefore refused rations, starving in dry seasons.[40] During a prolonged drought in the mid-1890s a number of runs closed down, including Mount Serle (which then became the camel depot). The Adnyamathanha were competing unsuccessfully with unemployed whites for work. The only source of paid work left to them was catching dingo pups for which they received rations, a form of payment they resented.[41]

The condition of the Aborigines during this drought in the North Flinders horrified many who saw them. It even prompted someone who was basically unsympathetic to the Aborigines ('I do not hold the blacks up as being anything more than lazy, useless beings') to write to the *South Australian Register* in their support. This correspondent pointed out that the dispenser of rations at Blinman (the local police trooper) was instructed not to issue rations to able-bodied men. He went on to say: 'Any person seeing the condition of so-called "ablebodied" men would have been filled with disgust for the powers that be . . . who are living upon the products of the soil taken from these unfortunates'.[42] The policeman from Beltana then went out to investigate the condition of the people at Mount Serle. He reported that the Aborigines had not had rations for several days but they were not starving. He suggested the reason they did not catch wallaby was because they were lazy, although they told him they had no shot or nets to catch them and their dogs were too weak to run. He assessed their condition as good, despite the death of four people in the previous months.[43]

McConville of Angepena run had a very different impression of local conditions. He said the drought was so severe there was no game in the Angepena hills and the people were close to starvation. The Aborigines had been forced to leave camp, leaving two old, decrepit women and two children behind because there were no rations. He pointed out that two years previously when Angepena, Artimore and Mount Serle runs were stocked, the young men had employment and supported the old ones, but the runs were now abandoned because of the drought.[44]

A caretaker in charge of Mount Serle camel depot described the Adnyamathanha as bold and threatening, lazy and independent. He said they refused to work for rations and demanded outrageous rates of pay. When the policeman from Blinman went to investigate the complaints he reported that the caretaker did not understand he was living with Aborigines who had worked and lived amongst Europeans all their lives. They depended on European foods but preferred to buy rations when work was available rather than accept government rations.[45]

By the 1890s the Adnyamathanha had integrated elements of Aboriginal and European economic life, which enabled them to maintain themselves independently in the Ranges. In drought years they were very vulnerable and came close to starvation, but most of the time the able-bodied had full employment and government rations fed those who could not maintain themselves. There was mutual economic dependence between the Adnyamathanha and the pastoralists. Women worked as domestics at homesteads and the men were skilled station workers. The stations throughout the Ranges had Adnyamathanha families camped within a few miles of the homesteads, but the European managers and stock workers did not concern themselves with how the people conducted their business at their camps, nor with their movements when they left the station. In these circumstances the Adnyamathanha maintained those aspects of their previous social and religious lives which were compatible with their new conditions. Throughout the nineteenth century they had pursued strategies to ensure not only that the community remained intact, but that their historical and cultural identity would be preserved and communicated to future generations.

There was no differentiation made among the Adnyamathanha between people of full and mixed descent. The Adnyamathanha, like other peoples of the Lake Eyre basin, followed matrilineal descent. All children born of an Adnyamathanha mother are Adnyamathanha irrespective of their father's affiliations. The children (as in many Aboriginal communities) were raised by their mother's Adnyamathanha husband and were considered his within the kinship system. The *Adnyamathanha Genealogy* compiled by two Adnyamathanha women does not acknowledge white fathers within family structures, only making passing reference to them in the descriptive text. The Adnyamathanha fathers who brought them up are the 'real' fathers.[46]

Throughout the first half of the twentieth century the numbers of people of mixed descent increased in relation to the number of people of full Adnyamathanha descent, but boys continued to be initiated and cultural knowledge continued to be transmitted.[47] The last person of full Aboriginal descent died in 1973. Occasionally white fathers tried to retrieve their children. For instance, on two occasions Beltana police attempted to 'arrest' children as 'neglected' and bring them under State control. On both occasions the mother and 'stepfather' refused to give up their children and it was subsequently determined they were not neglected as their 'stepfathers' had employment.[48]

Two ethnographers, Herbert Hale and Norman Tindale, who visited Mount Serle and Owieandana in the 1920s claimed the younger generation had little interest or knowledge of their ancestors' customs and that the language was rapidly falling into disuse.[49] They described the kinship system as two intermarrying classes with descent traced through the female line. Only two totemic lines survived. Linguists working with the Adnyamathanha in the 1970s describe a very similar social system operating, which suggests that Hale and Tindale underestimated the resilience of social and linguistic forms. Schebeck, who referred to *Mukunha* as clans rather than totems, listed fifteen clans, but believed all but three were extinct.[50] The matrilineal exogamous moiety system, on the other hand, has survived to the present and continues to influence Adnyamathanha marriages.[51]

Marriage and death rites, initiation and other ceremonies also continued, modified to suit changing circumstances.[52] C. P. Mountford claimed that the Adnyamathanha ceremonial leader revived the ceremonies in the early twentieth century by going to Eyre Peninsula to relearn some of the chants and forms which had been abandoned by the Adnyamathanha. This suggests a very deliberate strategy by the Adnyamathanha to maintain their cultural identity as well as their physical survival. Mountford also noted in the 1930s that the people were afraid the kinship system on which marriages were based would break down and lead to the extinction of their 'tribe'. They believed that the missionaries at Killalpaninna made the Diyari marry against the 'law' which resulted in their virtual extinction.[53]

Nonetheless they valued skills and knowledge acquired from Europeans. In 1914 the Royal Commission on The Aborigines travelled to Mount Serle. They interviewed D. Edginton, the caretaker of the camel depot, and two Aborigines, Frome Charlie and Susie Wilson (Wilton, married to Albert Wilton). The main concern of the Aborigines was that the Commission recommend that a school be established for their children:

> *Susie Wilson [Wilton]:* . . . we would like to have a school here, so that our children could be taught to read and write. We do not want them to live in the camps all their lives.
> *Q.:* What advantage would it be to your boys and girls if they were educated, and still remained in this locality?
> *[S. W.]* At present we do not know whether we get what we should. When we are paid for anything we do not know if the weight is right or if the money is right. We do not think we are cheated, but we would like to know for ourselves . . . We have no church here, but we would like to have houses like the white man. We could keep them tidy, and make them more comfortable than our wurlies. We would like our children to go to school, but we do not want them to go far away.[54]

The request for a school was ignored, which may have been fortunate for Adnyamathanha communal life. It is unlikely a school would have been supplied for them in the Ranges; more likely their mixed descent children would have been taken from them and sent south. But it is important to note that early in the century they were well aware of how they were disadvantaged without a basic European education, and wanted their children to improve their material circumstances.

Daily life

There is little documentary information on daily life in the Ranges. The following biographical sketches, drawn from oral history, convey an impression of the lives of a few Adnyamathanha in the early and mid-twentieth century.[55]

Bill Stubbs

Bill (Cecil) Stubbs' mother, Emily, was born at Mount Rose. Bill's father was a white man, Benjamin Stubbs, who had come to the North Flinders in search of gold. (He later returned to the south and ran a tree nursery in the Adelaide Hills.) Bill was born about 1890 at the Ring Neck Tree on Mount Lyndhurst station near the windmill and tank. His sister was born at Yankaninna. His mother worked as a cook on Mount Lyndhurst station and brought food home for the two children. The station was a ration depot at the time. When they were on the move Bill carried the swag. Emily married Nicholas Demell at the gum tree on the creek on the road between Angepena and Mount Serle. Emily and Nicholas had four children. The family moved around the Ranges to Mount Serle, Angepena, Depot Springs, Yudnamatana Mines. When Bill was old enough he worked on the stations. He camped out when doing station work, moving where the work took him.

In 1928 Bill married Mabel Johnson at Ram Paddock Gate. After his marriage he worked at Wooltana, Balcanoona, Wertaloona, Angepena and Mount Serle, where he worked with camels, breaking them in. Bill and Mabel had two daughters. When the girls were old enough to go to school the family moved to Blinman where Mabel had a job and they rented a house from her boss. Bill worked on the roads. Later they moved to Nepabunna.

Rufus Wilton

Rufus Wilton was born about 1910 at the Mount Serle camel depot. His father was George Edginton, the manager. His mother, Susan, later married Albert Wilton. The police attempted to take Rufus away from his mother at his father's direction. His mother used to paint him with black ochre so he would look as dark as the other children. When the family was at Mount Serle they camped at the Bullock Bush near the homestead. Rufus, with some help from a white man, Alf William, at Depot Springs, taught himself to read and write, even without the school his mother had requested in 1914.

When the people moved camp they always cleaned up the site so they could move back later. They burnt the wurlies and took everything else with them. They moved along a circular track from one well to the next. Their diet consisted of government

Rufus Wilton with Mavis Patterson, late 1930s.
(Courtesy of Mountford-Sheard Collection, State Library of South Australia.)

rations, damper and meat which they caught themselves—euros, rabbits, wallabies and, at Angepena, possums. The old women would collect seeds when they were on the plains, for instance at Wooltana, and grind them on a large rock.

Rufus married Ethel at Copley and they had eight children. Rufus worked on stations including Mount Serle, Umberatana, Wirrealpa, Wooltana, Balcanoona and Mount Fitton. He also won a contract to erect telegraph poles when the line was established through the Ranges. While he was away his family lived at Ram Paddock Gate and later Nepabunna. He worked at Leigh Creek for thirty years from the 1940s, at weekends he rode his bike to Beltana where his family rented a house from an Afghan.[56] The missionary at Nepabunna wanted Rufus to send his children back to the mission but Rufus insisted they attend a regular primary school, so he applied for exemption under the *Aborigines Act* on the advice of the policeman at Beltana. He was the first

Adnyamathanha to be exempted. As an exempted person he was not permitted to visit Nepabunna, but the missionary allowed him to visit his grandfather. While at Leigh Creek he joined the Buffalo Lodge whose pledges of secrecy, he claimed, had similarities to Aboriginal sacred business.

Rufus epitomised the Adnyamathanha ability to integrate elements of Aboriginal and European cultural values and education, while maintaining his economic independence. He was the first Adnyamathanha person known to have learned to read and write. The anthropologist, C. P. Mountford, noted on his trips to Nepabunna in the 1930s that Rufus was very keen to acquire further education and European skills. At the same time he was very conservative in cultural matters. He was fully initiated and stood with the Adnyamathanha men, who wanted to maintain the ceremonies, when the decision was taken to abolish them. He appreciated the United Aborigines Mission's role in saving his people from starvation during the depression, but was antagonistic to their Christian message and their attempts to undermine the initiation ceremonies. He was an informant of Mountford's, despite being a young man at the time, and this set a pattern of close cooperation with other researchers. His cultural and historical knowledge was extensive and he was determined to record this knowledge for posterity.[57]

Claude Demell

Claude was born in 1908 at Angepena. His parents were Emily and Nicholas Demell and Bill Stubbs was his stepbrother. His family lived at Mount Serle and later at Minerawuta (Ram Paddock Gate), while his father worked on stations around the Ranges, as a woolclasser, on the roads and as a tracker.[58] Claude began station work in 1920, working at Depot Springs, Wertaloona, Mount Serle, Balcanoona and for the Beltana Pastoral Company.

Claude married Ethel Ryan in 1937. The family lived at Nepabunna and Beltana while Claude was away working on the stations. He had no permanent dwelling when out working and received cooked meals from the homesteads. In 1958 the family moved to Blinman, where Claude continued to find station work and, in 1962, they moved to Quorn so that his children could go to high school. Claude was one of the last surviving initiated men and an elder, whose knowledge was highly respected in the 1980s.

These biographies attest to Adnyamathanha enterprise, independence and their belief that future survival would be determined by maintaining continuity with their past. The close-knit community insisted that their young people marry chosen partners and discouraged them from marrying outside the community, unless to a person within the same cultural bloc, such as Diyari or Pangkala.[59] The Adnyamathanha provide a sharp contrast to the early Poonindie people, who made a complete break with their past.

In 1923 the camel depot at Mount Serle was closed and reverted to a pastoral lease. The lessees, the Greenwood family, continued to distribute rations until they fell out with the Secretary of the Protection Board.[60] After the Greenwoods took over Mount Serle, the main Adnyamathanha camp moved to Minerawuta (Ram Paddock Gate), and so began a new era in Adnyamathanha history.

Notes

1 The Lutherans at Koonibba were very conscious of these different standards when they received Aborigines from the UAM mission at Ooldea.

2 For example, E. H. Spicer, *Perspectives in American Indian cultural change*, Chicago, 1969; Ted J. Brasser, *Riding on the frontier's crest: Mahican Indian culture and culture change*, Ottawa,1974.

3 E. H. Spicer, 'Types of contact and processes of change' in E. H. Spicer, *Perspectives*, p. 88.

4 Luise A. Hercus and Isobel White, 'Perception of kinship structure reflected in the Adnjamathanha pronouns', *Papers in Australian Linguistics*, no. 6, 1973, p. 50, C. P. Mountford, fieldnotes, vol. 20, Mountford-Sheard Collection, State Library of South Australia; B. Schebeck, 'The Atynymatana personal pronoun and the Wailpi kinship system', *Papers in Australian Linguistics*, no. 6, 1973, p. 23.

5 Luise Hercus, 'The status of women's cultural knowledge: Aboriginal society in north-east South Australia' in P. Brock (ed.), *Women, rites and sites: Aboriginal women's cultural knowledge*, Sydney, 1989, pp. 99 and 101. Adnyamathanha and Kuyani were Yura-Miru languages, (Adnyamathanha is the only language of this group to survive as a living language) while Yadliyawara was Yarli and Pirlatapa: Karna. L. Hercus, 'The status of women's cultural knowledge', p. 101.

6 Norman Tindale indicates the boundary between those peoples who circumcised and those who subincised ran through the territory of the present-day Adnyamathanha, with the Kuyani and Wailpi to the west of the line and the Yadliyawara and Pirlatapa to the east: N. B. Tindale, *Aboriginal tribes of Australia. Their terrain, environmental controls, distribution, limits and proper names*, Canberra, 1974, map.

7 Rufus Wilton, pers. com. 28/3/1984.

8 Bill Stubbs, pers com. 27/9/1982.

9 J. F. Hayward, 'Diary 1846–94' *Royal Geographical Society of Australia, South Australian Branch*, vol. 29, 1927, p. 107.

10 John Bowyer Bull, 'Reminiscences 1835–1894', n.d., Mortlock Library of South Australiana; GRG 24/6/3481, 3513, 3546.

11 J. F. Hayward, 'Diary', 1927, p. 98.

12 *Pastoral pioneers of South Australia*, vol. 1, Adelaide, 1974, p. 81b.

13 GRG 5/2/776/1857, SAPRO; John McKenzie, pers. com.

14 GRG 5/2/593/1857; GRG 5/2/130/1858; GRG 5/2/662/1858; GRG 5/2/514/1858.

15 GRG 5/2/514/1858.

16 SA Parliamentary Papers, 1865, no. 24.

17 *South Australian Register*, 12/7/1865.

18 P. Jones, 'Red ochre expeditions: an ethnographic and historical analysis of Aboriginal trade in the Lake Eyre Basin', (part 1), *Anthropology Society of South Australia Journal*, 22 (7), 1984, pp. 6 and 9; Rufus Wilton, pers. com.; A. W. Howitt, *Native tribes of south-east Australia*, London, 1904, p. 712; Robert Bruce, *Reminiscences of an old squatter*, Adelaide, 1902, p. 804 (facsimile copy, Adelaide, 1973).

19 Jones, 'Red ochre expeditions', p. 4 quoting a letter from Shanahan to Stirling, 26/12/1904, SA Museum archives, AA309.

20 Rufus Wilton and John McKenzie, pers. com., also see Jones, 'Red ochre expeditions', p. 8.

21 For example, GRG 5/2/1862/1753. They came from the region of the salt water lakes—Lake Eyre, Lake Hope, etc.

22 GRG 5/2/1863/306, 29/7/1863.

23 *Port Augusta Dispatch*, 9/6/1882, 3A; Jones, 'Red ochre expeditions', p. 10. An inquest was held into the killing and a verdict of justifiable homicide returned.

24 GRG 5/2/1844/1864, 12/7/1864; GRG 52/1/1/10/1869; GRG 52/1/14/11/1870.

25 GRG 5/2/1863/306, 6/10/1863; GRG 5/2 1864, 4/1/1864.

26 GRG 5/2/1863, 21/12/1863; *Port Augusta Dispatch*, 9/6/1882, see also Jones, 'Red ochre expeditions'.

27 S.A. Museum archive, AA 309, 26/12/1904.

28 GRG 52/1/1904/265, 1904/315; GRG 53/1/1905/40.

29 Henry Reynolds, *The other side of the frontier. Aboriginal resistance to the European invasion of Australia*, Ringwood, Victoria, 1982, pp. 166-9.

30 Pigeon (Jandamarra) of the Kimberley is another Aboriginal resistance fighter whose activities are well-documented, for example, in Howard Pederson, 'Pigeon: an Australian Aboriginal rebel', *Studies in Western Australian History*, no. 8, 1984.

31 A. W. Howitt, 1902, p. 47. Rufus Wilton believed Inabuthina was a Yadliawara man: pers. com.; GRG 5/2/1864, 15/1/1864.

32 John McKenzie, pers. com. Mount Serle Bob did not die until 1919: Christine Davis and Pearl McKenzie, *Adnyamathanha Genealogy*, Adelaide, 1985, p. 2.

33 For example, at Moolawatana, Parallana, Mt Serle, Frome Well, Mt Lyndhurst, Owieandana, Mt Freeling, Burr Well (Depot Springs), Wooltana, Balcanoona, Umberatana, Wirrealpa, Mt Fitton, Beltana and Wertaloona.

34 GRG 5/300/7, 15/9/1894, 8/8/1896, 2/11/1898.

35 *Report of the Select Committee of the Legislative Council upon 'The Aborigines'*, 1860, Appendix 2; Davis and McKenzie, *Adnyamathanha Genealogy*, p. vii and 1A.

36 GRG 23/1/1920/144; Herbert Basedow, First Medical Relief Expedition Report on the Far North, pp. 14 and 68.

37 See Davis and McKenzie, *Adnyamathanha Genealogy*.

38 GRG 52/1/1903/1.

39 GRG 52/1/1894/406.

40 GRG 52/1/1888/375, 1895/190.

41 GRG 52/1/1897/378.

42 *South Australian Register*, 27/3/1897.

43 GRG 52/1/1897/329.

44 GRG 52/1/1897/329.

45 GRG 52/1/1897/329.

46 Davis and McKenzie, *Adnyamathanha Genealogy*.

47 A census of people of mixed descent in South Australia in 1910 listed 9 people at Mt Serle, 12 at Wooltana and two families in Hawker (13): GRG 52/1/2/1910.

48 Davis and McKenzie, *Adnyamathanha Genealogy*, vi; GRG 5/300 vol 2, 6/6/1901, 1/1/1910. Rufus Wilton remembered the police coming to take him to his white father. He and another light-coloured child, Dick Coulthard, were blackened with ochre by their mothers so they would not be distinguished from the other children: pers. com. 1982.

49 Herbert M. Hale and Norman B. Tindale, 'Observations on Aborigines of the Flinders Ranges, and records of rock carvings and paintings', *Records of the South Australian Museum*, 3 (1), 1925, pp. 45, 46.

50 B. Schebeck, 'The Adnjamathanha personal pronoun and the "Wailpi kinship system" ' in Schebeck, Hercus and White, *Papers in Australian Linguistics*, no. 6, 1973, pp. 27-8.

51 Pearl McKenzie stated in the mid-1980s that there were still no wrong moiety marriages at Nepabunna: pers. com. 12/9/1987.

52 For example, see R. Ellis, 'The funeral practices and beliefs of the Adnjamathanha', *Journal of the Anthropological Society of South Australia*, 13(6), 1975.

53 C. P. Mountford, Fieldnotes, vol. 19, pp. 83, 98, Mountford-Sheard Collection. The Adnyamathanha use the term 'law' to refer to the body of ritual and social knowledge which governed their lives.

54 *Royal Commission on The Aborigines*, 1916, SAPP, 1917, p. 16. It is interesting to note that when Edginton was asked, 'Do you know of any instances when white men have interfered with the native women?' he answered, 'No. They marry amongst themselves, and there are no illegitimate

children'. Edginton himself had had a child, Rufus, by Susie Wilton, born in 1910: Rufus Wilton, pers. com. 1982.

55 Based on interviews with the author, unless otherwise indicated.

56 GRG 52/1/1941/17, 28/2/1942. Rufus Wilton owned a block of land at Copley but did not have the resources to build on it. His application for government assistance to purchase an iron house was refused: GRG 52/1/1947/36.

57 C. P. Mountford, Fieldnotes, vol. 20, 1939, p. 109. Rufus Wilton worked closely with staff of the Aboriginal Heritage Branch until his death and was particularly close to site recorder Craig Hoskyn.

58 Interview with researcher Adele Graham, 13/11/1984.

59 Molly Wilton, pers. com. 13/11/1985. Annie Coulthard said Marree people, possibly meaning Arabana people could not come into the Ranges without permission, they did not intermarry until after Nepabunna was established: pers. com.

60 Mrs 'Smiler' Greenwood, pers. com. 24/9/1982. They collected their rations in a buggy drawn by a donkey.

9

NEPABUNNA MISSION

The move to Ram Paddock Gate coincided with drought and the depression. There was little employment and the nearest ration distribution point was at Copley. The Adnyamathanha came close to starvation. They moved away from the homesteads that could not support them with work or rations, establishing their own settlement on land of significance to them, yet independent of Europeans. Ram Paddock Gate was close to the boundary of three stations but not associated with their homesteads. The Adnyamathanha chose not to be fringe dwellers at Copley, Blinman or the other more distant townships in the Flinders Ranges. They were careful not to be a burden on any of the pastoral stations. They maintained their communal cohesion, community pride and independence in the face of starvation. At Ram Paddock Gate the United Aborigines Mission missionary, Jim Page, offered the Adnyamathanha his support in 1929. They accepted him into the community. He came to their settlement, not they to his. He was joined by Harry Green, and later Fred Eaton succeeded him. Green later reminisced about the people he met at Ram Paddock Gate:

[people] who had previously been prosperous and useful workers on the stations around about but during the drought of 1925–1930 these poor people had fallen on bad times. There was no stock on the stations, they had lost their jobs and had just become wanderers again although they were all good tradesmen, excellent with motor cars, windmill experts, but we were sent there because the people were starving in the corner of a big sheep station . . .

They were wonderful people. In fact I still believe that they were the finest tribe of aborigines I have met. They were keen and industrious, highly intelligent. Some of them had been in charge of big projects in connection with the setting up of the North-South Telegraph line from Oodnadatta up to Alice Springs. They had big donkey teams and huge wagons of their own. They had sewing machines, motor cars (that wouldn't go), radios and yet, here they were starving . . .[1]

By the 1920s when the Adnyamathanha settled at Ram Paddock Gate they had been in contact with Europeans for seventy to eighty years. They had become familiar with the wage and ration systems. As early as the turn of the century they had stood their ground when the overseer at the camel depot had tried to make them work for rations. They spoke English, although Adnyamathanha was their first language. At Ram Paddock Gate they sank a well and built European-style huts of stone and mud with wooden uprights.[2] They used many European materials in their day-to-day living and no longer hunted with spears and boomerangs, although they supplemented rations with native foods. They hunted game when they could find it, using rifles, nets and dogs. They gathered local fruits, seeds and roots. They used sewing machines to make their own clothes. They had cars and taught themselves mechanical skills to maintain them. But when they could no longer obtain fuel, they adapted the car bodies and used them as wagons pulled by their donkeys. Every aspect of their lives showed their capacity to adapt and survive in the face of overwhelming odds.

Despite these adaptations to new economic conditions, ceremonial life continued to be central to their community. An archaeological study of the Ram Paddock Gate settlement in 1981 located the ceremonial grounds in relation to the dwellings.[3] Four *mulkara*, or first stage initiation grounds (an open ceremony attended by women and children) were closer to the settlement, and two *yandawuta*, or second stage initiation grounds, were further out. This indicates that during the period at Ram Paddock Gate, *mulkara* ceremonies were held on at least four separate occasions (each on a new ground) and *yandawuta* ceremonies on two occasions.

While the people were camped at Ram Paddock Gate, they established two burial grounds, one for each moiety, *araru* on one side and on the other *matheri*. When the people were more mobile there had been no need for specified areas to be set aside for burials as people were buried where they died, the camp was burned and the group moved on after a death. At Ram Paddock Gate they vacated the hut where someone died, but did not change camp so a burial ground became necessary. The graves show a mixture of Adnyamathanha and European influences. For example, they are oriented southwest with brush or stones at the head of each grave (Aboriginal practice), but are also fenced and have borders (European influence).[4]

The mythology associated with Adnyamathanha ceremonial and religious life was communicated to the young people, but to what extent it may have altered or adapted to changing circumstances is not known. Other beliefs also persisted. It was believed, for example, that a whooping cough epidemic at Ram Paddock Gate in which about seven children died was due to a grave being disturbed by two Adnyamathanha men who had no rights to disturb the grave.[5] They brought the bones to Ram Paddock Gate. One of these men lost two children in the epidemic and the other one. Thus the community to which the United Aborigines missionaries came was an Aboriginal community with a functioning religious and social life based on traditional forms and beliefs, surviving within the European economy and influenced by Europeans in most aspects of day-to-day living. No one in the community had received a European education.

When the first missionary came in 1929 he built a church in the settlement and a hut for himself across the Copley road from the main camp site, but otherwise made no

Nepabunna Mission.
(Courtesy of Mountford-Sheard Collection, State Library of South Australia.)

impact on the physical structure of the settlement.[6] Most important, he distributed rations to the hungry people and started teaching school. But within twelve months the settlement was forced to move.

While the advent of the missionaries saved the Adnyamathanha from starvation, it created other difficulties. The surrounding pastoralists were not pleased with the prospect of a mission. While they were happy to have Aboriginal workmen and their families camped on their land, they did not want a permanent community making inroads on their property. They began agitating to get the people moved. The lessees on whose property the Adnyamathanha were camped were particularly worried, threatening police action and destruction of all the Aborigines' livestock (mainly donkeys and goats) if they did not move. The missionaries applied to the State for land, but the government was slow to respond. They then negotiated directly with the lessee of Balcanoona station, who agreed to release some land to them under certain conditions.[7]

Before these negotiations were finalised the community had to leave Ram Paddock Gate. They moved to a temporary site at Boundary Gate, living in tents and make-shift accommodation. Finally they moved to a site that was to become their permanent home, the place known as Nepabunna, 'flat rock'. It had a creek flowing through it with a spring, but no large supply of permanent water. The Adnyamathanha for the first time in their existence had a permanent settlement, though on land bereft of traditional value. It was rocky ground, land on which they would not normally choose to camp.[8]

The missionaries who had come to an established settlement were now responsible for starting one from scratch, one in which they were in full control. No doubt this gave them added influence over the Adnyamathanha. This control was reinforced by the condition on which the land at Nepabunna was made over to the mission, that if the UAM withdrew the land would revert to the lessee. This was to give the missionaries great power over the people because if they did not co-operate, the missionaries could threaten to leave and the people believed they would lose their land.

The UAM missionaries ran the community from 1931 to 1973, when the government took over control of Nepabunna. Jim Page and Fred Eaton established the mission and after Page's suicide in 1931, Mr and Mrs Eaton ran the mission with assistance from others including R. M. Williams, who set up a leather workshop in a brushwood hut, where he taught some of the men leather work. He claimed in 1933 that the workshop supported eleven people. But the UAM would not allow him to continue his workshop unless the money went back to the mission society.[9] In 1934 Williams left the mission, having started an industry which was to become a multimillion dollar clothing and footwear business.

The Eatons ran Nepabunna Mission until the early 1950s when Bill Hathaway and his wife took over. Eaton is remembered by the people as a humane man who fought hard for the rights of the people under his control, although in a paternalistic way. He was a carpenter by trade and worked very hard to establish the mission, sinking wells and building houses and fences. He also tried to establish an economic base for the community by establishing mining ventures and trying to obtain more land on which to run stock. He strongly supported the Adnyamathanha man, Ted Coulthard, in his mining ventures.[10] The Hathaways seem to have been less easy-going. They were more distant in their relationship with the Adnyamathanha people and appeared less tolerant of the people's traditional culture. They penalised the people for speaking the Adnyamathanha language in front of them. They have also been blamed by some for ending the initiation ceremonies, although these had stopped before the Hathaways came to Nepabunna.[11] Bill Hathaway was not as able a handy man as Eaton; as a result the mission equipment and buildings became increasingly run down.

By the 1960s assimilationist demands for better living conditions for Aborigines in South Australia had given the Adnyamathanha the confidence to request government action to improve life at Nepabunna. They wrote to the Aborigines Department asking the government to take over the mission.[12] They complained of the continuing shortage of water, inadequate and run-down housing and demanded the freedom to run their own community free from any petty tyranny of the missionaries. This contrasts with the government takeover of Koonibba, which was initiated by the Church with strong support from the government. At Nepabunna it was the Adnyamathanha who took the initiative. In 1973 the government finally took control of the mission and today the Adnyamathanha have freehold title of the Nepabunna land.

Stone hut with pressed kerosene tin roof, Nepabunna, late 1930s.
(Courtesy of Mountford-Sheard Collection, State Library of South Australia.)

Daily life

The establishment of Nepabunna Mission brought relative security after many years of uncertainty as to where the Adnyamathanha community might be allowed to settle. The people worked with great enthusiasm but no financial support to build up their settlement, which was established at the depth of the depression when building materials were in short supply. The houses built on rocky outcrops were made from flattened kerosene tins, and on the southern campsite where there was some soil a few mud huts were constructed. The missionaries had slightly more substantial houses made of stone. The community also built a church building. Eaton made furniture for himself and showed others how to make it.

In 1954 the Nepabunna community wrote a letter of complaint to the Aboriginal Protection Board.[13] They were still living in houses made of rusty kerosene tins; the school was open only two hours a day so people were taking their children away; the old people were not getting sufficient rations and there was insufficient housing for young married couples. Few people went to church which had only fruit cases for seats. Conditions at Copley were no better. The letter ended with a plea for better housing and a chance for their children to learn to read and write.

When the welfare officer visited Nepabunna in 1958 the condition of the houses had further deteriorated. There were six people to each three-roomed cottage, living in squalid conditions. Although eight new cottages were built the next year, inadequate housing remained a major concern throughout the 1960s. The UAM lacked financial resources to increase or improve housing. The Adnyamathanha complained that the houses were totally inadequate for the extremes of cold and heat experienced in the area. They did not have verandahs and many had no guttering. The bathrooms and laundries were rudimentary and the houses lacked basic facilities such as cupboards and sinks. The houses had not been maintained for many years, despite the people paying rent for their accommodation. Most houses were overcrowded.[14]

Unlike Koonibba and Poonindie, Nepabunna did not provide employment, for it had never been envisaged as a self-supporting, independent community. The missionaries wanted to convert the people to Christianity, but it was not linked, as at the other two missions, to simultaneously 'civilising' them. The Adnyamathanha had already adopted those aspects of European life which were available to them and could be integrated into their own lives. The Adnyamathanha had well-established work patterns before the missionaries arrived. Eaton did encourage people to make some wooden artefacts which he marketed on their behalf.

During the depression rabbiting was a major source of work and food, although a few men managed to maintain employment on pastoral stations. By the 1940s and through the 1950s and 1960s stations employed most of the men and boys (many of the boys went out working in their early teens), although often at exploited rates of pay. In 1940 Eaton had talks with the local Australian Workers Union organiser and they agreed that Aboriginal people should be paid wages equal to whites. It was often the stations closest

Hut made of lime mortar on chicken wire, Nepabunna, late 1930s.
(Courtesy of Mountford-Sheard Collection, State Library of South Australia.)

to the mission which were most exploitative. In 1939 it was claimed that distant stations paid award wages of £2/12/6 per week and no keep, while stations closer to Nepabunna paid £1 to 35 shillings per week plus keep. In 1950 the policeman at Farina complained about this exploitation. He claimed there were unscrupulous station managers who cheated the Aborigines by paying them on paper, but then taking all their wages by charging them exorbitant prices for clothes and food. He quoted an example of one Aborigine who was denied wages for months because of this situation. He pointed out that other stations such as Witchelina paid Aboriginal stockmen equal wages. He negotiated a job for Jack Forbes at Witchelina ensuring he had a cottage and food for his family and was paid £7 per week.[15]

Some employment continued at the mines dotted around the Flinders; these included silver, lead, copper, barytes mines, as well as a talc mine at Mount Fitton. In 1940 Eaton arranged for people from the mission to mine silver and lead 10 miles from Nepabunna and in 1948 he established a barytes mine not far from the mission. This mine continued operating until 1957, employing men from the community. Some Adnyamathanha men worked their own mining claims from time to time, or in other ways were self-employed. Women obtained work as domestics at station homesteads or in nearby townships such as Blinman and Copley.

The opening of the Leigh Creek coalfields in the 1940s created alternative employment, not only work at the mines but on the roads and railway associated with them. However, the Electricity Trust of South Australia (ETSA), who worked the coalfields and built Leigh Creek township, banned Aborigines from the housing in the town. Aboriginal people employed by them or by associated industries were forced to camp at Copley or Beltana. The racist attitudes of many ETSA employees would have ensured that Aborigines would not have felt comfortable living in the Leigh Creek township even if it had been an option.[16]

Nepabunna acted as the dormitory of the community while men were away working. The mission was a place where people came to rest between jobs, or when they were old or sick, or as a haven for women and children while the men were absent. The mobility of families and, more particularly, the extremely erratic schooling which was available at Nepabunna, resulted in children receiving a very elementary education. The missionaries, first the Eatons and then the Hathaways, were not trained teachers nor were they able to devote themselves to teaching. They had all the responsibilities of running the mission and the school was low on their list of priorities. Few of the children at Nepabunna progressed beyond primary school until the Education Department took over the school in the early 1960s.

Eaton built a dormitory on the mission to enable parents to leave their children in school while they were away on the stations, but it was rarely used. Some people moved away from the mission so their children could attend regular primary schools in towns such as Copley, Beltana, Blinman and Hawker. Later on some moved away to ensure their children obtained a secondary school education. Children are now bussed into Leigh Creek South secondary school by the Education Department.

Nepabunna's extreme isolation, the UAM's lack of resources and the material poverty of the Adnyamathanha meant that living standards—even compared with other Aboriginal missions and stations—were low. The missionary distributed rations to the old and sick but these had to be supplemented by game and wild fruits and seeds. A woman who came to Nepabunna after living in institutions at Colebrook Home and Point Pearce was shocked by the poor quality of food.[17] Water shortages were an ongoing problem for the settlement; there was still no permanent reliable supply by the 1960s. Disposal of effluent was another problem. The rocky Nepabunna site not only made it difficult to drill for water and build houses, it made it difficult to put in a hygienic, modern effluent system. In 1945 a visiting policeman was horrified to find twenty huts and houses at the mission with no lavatories and people still using the creek beds for their effluent. He pointed out that illnesses spread by flies such as sore eyes and dysentery were prevalent in the community.[18] By the late 1940s the houses had been fitted with 'Hygieno' pans which had to be emptied regularly. This work was left to the women as the men were normally away. The women lacked the means to cart the effluent very far. Disposal of sewage in watershed areas close to residential areas was still a problem as late as 1967.[19]

Health care has been another continuing hardship for the community. By the time Nepabunna was established the Adnyamathanha had come to rely on European medicine. In the early days the journey to Copley was arduous, and Copley was only a stage on the way to the doctor at Hawker or the hospital at Port Augusta or Adelaide. Eaton failed to find a house in Copley in which people could stay on their way to seek medical attention, so the sick continued to have to camp out while they waited for the train south.[20] Eaton sent outspoken letters of complaint to the Protector of Aborigines about the inequities suffered by Aborigines. He pointed out in one such letter that 'his' people had to travel twelve hours by train, past two hospitals which would not accept them, before they could receive medical attention.[21]

The best medical attention and specialist procedures such as cataract operations were only available in Adelaide. For these purposes people (often old people) had to make the long trek to the capital. This caused great anxiety, both for the patients and their families. In 1943 the elderly Albert Wilton was sent to Adelaide for a cataract operation, which so alarmed his family that Eaton asked that he be sent back to Nepabunna if there was no hope for his recovery.[22]

Women still had their babies at home as late as the early 1960s. Mrs Forbes, a white woman who had married an Aboriginal man and lived at Nepabunna, was the midwife. The missionaries kept a register of births. The people depended on the missionaries for decisions about medical treatment as they controlled the transport to Copley and the radio receiver (which the people had helped buy) which enabled them to call the Flying Doctor Service. Since the missionaries were in control of the people's health they were sometimes blamed when people died.[23]

Biographical sketches reveal some of the ways in which the Adnyamathanha incorporated the mission into their lives in the Ranges.

Pearl and John McKenzie[24]

Pearl Wilton was born in 1922 at Burr Well station. Her father, Henry Wilton, was born at Mount Serle, her mother, May, at Burr Well station. Both May and Henry grew up at

Mount Serle station. Henry worked as a station hand at Burr Well and Wertaloona stations, returning to Mount Serle between jobs. They moved to Ram Paddock Gate when work was difficult to get, and then to Boundary Gate (for a few months) and finally Nepabunna. During the depression Henry obtained occasional work at Balcanoona fencing and crutching sheep and later worked at Burr Well station. Henry and May Wilton had few possessions—cooking utensils and a swag—and were therefore very mobile. They would set up camp in traditional camping areas as they moved from station to station in a landscape which had personal meaning to them marked by their birth trees, marriage tree and graves of family members who had died.

Pearl attended school at Nepabunna where she learned to read and write. She also became a Christian. Both her parents were important members of the community. Henry was a ceremonial leader and May was regarded as the senior woman of the Adnyamathanha. She passed both her knowledge and authority on to Pearl. Pearl in her turn has spent much time recording her knowledge, particularly the language and the Adnyamathanha community genealogy.[25]

Pearl married John McKenzie in 1941 at Nepabunna. John was the son of Fred and Jessie McKenzie, one of sixteen children. Fred's natural father was a Scotsman but he inherited from his Aboriginal father, Mount Serle Bob, the mantle of ceremonial leader. He was assisted by Henry Wilton, whose wife, May, was Mount Serle Bob's niece.

John and Pearl went to Wirrealpa station where John worked as a station hand, fencer and boundary rider. John also worked at Wertaloona station, and Martins Well. While John worked, Pearl was at home alone; they were always given a house to live in on the stations, except for Wertaloona where they lived in the shearers' quarters. They had five children, three of whom survived. In 1964 the McKenzies moved to Hawker. John first worked as a professional kangaroo shooter for Jesser Chiller. From 1970 he worked on the roads. John and Pearl McKenzie were of the generation that could remember the establishment of Nepabunna Mission. They spent their childhoods living in a manner similar to their parents, but during their adult lives came closer to the European modes of living in houses, accumulating possessions and living in one place.

Ted Coulthard

While most Adnyamathanha found work on pastoral stations, some established their own businesses. Ted Coulthard was the most enterprising. In 1924–25 he won a contract from the Vermin Board to put up a netting fence (dingo proof) from Angepena to Lyndhurst.[26] Although he based himself at Nepabunna later in life, he worked his own barytes mine and ran one hundred head of cattle and sheep in the 1940s, despite not having any land himself.[27] Ted and his brother Dick also had their own donkey teams which they used for contract work carting goods to and from the railhead at Copley. They carted wool clips, copper, fencing materials and, when the mission was established, they transported a windmill from Copley to Nepabunna, which took them three days.[28] At Nepabunna Ted established a garden. He grew fruit and vegetables despite the rocky ground and scarce water.

Fred McKenzie, late 1930s.
(Courtesy of Mountford-Sheard Collection, State Library of South Australia.)

Living conditions in Copley

By the 1940s Adnyamathanha people not only lived on stations, and at Nepabunna, but also in the towns dotted through the Flinders Ranges, including Copley, Beltana, Blinman and Hawker. In the mid-1940s there were a number of families living in Copley and Beltana, attracted by employment available in industries associated with the Leigh Creek coalfields. As they were barred from company housing in Leigh Creek, they set up camps in Copley in very similar circumstances to those the Koonibba people experienced at Ceduna and Wudinna. Attempts to buy houses or land in the town failed because no financial support or backing from the Aborigines' Department was forthcoming. The local white population did not like Aboriginal people camping in the middle of the township and the Aborigines were harassed by the local policeman. Walter and Andy Coulthard made a number of submissions to the Protector of Aborigines asking him to intervene on their behalf so they could settle somewhere permanently:

> I [A. Coulthard] have been working at Leigh Creek for approximately 12 months and have in that time been resident on the Copley Common with permission of the Lands Department and for the last 2 months I have been living in a house in the town. The local Police Constable has warned the owner of the house that if I did not get out he would have the house condemned. I have now sent my family out to Nepabunna and am camped on the common on my own. My children have been attending the Copley school and are now doing well in their schooling.
> Could you please come up here and see how we are being kicked around. I am liable to be kicked off the Common at any time. I am not the only aborigine receiving this treatment.
> Please send advice what to do. I cannot get a living at Nepabunna and do not wish to give up my present work and want my children to attend Copley school.[29]

Eventually in 1948 permission was granted for three families (Andy and Walter Coulthard and Maurice Johnson) to camp on the Copley Common Reserve north-east of the town (this permission did not extend to other people camping for periods of more than forty-eight hours in Copley). They now had somewhere to camp but no direct access to water. They had to pay 3 shillings per 100 gallons to have the water carted, costing them up to 9 shillings per week. The carter was unreliable and they often had to carry a bucket at least half a mile to get drinking water. Water was not made available to the campsite until August 1951.[30]

Changes in the missionary era

The missionaries who came to Nepabunna were not sophisticated people. They came from working-class backgrounds, some from skilled trades, others with no particular training or skills. The innovations they introduced into the lives of the Adnyamathanha were the preaching of Christianity, basic European schooling and white control. The Adnyamathanha accepted these changes. They were relieved to have someone able to negotiate on their behalf, and Eaton turned out to be a strong advocate for Aboriginal rights. Although the UAM introduced primary education at Nepabunna, it sent no trained teachers and unlike the Lutheran and Anglican missions, gave no special attention to the school. The store, which generated income, was given priority. The school was only run when the store was closed and other duties of the missionary did not get in the way. As a result classes were held for only an hour or two a day, if at all. Most of the early students did not get past junior primary level.

Many of the Adnyamathanha also accepted Christianity in this period. There does not seem to have been any strong antagonism to Christian teachings but many of the people, especially the men, did not believe that this excluded their own traditional religion. Some came into conflict with the missionary over this issue, a conflict partly documented by C. P. Mountford in fieldnotes of his visits to Nepabunna in 1937, 1939 and 1944. He went to Nepabunna to gather data on Adnyamathanha traditional culture and made special trips to observe the initiation ceremonies in 1937 and 1939. His interest in the

Adnyamathanha was, therefore, in direct conflict with that of the Eatons.[31] Mountford favoured the continuation of the ceremonies and his very interest in them was interpreted by Eaton as encouraging them. There was a mutual dislike between Eaton and Mountford, and strong moral disapproval on both sides. Mountford's observations must therefore be read cautiously. He described the church as constructed of pine logs and kerosene tins with bag windows and children's desks for seats. He found the service rather unorthodox, very different from the strict form of the Anglican services with which he was familiar:

> Before the service commenced the missionary, minus coat, and armed with a guitar strummed away at favourite evangelistic hymns and sang them in a low voice. The women slowly drifted in and sat in the front seats, accompanied by the children, while the men occupied the back seats. The seating accommodation consisted of old school desks on which everybody leaned. When the service commenced nobody stood to sing. Everybody sat down while the missionary called for suggestions for choruses. These were readily forthcoming and were sung (with little vigour) by the congregation. There were many choruses, interminable they seemed, a bible reading and a short address . . .
>
> At the completion of the service communion was given to all present. This is the service which is supposed to separate the believers from the non-believers. If a man takes part in a wilyeru ceremony, he is not supposed to be allowed to attend this service.[32]

Adnyamathanha initiation was a two-stage ceremony. After the first stage, when the boy was circumcised, he became *vadnapa*. After the second stage, which involved further mutilations to the body, he emerged *wilyeru*, a fully initiated man. Eaton especially objected to the second stage. His professed reason for trying to stop them was his abhorrence of the mutilations. Mountford believed his objections went further, suggesting that when the first missionary began preaching to the Adnyamathanha, an equivalent had to be found for the devil. As there was nothing evil like the devil in their mythology the missionary seized on the pivotal mythological character in the *wilyeru* ceremony, who was dreaded particularly by the women. The *wilyeru* ceremony then became associated with devil's work.[33] Whatever the reason, Eaton not only disapproved but refused the sacrament to any men in his congregation who attended the ceremony, thus forcing them to choose between the two religions.

Mountford found Nepabunna divided into two factions. A vocal minority favoured discontinuing the ceremonial life, putting the past behind them and adopting the ways of the whites. The rest wanted the ceremonies to continue. The second group was dominated by men who felt they were too old to change their ways, and feared what might happen to the Adnyamathanha if they stopped. Abandoning the old ceremonies might make them susceptible to the power of outside 'tribes', and break down their social system. The young men would not respond to their authority and the marriage rules would break down.[34]

The same generation of elders who had revived the ceremonies earlier was now having to decide whether they should modify or abandon the cultural forms they had worked so hard to maintain. If they continued them they might split the community. If they stopped them they would lose their cultural identity. In 1939 they decided on a compromise. They performed a *wilyeru* ceremony, but in modified form without the mutilations. Mountford claimed that this satisfied both factions in the community as well as the missionary. By

1944, however, the missionary was advocating the total abandonment of the ceremonies. Mountford wrote that Eaton had threatened to leave the Adnyamathanha, in which event they would lose their reserve, if they did not adopt Christianity and end their ceremonial life.[35] Mountford believed Eaton was therefore responsible for ending the ceremonies. In fact, another and final ceremony was held in 1947–48.

Mountford's views of the social changes occurring at Nepabunna were rather blinkered. He seems to have been oblivious to the pressures, apart from the missionaries, which were affecting the Adnyamathanha. Most of the men and some of the women were employed in the European economy and they could not always take time off to attend to ceremonial business. The initiation ceremonies in the 1930s and 1940s were held in late December during the Christmas holidays to fit in with their working lives. Use of alcohol was increasing and the elders did not want their sacred life tainted by drunken participants. A third factor was access to land. Although the Adnyamathanha still worked all over the Flinders Ranges and many lived for extended periods on the stations where they were employed, their access was increasingly restricted. They were known to be Europeanised and were not expected to move about the country as they had fifty years earlier, nor to remain sequestered in the bush for many days, as initiation ceremonies required. Dependence on European food also affected the way they related to a land which no longer directly sustained them. Finally, there were the debates Mountford had noticed about the ways in which their religious, social and cultural life should proceed.

The UAM prerequisites for conversion were less rigorous and more ad hoc than those of the denominational churches. The missionaries' attempts to convert the Adnyamathanha to Christianity succeeded better with some people than others. Women proved to be more susceptible to the Christian message than men and some families were more responsive than others.[36] Some of these families made their own independent decisions not to participate in the ceremonial life. This created problems as those who had not been initiated were not considered marriageable men. In one instance, when the father of a girl objected to her marrying an uninitiated man the young couple appealed to the Protector of Aborigines, who was willing to override parental authority and allow the marriage to go ahead.[37] This uncertainty and controversy over the ceremonies, and the increasingly Europeanised lifestyle made it much more difficult for the boys to go through the protracted ceremonies with the same commitment their forefathers had. The possibility that these boys would not be able to stand up to the rigours of initiation was another factor in the decision to end them.[38]

The missionaries were not in a position to stop the Adnyamathanha ceremonial life but there is no doubt they used their influence to try to put an end to cultural forms which they believed were 'devil's work'. However, had secular authorities rather than missionaries been in charge at Nepabunna the ultimate outcome might not have been very different. The Protector of Aborigines was not as vehement or morally judgemental as the UAM missionaries, but he also held that the ceremonies would and should end. He believed this was inevitable and would happen with only minimal intervention from outside.[39] He was prepared to protect boys from the elders of a community if he believed the boys were being initiated against their will and to intervene in marriage arrange-

An Aboriginal camp with women in mourning, North Flinders Ranges.
(Courtesy of W. B. Sanders Collection, Mortlock Library of South Australiana.)

ments. It seems unlikely that, with these internal and external pressures on the Adnyamathanha, the ceremonial life, which had already been modified, would have ultimately survived.

Once the decision to end the ceremonies had been taken, other changes followed. Until the mid-1950s all marriages among the Adnyamathanha were 'firestick' marriages performed in the traditional manner; from the mid-1950s on, all marriages were performed according to European forms. The missionaries had recognised Adnyamathanha marriages but the government did not and would not pay child endowment to those they insisted on classifying as 'unmarried' mothers.

When the Adnyamathanha moved to Nepabunna they established two cemeteries, an *araru* and a *matheri*, as they had at Ram Paddock Gate. By the mid-1950s, a third cemetery was used where people were buried regardless of moiety. Ceremonies associated with death and burial gradually changed and disappeared, such as abandoning a house where a death occurred, building a wind-break at the head of the grave, lighting fires between the grave and the camp or settlement. (These ceremonies had been performed to prevent the spirit of the dead person from returning to haunt the living in the first three days after burial.)

The moiety system prevailed in determining categories of appropriate marriage partners until the 1950s when people began marrying outside their own community. Mountford claimed that Eaton had deliberately tried to undermine the Adnyamathanha marriage system by encouraging non-conforming marriages, but if he did, he was only partly successful. In the one documented case of a girl marrying an uninitiated man in the 1940s (cited above), the couple had to move away from Nepabunna to get married, even though they were conforming to the moiety system. On the other hand there were a number of men at Nepabunna without wives because the system of arranged marriages was breaking down and there were no women in appropriate relationships available to them.[40] The marriage rules really disintegrated (apart from the exogamous moiety rule) after the ceremonies ended and the Eatons had left Nepabunna.

By the time the Hathaways arrived at the mission in 1954 European practices informed most aspects of the Adnyamathanhas' lives. However what remained of older patterns was still strong, and continued to ensure that the Adnyamathanha were a distinctive community with a strong identity. They kept their language, in spite of the missionaries, but the children now learned English as their first language and were no longer fluent in Adnyamathanha. The mythology was still a vibrant part of community life and the sites associated with the mythologies were important to the people. On the other hand, their association with the land was further undermined by the virtual end to employment on pastoral stations in the 1970s. This meant that Adnyamathanha children could not have the same access to the land, and therefore the knowledge of the land, that their parents had had.

Assessing the influence of the mission on the Adnyamathanha is a complex business. The missionaries were concerned to save the Adnyamathanha and to Christianise them; on both counts they were largely successful. But their success had conflicting and contradictory outcomes. They probably rescued the Adnyamathanha from starvation and certainly protected them from being dispersed by negotiating a place for a permanent settlement. Without the UAM's intervention it is possible the Aboriginal people of the north Flinders Ranges might not have been able to maintain their strong group identity. They would eventually have been forced to move to the fringes of nearby towns or south to Port Augusta. It is possible the government would have intervened and removed their children if they had not been able to maintain them. The children were all of mixed descent by the 1930s and therefore could legally be removed from their mothers. Ironically the missionaries' intervention thus actually saved Adnyamathanha culture, language and identity, which they were working to suppress.

Unlike the communities at Poonindie and Koonibba, these people had extensive contact with Europeans before the advent of the missionaries. The Adnyamathanha already had eighty years of experience of this foreign culture and economy. They were, therefore, in a better position than some other mission Aborigines to decide whether to become Christians or not. Rejecting Christianity did not mean an individual was rejecting all aspects of European life. The retention of their own religious life on the other hand was not an individual but a communal decision. The balance of community attitudes changed in the 1940s and the decision was taken to abandon the ceremonial life, which was becoming less and less the focal point of Adnyamathanha life. A number of individuals felt keenly that this communal decision meant their personal options were restricted. They could choose not to be Christians but they could not choose to engage in their own religious rites.

The post-mission era

Nepabunna was taken over by the government ten years after Koonibba, enabling the Adnyamathanha to escape doctrinaire application of government assimilation policies, and to benefit from the new policies of self-determination. Like many other Aboriginal communities they moved from a regime where they had no formal authority to a self-government. They had to learn to deal with a variety of government departments, to apply for funds and to manage them when they came. Many adults had only limited literacy skills as a result of their inadequate schooling in the mission era.

Adnyamathanha who have moved away from Nepabunna to towns in the Flinders Ranges, south to Port Augusta and as far as Adelaide, nevertheless maintain strong community ties and a keen interest in their cultural identity. This interest has linked up to the heritage concerns of the late twentieth century. The community has worked closely with the Aboriginal Heritage Branch of the Department of Environment and Planning in South Australia. It was the first Aboriginal community to use this government resource to record sites of significance and other aspects of its culture.[41] It was the first Aboriginal community to negotiate to have its own people employed as field staff in the Aboriginal Heritage Branch. The community elders were involved in the staff selection process. It was the first to cooperate with the National Parks and Wildlife Service and establish a training programme for Adnyamathanha rangers in national parks in the Flinders Ranges. The community has worked with linguists and the Education Department on Adnyamathanha language programmes for their children. The Education Department has also produced, in cooperation with the community, a course on the Adnyamathanha people for Aboriginal studies courses. The Adnyamathanha have a rock/country and western band which performs songs in Adnyamathanha as well as English. Their people act as guides to educational and tourist groups who visit the Ranges.

The Adnyamathanha have, therefore, very deliberately set out to preserve and record their culture for their descendants and ensure their children grow up with a knowledge of and a pride in being distinctly Adnyamathanha. This is a different strategy from that pursued by many Aboriginal people, who in the late twentieth century see land rights as the only alternative to cultural extinction.[42] However, the Adnyamathanha too have agitated for control over land. They attempted to gain control over the area that is now the Gammon Ranges National Park. When that failed they negotiated for their rangers to oversee the park. They control the Nepabunna land through the Aboriginal Land Trust and have gained control of two pastoral leases at Mount Serle and Nantawarrina. The Mount Serle lease is administered by a community council, the Artoowarrapunna Council.[43]

These new responsibilities, the loss of the last generation of initiated men and women and the impingement of the bureaucratic world on the Adnyamathanha have caused tensions in the community that did not previously exist. Young, educated people are now given authority through government positions which was previously held by the elders. There are also tensions between those who live at Nepabunna, and those who have temporarily or permanently moved away but still believe they have a stake in the settlement. Some of these differences relate to family and religious affiliation (a number of families are strongly committed Christians, while other families never accepted Christianity).

Nevertheless, the urge to maintain a strong Adnyamathanha identity has kept the differences in check.

Although the transition from paternalistic control of the mission to self-governing community has been as difficult for them as for other Aboriginal communities, the Adnyamathanha experience of institutionalisation has been much less intense. Through the forty years of mission control many aspects of Adnyamathanha life changed, but these changes occurred with their acquiescence and could be controlled by the people who had a focal point for communal action at Nepabunna. It would have been more difficult to make and implement communal decisions if the Adnyamathanha had been dispersed in fringe camps. The institution has therefore had an important but transitional impact on the Adnyamathanha.

Notes

1 Harry Green, 'Harry Green Remembers', unpublished typescript in the possession of his widow, Marion Green, pp. 2–3.
2 Heritage Unit, Department of Environment, *Minerawuta (Ram Paddock Gate)*, Adelaide, 1981, p. 6.
3 Heritage Unit, *Minerawuta*, p. 5.
4 Heritage Unit, *Minerawuta*, p. 19.
5 Annie Coulthard, 1984, pers. com.
6 Heritage Unit, *Minerawuta*, p. 7 (plan of site).
7 These conditions included: putting up a sheep and donkey-proof fence; ensuring the camp was not near other station boundaries; dogs to be kept in check; land to revert to the lessee if the UAM abandoned the mission: GRG 52/1/1930.
8 Rufus Wilton, pers. com.
9 GRG 52/1/1933, SAPRO; Rufus Wilton, pers. com.
10 Although one informant claimed Eaton jumped one of Ted Coulthard's claims: Molly Wilton, pers. com.; another said Greenwood jumped Ted's claim: Clem Coulthard, pers. com. which is confirmed by documentary evidence GRG 52/1/1941/17 2/11/1941.
11 For example, Clem Coulthard, pers. com.
12 GRG 52/1/1966/1159.
13 GRG 52/1/1954/64.
14 GRG 52/1/1957/165, 3/9/1958, 15/4/1959; GRG 52/1/1966/1159.
15 GRG 52/1/1940 2/8/1940; GRG 52/1/1939/43 3/6/1939; GRG 52/1/1947/62 22/6/1950.
16 The first Adnyamathanha to be employed as a permanent employee and given accommodation in Leigh Creek was Don Coulthard in the late 1970s: Don Coulthard pers. com.
17 GRG 52/11949/42 14/8/1949.
18 GRG 52/1/1945/33 27/12/1945. Penhall, the Secretary to the Protection Board, replied that there would be no point supplying conveniences as they would not be used!
19 GRG 52/1/1945/33 4/2/1946; GRG 52/1/1966/1599.
20 GRG 52/1/1946/26 20/4/1946.
21 GRG 52/1/1950/42 17/2/1950.
22 GRG 52/1/1943/7 20/3/1943 (he died in 1945).
23 For example, GRG 52/1/1949/42.
24 Based on interviews with Pearl and John McKenzie.
25 Pearl has worked with the linguist, Dorothy Tunbridge (whose chief informant was Annie Coulthard, John McKenzie's sister) and published the *Adnyamathanha Genealogy* through the Aboriginal Heritage Branch.

26 Molly Wilton (née Coulthard), pers. com. 13/11/1985; Clem Coulthard, pers. com. This was part of the dog (dingo) proof fence which traversed South Australia.

27 Molly Wilton, pers. com. 13/11/1985. Clem Coulthard believed Ted was given land by Greenwood from Mt Constitution to Mt Rowe on which he ran his stock in lieu of payment for the fence Ted built, but there are no corroborating sources for this.

28 Clem Coulthard, pers. com.

29 GRG 52/1/1948/36 1/5/1948.

30 GRG 52/1/1948/36 2/8/1948, 30/11/1948; GRG 52/1/1951/44 1/8/1951.

31 Mountford, Fieldnotes, vols. 19 and 20, Mountford-Sheard Collection, State Library of South Australia. Antagonism between missionaries and anthropologists is not uncommon. Ronald and Catherine Berndt, who spent six months at Ooldea had an uneasy relationship with the UAM missionaries, Harry and Marion Green: Marion Green, pers. com.

32 Mountford, Fieldnotes, vol. 20, pp. 87 and 89.

33 Mountford, Fieldnotes, vol. 20, p. 83.

34 Mountford, Fieldnotes, vol. 20, pp. 28 and 83.

35 Mountford, Fieldnotes, vol. 20, p. 73, and vol. 51, p. 25.

36 Women were also more eager to end the ceremonies than the men: Gertie Johnson and Roma Wilton, pers. com.

37 GRG 52/1/1948/36.

38 Gertie Johnson and Roma Wilton, pers. com.

39 GRG 52/1/1947/62.

40 Mountford, Fieldnotes, vol. 19, p. 99.

41 Apart from recording and registering large numbers of Adnyamathanha sites, the branch has published various texts for the Adnyamathanha: Heritage Unit, Department of Environment, *The Flinders Ranges an Aboriginal view*, Adelaide, 1980; Heritage Unit, Department of Environment *Minerawuta (Ram Paddock)*, Adelaide, 1981, Davis and McKenzie, *Adnyamathanha Genealogy*, Adelaide, 1985; Brock, *Yura and Udnyu: A history of the Adnyamathanha of the North Flinders Ranges* Adelaide, 1985. The linguist, Dorothy Tunbridge, has also worked with the community and produced two publications, *Artefacts of the Flinders Ranges*, Port Augusta, 1986, and *Flinders Ranges Dreaming*, Canberra, 1988.

42 This issue is discussed in great detail by Jane Jacobs in her MA thesis, 'Aboriginal Land Rights in Port Augusta', University of Adelaide, 1983.

43 Nantawarrina lease was bought by the government and transferred to the Aboriginal Lands Trust in 1974. Mount Serle was purchased by the Aboriginal Development Commission in 1981 and the lease transferred to the Artoowarrapunna Council in 1989.

10

THE GHETTO EXPERIENCE AND SURVIVAL

Historian, Bain Attwood, has suggested in his book, *The Making of the Aborigines*, that Aborigines in their colonial situation had changes imposed on them which they did not seek: 'I thought it necessary to emphasise the ways in which Aborigines in colonial Australia were "made" more than they "made" themselves'. He discerns through the interaction of Aborigines and Europeans the development of a common Aboriginal consciousness, which did not previously exist.[1]

There is no disputing that the colonial experience has had a far reaching impact on Aborigines and profoundly affected the way that they perceive themselves. But Attwood understates the degree to which Aborigines made themselves in response to the pressures of colonisation. The communities examined in this book, which do not diverge dramatically from his example of the Moravian mission at Ramahyuck in Victoria, suggest that Aborigines were adapting to changing circumstances as they happened. The people who went to Poonindie and Koonibba or lived in the Flinders Ranges may not have identified themselves as Aborigines in the sense that we now understand the word. They did not identify with indigenous people in the other Australian colonies, nor with other peoples in southern Australia. Nevertheless, they understood that at their local level they had to redefine themselves if they were to survive. This understanding was not imposed on them, they chose it over other options. Those who chose not to redefine themselves may well have been those who did not ultimately survive. I suggest that we should see Aborigines making themselves rather than being made. C. D. Rowley has pointed out that: 'It was inevitable that [institutionalised] people should come to regard these places [institutions] as their own. Much of what has been loosely accepted as "tribal" loyalty is really the result of common history and experience as inmates of these places . . .'[2]

This loyalty was not an accidental outcome. It was a conscious choice made by those people who moved to the mission and stayed (this does not, of course, apply to people who were rounded up and forced on to distant institutions). There is evidence from many parts of Australia that Aborigines successfully resisted attempts to move them to places to which they did not want to go, and to make them associate with people with whom they did not want to associate.[3]

This changing self-definition did not necessarily depend for its maintenance on an ongoing association with an institution. The Adnyamathanha exemplify a community who expanded its self-definition of Yura, the people, to encompass neighbouring groups, without the support of an institution or settlement. In Victoria the Aborigines at Framlingham, who were dispersed in the late nineteenth century, retained their strong identification with that government station for a century after they were removed.[4] The process of Aborigines redefining themselves continues. Many Aboriginal people now define themselves at the regional rather than the national or local level. There are the Kooris of south-eastern Australia, the Nungas of southern South Australia and the Nyungar of south-western Western Australia. The Anangu or Pitjantjatjara also encompass peoples who previously defined themselves in smaller units.

While missionaries were not in a position to coerce Aborigines to join their institution, once the Aborigines had forged an emotional link and established a dependency on the mission the missionary or superintendent did have power over them. The balance of the power relations changed over time, as did the attitudes of both Aborigines and staff to the institution. The first generation knew a life away from the institution, they could leave if they were not happy. The missionary had an evangelical drive to establish his settlement and encourage potential converts to stay there. But the second generation of Aborigines who grew up on the mission never experienced a separate existence, nor did many of them have the comfort of an alternative world view to that offered by the institution. The staff were no longer idealistically converting the 'heathen', but baptising and confirming children and controlling 'inmates'. There was no longer an ultimate goal, merely a continuation of present circumstances. There was an emphasis on discipline and control for its own sake. Staff authority depended on their charges remaining 'children', never having responsibilities, never being allowed to establish themselves independently.[5] It was difficult for the 'inmates' to escape from the institution because they had no support systems outside. The implementation of assimilation programmes in the 1950s and 1960s presented Aborigines with a viable alternative to institutional life for the first time and many took the opportunity to move away permanently.

Initially the advantages of the missions outweighed the disadvantages. They offered a source of ready food; a secure place to camp; steady employment; a refuge for the old and sick, some health care, a refuge for children and the opportunity to gain literacy and numeracy skills. Perhaps most important, the missions offered a permanent settlement where the Aborigines could re-establish kin ties and strong communal links which were under threat, if not already destroyed. An alternative set of beliefs and ceremonies were offered which were relevant to their changing circumstances and helped to make sense of the devastation and huge loss of life that they sustained. The institution also acted as mediator between Aborigines and the outside world. Weighed against these advantages was the paternalism, which at best offered protection but entailed constant supervision, control and punishment. The Aborigines were in a perpetual state of uninitiated children, never able to attain adult status. They were regarded as irresponsible and unreliable in an unredeemable state of inferiority. Conversion to Christianity, while raising their status did not bring them equality with Europeans. These institutions, which were established with Aboriginal labour, never belonged to the Aborigines. The land they farmed gained in value, but they did not benefit. The fate of Poonindie epitomised this trend repeating the pattern of the original usurping of their lands.

Nepabunna was an exception to this pattern. The small parcel of rocky land was not economically viable. The mission was never planned to be self-sufficient but rather a dormitory for Aboriginal workers and their families. While the Adnyamathanha suffered under the paternalism of the missionaries, they were not economically exploited by them.

Mission success or failure?

I will use Axtell's distinction between the missionary view and the Aboriginal perspective of the success or failure of missions to consider the role of these institutions and their impact on Aboriginal people.

It is difficult to judge success in mission terms. Is success based merely on conversion statistics, or rather on the production of independent Christian workers? All three missions succeeded in converting at least some of their charges to Christianity. Poonindie and Koonibba also succeeded in their aim of 'civilising', that is inculcating European attitudes towards dress, accommodation, education, work and morality. But this process was then subverted by the institution itself, so that one finds this pattern emerging: 'uncivilised heathen' → 'civilised' Christian → institutionalised 'inmate' or fringe dweller.

If producing independent, Christian workers was the ultimate goal then there were few successes during the life of each mission. Examples which spring to mind are the Solomon brothers at Poonindie; Dick Davey who moved from Koonibba to Port Lincoln where he and his family established themselves in a house in the town and remained church-going Christians; and Yari and Lena Miller and family, who established themselves in Ceduna after being converted at Koonibba. But the majority of converts remained institutionalised (particularly at Poonindie) or abandoned an active interest in the Church when they moved away from the mission.

Different criteria must be used to assess success or failure in Aboriginal terms. Axtell argues that, '[t]he elemental fact of ethnic survival is all important in assessing success or failure of mission efforts from the native perspective.'[6] In his study of the 'praying towns' of New England Axtell notes that the missionaries were most successful when the colonists had most decimated and endangered the survival of the group being proselytised. But paradoxically the Indians were most successful in fulfilling their goals, either when their cultural resources and sovereignty were unimpaired and they could pick and choose from the missionaries' offerings, or when their cultural and social needs were so great that they opted for the life of the group by forming a praying town rather than splintering into vulnerable fragments.[7] Axtell emphasises that the success of the missionary endeavour was determined by the Indians' assessments of their best strategies for communal survival.

The peoples who were attracted to the three South Australian missions under study can be described in the same terms. The first generation of people who went to Poonindie were decimated and endangered. The Adnyamathanha had their cultural resources relatively unimpaired, while those people who went to Koonibba could be described as having social and cultural needs which pushed them into the life of the group, rather than becoming vulnerable fragments.[8] I consider each case separately in terms of the community's perceived needs and the action taken to ameliorate them. The argument can be taken one step further by asking what use do the colonised make of Christianity once they adopt it? Does it represent submission to the dominant ideology, or is it used selectively to bolster ideological resistance to the missionaries and the culture they represent?[9]

Poonindie

The people who chose to go to Poonindie came from regions where large numbers had already died. Their survival was in doubt. Contemporary European observers believed that by the 1860s the Adelaide and upper Murray River people had virtually become extinct. Yet the death rate among people at Poonindie during the first ten years was extremely high. Had they changed their circumstances without improving their prospects of ethnic survival? Some of their kin on the River Murray believed the Poonindie people had done this. They refused to go with missionary Holden in 1869 because they believed they would be going to their deaths. Ultimately enough people survived and produced children at Poonindie to build up a stable, close-knit community.

The early years engendered a strong sense of achievement among both European staff and Aborigines. The Aborigines were no longer marginalised as they had been in Adelaide, but central to the establishment of a farming enterprise. They learned quickly and well; their level of skill was equal to that of non-Aboriginal workers. Poonindie was a communal enterprise which generated a communal pride, reinforced by the Aborigines' sporting prowess. Poonindie in the 1860s and 1870s was an Aboriginal success story, but this achievement was later eroded by continued institutionalisation and was followed by the tragedy of closure and loss of land, a tragedy experienced by many other Aborigines who helped establish institutions in Western Australia, Victoria and New South Wales.

The lack of any reference by Mathew Hale to Aboriginal ritual or beliefs competing with his own evangelical agenda suggests the Aborigines who came and stayed at Poonindie had rejected these along with their past lives. The missionary's task was, therefore, simplified. He had to convince his converts of the rightness of his beliefs without first undermining theirs. In these circumstances he achieved a high rate of genuine conversions. Christianity was part of the political, social and economic package offered and accepted. People came to the mission on an individual basis, they could not revert to an alternative communal or ritual life. Christian myths and explanations of life and death were the only ones available to make sense of the threat and reality of early death. When they died, Christian mourning and burial customs were the only ones available. If they wanted to marry, it had to be at a Christian ceremony. Conversion was a further submission to the new world order they had adopted.

Koonibba

The choices facing people at Koonibba were not so clear cut. The devastation of their communal lives had not been so thoroughgoing. Encroachment over their lands was more gradual, allowing time for adjustment. It may have exacerbated population movements which were already occurring and hastened the process of conciliation between different Aboriginal cultural and language groups. Pastoralism and kangaroo hunting did not affect the people as dramatically as urban development did those of the Adelaide Plains. It was the westward movement of the agricultural frontier which called for more drastic responses from the Wirangu and Kokatha as they faced the danger of 'splintering into vulnerable fragments'.[10] Koonibba offered a secure base at which the process of the redefinition of kinship ties could continue. It contrasts with Poonindie which attracted individuals who formed a new community with no antecedents in Aboriginal society. This process of renewal and expansion continued during the life of the mission. Up to the 1950s new groups continued to come to Koonibba. First they came from the coastal region, then from Fowlers Bay, the Gawler Ranges and finally from the north via Ooldea. (It is worth noting that the Ooldea adults who went to Koonibba made that decision freely, while those who went to Yalata had been forced to leave Ooldea in the 1950s and became an uprooted and dispossessed community.)

The early pattern of conversion suggests it was motivated by political and social accommodation with the mission authorities.[11] The mission was ridiculed and criticised by non-Lutheran white farmers in the region, indicating that accommodation was specifically to the mission rather than to the entire colonial society. There is no documentation on how the Aboriginal ceremonial and ritual practices ended. It is likely that as the mission claimed control of the children, there were no new initiates to maintain ceremony and ritual, which then died with the last initiated generation.

Christianity and the 'civilising' mission were strongly linked at Koonibba. So, while there is some evidence of syncretism and rejection of Christianity and its concomitant 'civilisation', the vast majority of people were church-going Lutherans while they remained at the mission. When the government took over at the same time as alcohol became readily available, many people associated the loss of their Christian community with alcoholism and social trauma.

Institutionalised attitudes and dispersal policies coincided at Koonibba in the 1920s and 1930s creating conflicting pressures and expectations. Good Christian behaviour could no longer be rewarded as it had been when Koonibba functioned as a total institution. Expectations, which had been encouraged by the Church, that Koonibba was a permanent and stable home were not met, causing alienation and disillusionment among the people. As with Poonindie, Koonibba's inability to offer viable alternatives to institutionalisation limited its longterm promotion of an independent Koonibba people. One of the few escape routes from institutionalisation or marginalisation in fringe camps was that offered by the high standard of education, which by the 1950s enabled some to leave the mission to further their studies and establish themselves independently in the general community.

The longevity of the Koonibba community was an historical accident, rather than the fulfilment of long-term objectives held by Church or government.[12] Yet the people, by their persistent attachment to Koonibba, eventually won control and ownership of its land.

Nepabunna

Nepabunna was important to the Adnyamathanha because it provided them with their own settlement. This permanent village was not imposed by the missionaries, the Adnyamathanha had already established a settlement of their own at Ram Paddock Gate, but it lacked security of tenure. If the missionaries had done nothing but negotiate the Nepabunna land and provide rations during the depression, they would have succeeded in fulfilling the Adnyamathanhas' most pressing requirements. They were determined to stay in their own country and had refused to move to establish fringe camps at the townships of Blinman or Copley where they could have obtained rations. Had they been provided with their own reserve land, they would have had no need of the mission. They could have run their own stock and continued working on pastoral stations. The establishment of the mission did not have a major impact on the pattern of their lives. They continued their stock work, their mining activities and any contract work they could pick up. Now instead of wives and children moving from station to station with the men, many chose to stay at Nepabunna.[13] The major changes that came to the Adnyamathanhas' lives in the 1930s and 1940s were the result of economic and industrial changes—the establishment of the Leigh Creek coalfields and the introduction of roads and railway. Later came the loss of employment on pastoral stations as a result of increased mechanisation and the introduction of an equal wages award. The Adnyamathanha were in a position 'to pick and choose from the missionaries' offerings'.[14]

In contrast to the experiences of Poonindie and Koonibba people, the Adnyamathanha were not presented with Christianity as part of a 'civilising' package. Initially a number were prepared to embrace Christianity. They felt some obligation to the missionaries who had helped them but did not anticipate that it would affect their pre-existing beliefs and ritual life. When the missionaries insisted that they had to choose between the two religions, they lost a number of potential converts and created lingering resentments among some of the Adnyamathanha. Once the decision to end the ceremonies had been taken, there was no impediment to conversion to Christianity but there were few advantages for the Adnyamathanha. It did not affect their ability to obtain work or move on and off the mission, nor was it linked to other material aspects of life such as the availability of food, clothing or education. The end of the ceremonies also signalled the end of other rituals such as those associated with death and marriage, but these changes would have occurred eventually without the intervention of the missionaries, for it was the Adnyamathanha who determined the rate at which they could accommodate change. The missionaries tried hard to discourage the use of Yura Ngawarla (Adnyamathanha language), penalising those who spoke it publicly. But the Adnyamathanha chose to retain their language and it survived the missionary era, although not as the primary language of daily communication.

A period when institutionalised attitudes dominated the community was not fully experienced at Nepabunna, partly because the mission was relatively shortlived but also because the missionaries never attained the same control over people's lives as at Koonibba and Poonindie. Nor did it provide the same level of services as the more affluent institutions. There were three reasons why people left Nepabunna. The two major ones were to move closer to sources of employment and to obtain a better education for their children. The third reason was to escape the supervision and interference by the missionaries in their personal lives. When the missionaries could no longer benefit the Adnyamathanha, when they became more of a liability than an asset, they were asked to leave. The missionaries did not make the community, but sustained it at a particular point in its history.

Aboriginal agency

Evaluating Aboriginal agency is controversial and will continue to be so as it relies on a very careful reading of the evidence. This documentary evidence is not only held by the dominant colonial power, as Henrietta Fourmile has noted, but it is also produced by those in power.[15] These records are by and large a day-by-day accounting. The missionaries, police and public servants are not concerned with the internal consistency of their reports over time. The historian is in a position to assess these records over the long term, to compare the views expressed at one point in time with those presented at an earlier or later date. Personal biases and prejudices are revealed by this process in a way that the author of a document could never have anticipated.

In most mission archives, the first conversions are described in great detail, later ones are barely mentioned. The missionary sees what he wants to see. For him these early recruits are the measure of his success or failure. It is difficult to extract an Aboriginal perspective, but the historian can build up biographical sketches based on missionary and government records in which patterns emerge. At Koonibba the pattern of acquiescence and resistance is very obvious—the embracing of the Christian message one day followed by a distancing and then reassessment. Other indications of the turmoil created by these pressures emerge in the reports of volatile behaviour among the early converts and their wild swings in mood.

The biographies reveal Aboriginal attitudes towards conversion to Christianity, as well as to other aspects of the 'civilising' package. Poonindie biographies reveal a pattern of readiness to work and establish a community, but hesitancy to adopt European modes of personal interaction. Koonibba biographies show the early converts were on the periphery of Aboriginal cultural life. They came from other areas, or had spent time with Europeans. Unfortunately there is no information on the motivations for conversion of a few Aboriginal elders such as Jack Jebydah, Yarrie Tchuna and Colona Tom (a death-bed conversion, perhaps an explanation in itself).

The biographies also help illuminate the ways in which people's lives changed over time, from pre-mission days to life on the institution, their movements on and off the missions, and the role the institution played in their lives. For some the mission became a permanent home. Micky Free exemplifies this response. But for most it was a base from which people might go in search of work, as did Jimmy Richards, John and Emanuel Solomon, Claude Demell and Ted Coulthard. For others it was a staging post in their lives from which they moved out into the community, as with Pearl and John McKenzie, Rufus Wilton, Robert Betts, Yari and Lena Miller and Daniel Limberry. These various responses belie the impression missions often present as totally controlling all aspects of Aborigines' lives. Some children's homes and dormitories might seem like prisons but for most adults a major fear was being banned, rather than being retained on the institution. The institutions featuring in this study were very different from the prison-like Moore River Settlement in Western Australia, the ultimate segregationist ghetto.[16]

This study also indicates that despite the common experiences of contending with discrimination, racial prejudice and bureaucratic controls over their lives (by government and/or church), Aborigines' individual and communal experiences have been very different. Their responses to colonial situations have had to be flexible as each new historic period has presented them with new obstacles to overcome. Institutional ghettos played a necessary role in survival, first consolidating their communities and secondly as havens against the racism of non-Aboriginal society which repeatedly set them up to fail.

The physical environment—natural and manmade—also influenced Aboriginal responses to colonialism. The natural environment facilitated Aboriginal resistance in some areas more than others. The Adnyamathanha's use of the rugged Ranges exemplifies Aboriginal superiority in conditions where European technological advantages were neutralised by Aboriginal knowledge of the terrain. But in the long term, it was European modifications to the natural environment which determined Aboriginal responses to colonialism. Urbanisation had immediate and catastrophic effects on Aboriginal life. Agriculture also forced Aborigines off their lands, except where land was reserved for their use; but non-Aboriginal society would not accept Aborigines as farmers, so to maintain themselves by agriculture they had to move on to a mission or government station. Pastoralism offered a wider range of Aboriginal options, as they were able to maintain a degree of independence which was impossible where other land uses predominated.

A re-assessment of the common assumption that Aborigines were antipathetic to work is needed. Aborigines had to learn European work practices despite the obstacles that were put in their way. Each time they proved themselves through the success of their own endeavours, the evidence had to be removed so the myth of the lazy, apathetic parasite could be sustained.[17] Aborigines appeared to succeed better in the pastoral industry than elsewhere because the early industry depended on their labour and therefore could not afford to subvert them as happened in agricultural and urban environments. The three case studies reveal no evidence of Aboriginal parasitism. The Adnyamathanha had a persistent record of high employment in the Flinders Ranges which was not affected by the establishment of Nepabunna. At Poonindie and Koonibba, Aborigines began working as soon as they joined the mission, but were often enticed away by the offer of higher wages elsewhere. They understood that work is rewarded and were not prepared to work unless wages, rations or some other material benefit were offered. Yet they were consistently paid at a lower rate than European workers and then accused of not being motivated.

When Koonibba ended its policy of full employment Aborigines left the mission to look for work. The plan to move the Aboriginal reserve from Ceduna/Thevenard to

Denial Bay in 1945 upset them because it would have removed them from the source of employment for which they had come to Ceduna in the first place. The Adnyamathanha moved away from Nepabunna because there was no employment in the area and no decent schooling for their children. This is not the behaviour of parasites but of people determined to be independent. Another theme which runs consistently through the evidence is the strong desire of Aborigines for land of their own. They were not asking for land so that they could return to a hunter-gatherer economy, but to farm.

Aboriginal reactions to the dismemberment of Poonindie were quite unambiguous. They wanted to farm land for themselves, either alone or cooperatively. Many Poonindie people stubbornly persisted in their attempts to gain access to farm land, their efforts continuing over a decade after Poonindie was disbanded. The evidence from Koonibba is very similar. From the earliest days Aborigines requested land to share-farm, but the marginality of the land as agricultural land made it impossible for them to maintain themselves on the small parcels they were given. When Koonibba was under threat of being sold in 1931, the Koonibba people's reaction mirrored the experience of Poonindie forty years earlier. They asked that the land be given to them to farm. The failure of the Poonindie and Koonibba people to gain access to farm land is not surprising in the context of the policies of the governments of the time and the attitudes of the non-Aboriginal society.

From the earliest days of the colony of South Australia small parcels of land were set aside for Aborigines, but never given to them. By 1860 forty-two reserves had been established (ranging from 52 to 240 acres excluding Poonindie), but thirty-six of them had been leased out to non-Aborigines.[18] By 1916 there were ninety-seven reserves, sixty-four of which were leased or sold to non-Aborigines.[19] Only 1,784 acres were directly leased to Aboriginal people.[20] Although the 1911 *Aborigines Act* acknowledged that Aborigines should be encouraged to establish their own farms, it limited the size of such farms to 160 acres, not a sustainable farm block in most parts of the State. The Poonindie lands were one of the few viable agricultural holdings available to Aborigines but as soon as they proved themselves as agriculturalists, the land was taken away. One can only conclude that the non-Aboriginal society was determined to make Aborigines parasitic and undermine their attempts to become independent.

Crucial to Aboriginal farming and stock work was the Aborigines' ability to learn new technical skills and apply new technologies to their own lives. The Adnyamathanha stand out because of the particularly deprived conditions in which they lived.[21] Prior to 1930 they had no institutional patronage, the government supplied the unemployed with basic rations; apart from that anything they acquired or any skills they learned were through their own endeavours. Most of these were learned on the job—horse work, use of explosives, maintenance of windmills, sewing, cooking in the European manner. Others showed quite remarkable ingenuity and adaptability. Men who had never learned to read could pull a car engine apart and put it together again; when fuel was unavailable, the cars were not abandoned but used as wagons, pulled along by their very useful donkeys. Donkey teams were put to a great variety of uses, carting machinery, minerals, wool clips. The Adnyamathanha were major suppliers of transport in the northern Flinders Ranges over a number of years.

Donkey team pulling car body, Nepabunna, late 1930s. When fuel was unavailable, or the engine ceased functioning, the Nepabunna people used the car body as a wagon.
(Courtesy of Mountford-Sheard Collection, State Library of South Australia.)

Similar adaptations characterised Poonindie and Koonibba people. Jimmy Richards at Koonibba was an extremely skilled tradesman who could turn his hand to almost any trade. Others learned to handle horses and bullock teams or became top class shearers. The Kokatha and Wirangu appreciated the uses of the written word long before they could read or write themselves, utilising it to promote their own ceremonial and communal life. Koonibba people were quick to aquire cars when they became available on the west coast to increase their options for employment. The effects of this innovation were immediately felt by the farm manager who had to contend with labour shortages at the mission as a result of this new mobility of his Aboriginal workforce.

Aborigines did not establish the institutional ghettos which dominated their lives for so many years, but neither did they avoid them. Aborigines associated themselves with missions in the early years of their establishment because they fulfilled their urgent needs. They offered them protection from a hostile world, access to rations, and education and training in European skills. Later the missions became self-perpetuating institutions. They became increasingly restrictive, emphasising discipline rather than training for employment. They became ends in themselves instead of a means to an end. Many Aboriginal people associated with them succumbed to the hopelessness of their position and took on the attitudes and behaviour of the institutionalised. Others used the mission as a periodic retreat when unemployed or in need of medical services or education for their children. A few moved away to try to establish themselves independently in the general community. Despite the changing role of the missions and the varied Aboriginal responses to them, their legacy to Aboriginal communal identity has been consistent and profound. They created the circumstances for Aborigines to establish large, close-knit communities based on shared experiences, intermarriage and association with land with which they identified. Some of these communities and the land with which they were associated had continuities with the pre-colonial past, others did not. Their importance to contemporary Aboriginal identities is based on shared institutional experiences, enforced separation from the non-Aboriginal population and the ability of Aborigines to use these circumstances to aid their ongoing survival.

Notes

1 Bain Attwood, *The making of the Aborigines*, Sydney, 1988, pp. 148, 150.

2 C. D. Rowley, *Outcasts in white Australia*, Canberra, 1972, p. 63.

3 For example, Christopher Anderson, 'A case study in failure: Kuku-Yalanji and the Lutherans at Bloomfield River 1887–1902', in Tony Swain and Deborah Bird Rose (eds), *Aboriginal Australians and Christian missions. Ethnographic and historical studies*, Bedford Park, South Australia, 1988 (Kuku-Yalanji in north-eastern Cape York Peninsula); Jan Critchett, *Our land till we die: a history of the Framlingham Aborigines*, Warrnambool, 1980 (Framlingham, Victoria); Diane Barwick, 'Coranderrk and Cumeroogunga' in T. Scarlett Epstein and David H. Penny (eds), *Opportunity and response*, London, 1972 (Coranderrk, Victoria); Peter Biskup, *Not Slaves, not citizens: the Aboriginal problem in Western Australia 1898–1954*, Brisbane, 1973 (Forrest River, Western Australia).

4 Diane Barwick, 'An assessment of the cultural and historical significance to the present Aboriginal community of the land reserved at Framlingham in 1861', Report to the Land Conservation Council, Melbourne, 1979, p. 3.

5 Compare evidence from missionaries and mission societies to the 1913–16 Royal Commission, which presented people of mixed descent as descended from Aborigines 'practically animals crawling in the bush' (p. 18) and as dependent children, with evidence from neighbouring farmers and others reliant on Aboriginal labour: 'The training of the natives should go on, not with the object of keeping them at the stations, but with the object of getting them on to land of their own' (p. 13).

6 James Axtell, 'Some thoughts on the ethnohistory of missions', *Ethnohistory*, 29 (1), 1982, p. 37.

7 Axtell, 'Some thoughts', p. 39.

8 This became the fate of many Kokatha people who did not base themselves at Koonibba. They moved from place to place in small groups with little community cohesion and were vulnerable to dispersal and extinction: Jane Jacobs, 'Aboriginal land rights in Port Augusta', unpublished MA thesis, University of Adelaide, 1984, pp. 215–16.

9 David Trigger, in his study of Doomadgee mission in the north-west of Queensland, explores the concept of the political significance of Christianity in different colonial situations: 'Christianity, domination and resistance in colonial social relations. The case of Doomadgee, northwest Queensland', in Swain and Rose, (eds), *Aboriginal Australians and Christian missions*, p. 214.

10 Axtell, 'Some thoughts', p. 39.

11 Trigger, 'Christianity, domination and resistance', p. 230.

12 In 1916–17 the government planned to take over the mission; in 1931 the mission was put up for sale, but no buyers came forward; in 1963 when the government did take over it planned to disperse (assimilate) the people with the long-term goal of closing the station.

13 Fay Gale, *A study of assimilation. Part Aborigines in South Australia*, Adelaide, 1964, p. 178.

14 Axtell, 'Some thoughts', p. 39.

15   Henrietta Fourmile, 'Who owns the past?—Aborigines as captives of the archives', *Aboriginal History,* 13(1), 1989.

16   Anna Haebich, *For their own good: Aborigines and government in the southwest of Western Australia 1900–1940,* Perth, 1988; Peter Biskup, *Not slaves, not citizens.*

17   For example, Poonindie, Coranderrk in Victoria and the Aborigines of the south-west of Western Australia.

18   Fay Gale, *A study of assimilation,* p. 154, quoting figures from the 1860 Select Committee on The Aborigines, Adelaide.

19   Fay Gale, *A study of assimilation,* p. 155, quoting figures from the 1913–16 Royal Commission on The Aborigines Report.

20   Royal Commission on The Aborigines, Final Report, 1916, appendix A, p. 44.

21   In 1983 I visited Wooltana station with an elderly Adnyamathanha woman who had lived there for many years. We visited the ruins of her old camp and there were the remains of her sewing machine among the other debris.

Select Bibliography

Archival sources

Flinders Ranges:

Beltana Police Station Journal and Letterbook, SAPRO GRG 5.
Bull, J. B., Reminiscences 1835–94, Mortlock Library of South Australiana.
Commissioner of Police Office correspondence files, SAPRO GRG 5.
Mount Freeling Police Station Journal, SAPRO GRG 5.
Mountford-Sheard Collection, Flinders Ranges Notebooks, State Library of South Australia.
Police Officers records, SA Police Department archives.
Port Augusta Police Station Letterbook, SAPRO GRG 5.
South Australian Aborigines Department, correspondence received, SAPRO GRG 52.
South Australian Chief Secretary's Office, correspondence received, SAPRO GRG 24.
South Australian Lands Department, Mount Serle station, SAPRO 1324/14.
South Australian Lands Department, Mount Serle maps and plans 1855, 1860, 1865, 1930–39.
South Australian Museum Archives, accession nos. 162, 642, 2286.
South Australian Protector of Aborigines correspondence received Outletter book and Reports SAPRO GRG 52.

Poonindie:

Mathew Hale's private papers on microfilm, original at Bristol University archives, England. The papers include Hale's diary and letters received by Hale when he was at Poonindie and in the mid-1890s when the institution was closed down. The microfilm is catalogued in the Private record group (PRG) 275, the contents still carry the Bristol University accession numbers. Mortlock Library of South Australiana.

Church of England Poonindie papers—Society record group (SRG) 94/W83 (the collection had not been catalogued, so series list numbers are not cited, dates of all correspondence and papers are cited). The collection includes correspondence and reports to the trustees, financial statements and receipts and population returns from the 1860s to the 1880s. Mortlock Library of South Australiana.

J. D. Somerville collection comprises six volumes of bound records relating to Poonindie copied under the direction of J. D. Somerville in the 1930s. The records are culled from government archives, newspapers, Church of England diocesan papers, parliamentary papers etc. Somerville was researching the history of Poonindie and was particularly interested in tracing what happened to the money which was put in trust when Poonindie was closed. The collection is catalogued as 1380. Mortlock Library of South Australiana.

Gertrude M. Farr. 'History of Poonindie mission', typescript, A1171 B10, Mortlock Library of South Australiana.

Protector of Aborigines and Aborigines Department records 1850–1925 SAPRO GRG 52/1; 52/7.

Chief Secretary's Office records SAPRO GRG 24/6.

South Australian Department of Lands, discontinued survey diagram books.

South Australian Department of Lands, perpetual lease books.

St Thomas Church of England, Port Lincoln, Poonindie births, deaths and marriages records.

Point Pearce Community Council, births, deaths and marriages records 1880s–1960s.

Point McLeay Community Council, births, deaths and marriages records 1850s–1960s.

Koonibba:

Lutheran Church archives, Aboriginal Mission Board minutes of meetings (German and English).

——— Koonibba record boxes (uncatalogued).

——— *Der Lutherische Kirchenbote für Australien* 1898–1917 (German language newspaper).

——— *Australian Lutheran* 1913–1933 (English language newspaper).

——— General Synodical Reports, Ecumenical Lutheran Church of Australia.

Protector of Aborigines and Aborigines Department records SAPRO GRG 52/1.

Herbert Basedow, first and second medical relief expeditions SAPRO GRG 23/1/144/1920.

Surveyor-General's Office 2487/1905.

South Australian Museum, Norman Tindale, fieldnotes, 1939.

Oral sources

Extensive interviews over many years were undertaken with Adnyamathanha and Koonibba people, as well as with a few people whose parents and grandparents had had an association with Poonindie. Non-Aboriginal people who were involved with the communities under study were also interviewed. Selection of interviewees was influenced by recommendations made by Aboriginal community members. Generally older people with the greatest historical knowledge and authority were suggested, but the selection was also influenced by the desire to maintain a balance of opinion from within the communities—Christians/non-Christians, representatives from different families or factions within the community etc.

Most Aboriginal people interviewed felt ill at ease when asked if they agreed to be taped. Notes of interviews were therefore taken and return visits arranged to ensure accuracy and gain approval for use of material thus collected. Draft copies of the community histories were sent back to community organisations as well as knowledgeable individuals for feedback on accuracy and sensitivity of material used before a final version was written.

Published sources

Newspapers:

Observer.
Port Augusta Dispatch 1878, 1882.
South Australian Register.
West Coast Sentinel.

Parliamentary publications

An Act to empower His Majesty to erect South Australia into a British Province or Provinces, and to provide for the colonization and Government thereof (1834).
Protector of Aborigines Reports.
Report of the Select Committee of the Legislative Council Upon the Aborigines 1860.
South Australian Government Gazette 1853, 1856–66, 1874, 1876, 1878, 1894, 1935.
South Australian Parliamentary Papers (SAPP) 1856 (no. 193) 1858–59 (including no. 177), 1859 (no. 30 Report on Poonindie mission), 1869 (no. 9) 1887, 1891.
South Australian Parliamentary Papers, Legislative Council 21/11/1894; 5/9/1895.
South Australian Parliamentary Papers, *Poonindie Exchange Act* (1895) no. 631.
South Australian Parliamentary Papers, Statistical Register of South Australia 1860–1900.
South Australian Yearbook 1872.

Books, articles and theses

Aboriginal Heritage Section, Department of Environment and Planning, *Yura Newsletter*, 1, 1977–78.
Anderson, Christopher, 'A case study in failure: Kuku-Yalanji and the Lutherans at Bloomfield River, 1887–1902' in Tony Swain and Deborah Bird Rose, *Aboriginal Australians and Christian missions*, Australian Association for the Study of Religions, Bedford Park, South Australia, 1988.
A piece of God's history: Koonibba 1901–1976, Adelaide, 1976.
Atkinson, Wayne, Langton, Marcia, Wanganeen, Doreen and Williams, Michael, 'Celebration of resistance to colonialism', *Black Australia*, 2, 1985.
Attwood, B. M., 'Blacks and Lohans: a study of Aboriginal European relations in Gippsland in the nineteenth century', PhD thesis, University of Melbourne, 1984.
Attwood, Bain, *The making of the Aborigines*, Allen and Unwin, Sydney, 1989.
Axtell, James, 'The invasion within. The contest of cultures in colonial North America' in James Axtell, *The European and the Indian. Essays in the ethnohistory of colonial North America*, New York, 1981.
Axtell, James, 'Some thoughts on the ethnohistory of missions', *Ethnohistory* 29 (1), 1982.
Barwick, Diane, 'Coranderrk and Cumeroogunga' in T. Scarlett Epstein and David H. Penny (eds), *Opportunity and response*, London, C. Hurst, 1972.
Barwick, Diane, Urry, James and Bennett, David, 'A select bibliography of Aboriginal and Islander history and social change: theses and published research to 1976', *Aboriginal History*, 1 (2), 1977.
Barwick, Diane, 'An assessment of the cultural and historical significance to the present Aboriginal community of the land reserved at Framlingham in 1861', Report to the Land Conservation Council, Melbourne, 1979.
Basedow, H., 'Burial Customs in the Northern Flinders Ranges of South Australia', *Man*, 26, 1913, pp. 49-53.
Bell, Diane and Ditton, Pam, *Law the old and new. Aboriginal women in Central Australia speak out*, Central Australian Aboriginal Legal Aid Service, Canberra 1980.
Bennett, Scott, *Aborigines and Political power*, Allen and Unwin, Sydney, 1989.

Berndt, R., 'Tribal Migrations and the Myths Centring on Ooldea, South Australia', *Oceania*, 12 (1), 1941.

—— (ed.), *Aborigines and change: Australia in the '70s*, AIAS, Canberra, 1977.

—— 'Traditional Aborigines' in C. R. Twidale, M. J. Tyler, and M. Davies (eds) , *Natural history of Eyre Peninsula*, Adelaide, 1986.

Bickford, Anne, 'Contact history: Aborigines in New South Wales after 1788', *Australian Aboriginal Studies*, no. 1, 1988.

Biles, David, 'Aborigines and prisons: a South Australian study', *Australian and New Zealand Journal of Criminology*, 6 (4), 1973.

Biskup, Peter, *Not slaves, not colonists: the Aboriginal problem in Western Australia 1898–1954*, University of Queensland Press, St Lucia, 1973.

Blu, Karen I., *The Lumbee problem: the making of an American Indian people*, Cambridge University Press, New York, 1980.

Brady, Maggie and Palmer, Kingsley, 'Dependency and assertiveness. Three waves of Christianity among Pitjantjatjara people at Ooldea and Yalata' in Tony Swain and Deborah Bird Rose (eds), *Aboriginal Australians and Christian missions. Ethnographic and historical studies*, Australian Association for the Study of Religions, Bedford Park, South Australia, 1988.

Brasser, Ted J., *Riding the frontier's crest: Mahican Indian culture and culture change*, Ottawa, 1974.

Brauer, A., *Under the southern cross. The history of the Evangelical Lutheran Church of Australia*, Adelaide, 1985.

Brock, M., 'A comparative study of government policies towards Aborigines and Africans in South Africa', BA (Hons) thesis, University of Adelaide, 1969.

Brock, P., *Yura and Udnyu. A history of the Adnyamathanha of the North Flinders Ranges*, Wakefield Press, Adelaide, 1985.

—— (ed.), *Women, rites and sites: Aboriginal women's cultural knowledge*, Allen and Unwin, Sydney, 1989.

Brock, P. and Kartinyeri, D., *Poonindie. The rise and destruction of an Aboriginal agricultural community*, SA Government Printer, Adelaide, 1989.

Broome, Richard, *Aboriginal Australians. Black response to white dominance 1788–1980*, Allen and Unwin, Sydney, 1982.

Bropho, Robert, *Fringedweller*, Alternative Publishing Cooperative, Sydney, 1980.

Bruce, Robert, *Reminiscences of an old squatter*, Libraries Board of South Australia, Adelaide, (facsimile copy, 1973) Adelaide, 1902.

Bruner, Edward M., 'Mandan' in Edward H. Spicer (ed.), *Perspectives in American Indian cultural change*, University of Chicago, Chicago, 1969.

Bull, J. W., *Early experiences of colonial life in South Australia*, (facsimile copy), Libraries Board of South Australia, Adelaide, 1978.

Butlin, Noel, *On our original aggression. Aboriginal populations of south eastern Australia*, George Allen and Unwin, Sydney, 1983.

Cassidy, Julie, 'The significance of the classification of a colonial acquisition: the conquered/settled distinction', *Australian Aboriginal Studies*, no. 1, 1988.

Cawthorne, W. A., 'Rough notes on the manners and customs of "The Natives"', 1844 *Proceedings of the Royal Geographical Society of Australia South Australian Branch*, 27, 1926.

Corris, Peter, 'Ethnohistory in Australia', *Ethnohistory*, 16 (3), 1969.

Critchett, Jan, *Our land till we die: a history of the Framlingham Aborigines*, Warrnambool Institute Press, Warrnambool, 1980.

Curr, E. M., *The Australian Race*, vol. 2, Government Printer, Melbourne, 1886.

Davis, Christine and McKenzie, Pearl, *Adnyamathanha Genealogy*, Department of Environment and Planning, Adelaide, 1985.

Davis, J. W., 'Poonindie Aboriginal station 1850–1895: a study in race relations', BA (Hons) thesis, University of Adelaide,1971.

De Lawyer, A., 'Davenport and Umeewarra since 1937', BA (Hons) thesis, University of Adelaide, 1972.

Eckermann, C., 'Aboriginal Missions; the Church's problem child', *Australian Lutheran*, 1958–9.

Edwards, Meredith, *Tracing Kaurna Descendants: the saga of a family dispossessed*, Education Department, Adelaide, 1986.

Elkin, A. P., 'Civilised Aborigines and native culture', *Oceania*, 6 (2), 1935.

–––––– 'Reaction and interaction: a food gathering people and European settlement in Australia', *American Anthropologist*, 53, 1951.

Ellis, R., 'Aboriginal man in the Ranges', *The future of the Flinders Ranges. Proceedings of a seminar*, 1–6, Adelaide, 1972.

–––––– 'The funeral practices and beliefs of the Adnjamathanha', *Journal of the Anthropological Society of South Australia*, 13 (6) 1975.

Faull, J., *Life on the Edge. The Far West Coast of South Australia*, District Council of Murat Bay, Adelaide, 1988.

Felton, P. E., 'Aboriginal employment problems in Victoria' in Ian G. Sharp and Colin M. Tatz, *Aborigines in the economy*, Jacaranda Press, Melbourne, 1966.

Fenton, William N., 'Fieldwork, museum studies, and ethnohistorical research', *Ethnohistory*, 13, 1967.

Foster, Robert, 'Feasts of the full-moon: the distribution of rations to Aborigines in South Australia 1836–1861', *Aboriginal History*, 13 (1) 1989.

Fourmile, Henrietta, 'Who owns the past? Aborigines as captives of the archives', *Aboriginal History*, 13 (1) 1989.

Foxcroft, E. J. B., *Australian native policy: its history especially in Victoria*, Melbourne University Press, Melbourne, 1941.

Gale, Fay, *A study of assimilation: part Aborigines in South Australia*, Libraries Board of South Australia, Adelaide, 1964.

–––––– 'The history of contact in South Australia' in J. W. Warburton (ed.) *Aborigines of South Australia: their background and future prospects*, Department of Adult Education, University of Adelaide, 1969.

–––––– 'Roles revisited: the women of southern South Australia' in P. Brock (ed.), *Women, rites and sites: Aboriginal women's cultural knowledge*, Allen and Unwin, Sydney, 1989.

Gara, T., 'Ooldea Soak', *Journal of the Anthropological Society of South Australia*, 25 (4) 1988.

–––––– 'Mullawirraburka: "King John" of the Adelaide tribe', unpublished manuscript n.d.

Gascoyne, J., *Far West Football 1906–1986*, Ceduna, 1986.

Gibbs, R. M., 'Humanitarian theories and the Aboriginal inhabitants of South Australia to 1860', BA (Hons) thesis, University of Adelaide, 1959.

Gillen, F. J., *Gillen's diary: the camp jottings of J. F. Gillen on the Spencer and Gillen expedition across Australia 1901–1902*, Libraries Board of South Australia, Adelaide, 1986.

Goodall, Heather, 'An intelligent parasite: A. P. Elkin and the white perceptions of the history of Aboriginal people in New South Wales', unpublished paper presented at the Australian Historical Association Conference, 1982.

Graham, Doris May and Wallace, Cecil, *As we've known it. 1911 to the present*, Aboriginal Studies and Teacher Education Centre, SACAE, Adelaide, 1987.

Griffin, T. and McCaskill, M. (eds), *Atlas of South Australia*, Wakefield Press, Adelaide, 1986.

Haebich, Anna, *For their own good: Aborigines and government in the southwest of Western Australia 1900–1940*, University of West Australia Press, Perth, 1988.

Hale, Herbert M. and Tindale, Norman B., 'Observations on Aborigines of the Flinders Ranges, and records of rock carvings and paintings', *Records of the South Australian Museum*, 3 (1) 1925, pp. 45-60.

Hale, Mathew, *The Aborigines of Australia being an account of the institution for their education at Poonindie, in South Australia*, SPCK, London, 1889.

Harms, E. and Hoff, C. (eds), *Koonibba: a record of 50 years work among the Australian Aboriginals by the Evangelical Lutheran Church of Australia 1901–1951*, Adelaide, 1951.

Hartwig, M. C., 'A progress of white settlement in the Alice Springs district and its effect upon the Aboriginal inhabitants', PhD thesis, University of Adelaide, 1965.

Hasluck, Paul, *Black Australians: a survey of native policy in Western Australia 1829–1897*, Melbourne University Press, 1942.

Hassell, Kathleen, *The relations between the settlers and Aborigines in South Australia, 1836–1860*, Adelaide, 1966.

Hayward, J. E., 'Diary 1846–56', *Royal Geographical Society of Australia, South Australian Branch*, 29, 1927.

Hemming, Steve, 'Conflict between Aborigines and Europeans along the Murray River from the Darling to the Great South Bend 1830–1841', BA (Hons) thesis, University of Adelaide, 1982.

Hercus, Luise and White, Isobel, 'Perception of kinship structure reflected in the Adnjamathanha pronouns', *Papers in Australian linguistics*, Pacific Linguistics Series A 36, 1973.

Hercus, Luise and Sutton, Peter, *This is what happened*, Aboriginal Studies Press, Canberra, 1986.

Hercus, Luise, 'The status of women's cultural knowledge: Aboriginal society in north-east South Australia' in P. Brock (ed.), *Women, rites and sites: Aboriginal women's cultural knowledge*, Allen and Unwin, Sydney, 1989.

Heritage Unit, Department for the Environment, *The Flinders Ranges. An Aboriginal View*, Department of the Environment, Adelaide, 1980.

—————— *Minerawuta (Ram Paddock Gate)*, Department for the Environment, Adelaide, 1980.

Hickerson, Harold, *The Chippewa and their neighbors: a study in ethnohistory*, Holt, Rinehart and Winston, New York, 1970.

Howitt, A. W., *Native tribes of south-east Australia*, Macmillan, London, 1904.

Hull, I. V., *The rise and fall of Beltana*, Adelaide, 1973.

Hunt, J. M., 'Schools for Aboriginal children in the Adelaide district 1836–1852', BA thesis, University of Adelaide, 1971.

Inglis, Judy, 'Aborigines in Adelaide', *Journal of the Polynesian Society*, 1961.

Jacobs, J. M., 'Aboriginal land rights in Port Augusta', MA thesis, University of Adelaide, 1983.

Jenkin, Graham, *Conquest of the Ngarrindjeri*, Rigby, Adelaide, 1979.

Johnson, Colin, 'Captured discourse, captured lives', *Aboriginal History*, 11 (1).

Jones, P., 'Red ochre expeditions: an ethnographic and historical analysis of Aboriginal trade in the Lake Eyre Basin, (parts 1 and 2), *Anthropology Society of South Australia Journal*, 22 (7 & 8), 1984.

Kartinyeri, Doreen, *Rigney family genealogy*, University of Adelaide, 1983.

—————— *Wanganeen family genealogy*, University of Adelaide, 1985.

Koonibba jubilee booklet 1901–1926, Adelaide, 1926.

Langford, Ruby, *Don't take your love to town*, Penguin, Ringwood, Victoria, 1988.

Linton, Ralph (ed.), *Acculturation in seven American Indian tribes*, Peter Smith, Gloucester, Mass., 1940.

Long, J. P. M., *Aboriginal settlements: a survey of institutional communities in eastern Australia*, ANU Press, Canberra, 1970.

McConvell, P. 'The role of Aboriginal language in story: a comment on Shaw', *Australian Aboriginal Studies*, 2, 1985.

McGrath, Ann, *Born in the cattle: Aborigines in the cattle country*, Allen and Unwin, Sydney, 1987.

—————— 'Humanity and objectivity before the claims of history', *Australian Book Review*, no. 119, April 1990, pp. 34–5.

McLean, J., 'Police experience with the Natives. Reminiscences of the early days of the colony', *Royal Geographical Society of Australia, South Australian Branch*, 6, 1903.

McQueen, Humphrey, *A new Britannia*, Penguin, Ringwood, Victoria, 1982.

Mattingly, Christobel, and Hampton, Ken (eds), *Survival in our own land. Aboriginal experiences in South Australia since 1836*, Wakefield Press, Adelaide, 1988.

Meinig, D. W., *On the margins of the good earth. The South Australian wheat frontier 1869–1884*, Rigby, Adelaide, 1970.

Mincham, Hans, *The story of the Flinders Ranges*, Adelaide, 1977.

Miller, James, *Koori: a will to win. The heroic resistance, survival and triumph of Black Australia*, Angus and Robertson, Sydney, 1985.

Mol, Hans, *The firm and the formless. Religion and identity in Aboriginal Australia*, Wilfred Laurier University Press, Waterloo, Ontario, 1982.

Morris, Barry, 'From underemployment to unemployment: the changing role of Aborigines in a rural economy', *Mankind*, 13 (6), 1983.

Mountford, C. P. and Harvey, Alison, 'Women of the Adnjamathanha tribe of the North Flinders Ranges', *Oceania*, 12, 1941.

Muecke, S., Rumsey, A. and Wirrunmurra, B., 'Pigeon the outlaw: history as texts', *Aboriginal History*, 9 (1), 1985.

Narogin, Mudrooroo (Colin Johnson), *Writing from the fringe. A study of modern Aboriginal literature*, Hyland House, South Yarra, 1990.

Ngabidji, Grant as told to Bruce Shaw, *My country of the pelican dreaming*, Aboriginal Studies Press, Canberra, 1981.

Pastoral pioneers of South Australia, vols 1 and 2, Lynton Publications, Blackwood, South Australia, 1974.

Pedersen, Howard, 'Pigeon: an Australian Aboriginal rebel', *Studies in Western Australian History*, 8, 1984.

Platt, J. T., 'Some Notes on Gugada and Wirangu', *Australian Aboriginal Studies*, 23, 1970, pp. 59-63.

Price, A. Grenfell, *White settlers and native peoples: an historical study of racial contacts in the United States, Canada, Australia and New Zealand*, Georgian House, Melbourne, 1950.

Read, Peter, and Japaljarri, E. J., 'The price of tobacco: the journey of the Warlmala to Wave Hill, 1928', *Aboriginal History*, 2 (1), 1978.

Reece, R. H. W., *Aborigines and colonists: Aborigines and colonial society in NSW in the 1830s and 1840s*, Sydney University Press, Sydney, 1974.

Reynolds, Henry and Loos, Noel, 'Aboriginal resistance in Queensland', *Australian Journal of Politics and History*, 22 (3), 1976.

Reynolds, Henry, *The other side of the frontier. Aboriginal resistance to the European invasion of Australia*, Penguin, Ringwood, Victoria, 1982.

——— *The law and the land*, Penguin, Ringwood, Victoria, 1987.

Richardson, Norman A., *The pioneers of the north-west of South Australia 1856–1914*, (facsimile copy, Libraries Board of South Australia, 1969), W. K. Thomas, Adelaide, 1925.

Roughsey, Elsie (Labumore), *An Aboriginal mother tells of the old and the new*, McPhee Gribble/Penguin, Fitzroy, Victoria, 1984.

Rowley, C. D., *The destruction of Aboriginal society*, ANU Press, Canberra, 1970.

——— *The remote Aborigines*, ANU Press, Canberra, 1971.

——— *Outcasts in white Australia*, ANU Press, Canberra, 1972.

Russo, George, *Lord Abbot of the wilderness. The life and times of Bishop Salvado*, Polding Press, Melbourne, 1980.

Ryan, Lyndall, *The Aboriginal Tasmanians*, University of Queensland Press, St Lucia, 1982.

Schebeck, B., 'The Atynymatana personal pronoun and the Wailpi kinship system' *Papers in Australian Linguistics*, Pacific Linguistics Series A 36, ANU, Canberra, 1973.

——— 'Texts on the social system of the Atynyamatana people with grammatical notes', Pacific Linguistics Series D 21, ANU, Canberra, 1974.

Schebeck, B., Hercus, L. and White, M., *Papers in Australian Linguistics*, 6, ANU, Canberra, 1974.

Schmiechen, H. J., 'The Hermannsburg Mission Society in Australia 1866–1895', BA (Hons) thesis, University of Adelaide, 1971.

Schürmann, C., 'The Aboriginal Tribes of Port Lincoln in South Australia, their mode of life, manners, customs etc.', in J. D. Woods, *The Native Tribes of South Australia*, E. S. Wigg and Son, Adelaide, 1879.

Schurmann, Edwin A., *I'd rather dig potatoes*, Lutheran Publishing House, Adelaide, 1987.

Short, Augustus, *The Poonindie mission described in a letter from the Lord Bishop of Adelaide to Society for the Propagation of the Gospel*, London, 1853.

———— *A visit to Poonindie and some accounts of that mission to the Aborigines of South Australia*, Adelaide, 1872.

Simmons, Williams S., 'Culture theory in contemporary ethnohistory', *Ethnohistory*, 35 (1), 1988.

Spicer, Edward H. (ed.), *Perspectives in American Indian cultural change*, Chicago University Press, Chicago, 1969.

Spicer, Edward H., 'Types of contact and processes of change' in Edward H. Spicer (ed.), *Perspectives in American Indian cultural change*, Chicago University Press, Chicago, 1969.

Stanner, W. E. H., 'Continuity and change among Aborigines' (1958) in *White man got no Dreaming: essays 1938–1973*, ANU Press, Canberra, 1979.

Sullivan, Jack as told to Bruce Shaw, *Banggaiyerri: the story of Jack Sullivan*, Aboriginal Studies Press, Canberra, 1982.

Swain, Tony and Rose, Deborah, Bird (eds), *Aboriginal Australians and Christian missions. Ethnographic and historical studies*, Australian Association of the Study of Religions, Bedford Park, South Australia, 1988.

Swanson, Maynard W., 'The sanitation syndrome: bubonic plague and the urban Native policy in the Cape 1900–1901', *Journal of African History, 18, 1977.*

Tindale, Norman B., *Aboriginal Tribes of Australia*, ANU Press, Canberra, 1974.

Tolmer, Alexander, *Reminiscences of an adventurous and chequered career at home and at the Antipodes*, Sampson, Low, Marston, Searle and Rivington, London, 1882.

Tonkinson, Robert, *The Jigalong mob: victors of the desert crusade*, Benjamin/Cummins, Menlo Park, California, 1974.

Tregenza, John, 'Two notable portraits of South Australian Aborigines', *Journal of the Historical Society of South Australia*, 12, 1984.

Trigger, Bruce G., 'Ethnohistory: problems and prospects', *Ethnohistory*, 29 (1), 1982.

Trigger, David S., 'Christianity, domination and resistance in colonial social relations: the case of Doomadgee, northwest Queensland' in Tony Swain and Deborah Bird Rose (eds), *Australian Aborigines and Christian Missions*, Australian Association of the Study of Religions, Bedford Park, South Australia, 1988.

Tunbridge, Dorothy, *Artefacts of the Flinders Ranges*, Pipa Wangka, Port Augusta, 1986.

———— *Flinders Ranges Dreaming*, Aboriginal Studies Press, Canberra, 1988.

Turner, V. E., *Pearls from the deep. The story of Colebrook Home for Aboriginal children, Quorn*, Hunkin, Ellis and King, Adelaide, 1936.

Vansina, Jan, 'For oral tradition (But not against Braudel)', *History of Africa*, 5, 1978.

Walsh, P. B., 'The problem of native policy in South Australia in the nineteenth century. With particular reference to the Church of England Poonindie mission 1850–1896', BA (Hons) thesis, University of Adelaide, Adelaide, 1966.

White, Richard, *Inventing Australia: images and identity 1688–1980*, George Allen and Unwin, Sydney, 1981.

Wirth, Louis, *The Ghetto*, University of Chicago Press, Chicago, 1928.

Woods, J. D., *The Native Tribes of South Australia*, E. S. Wigg and Son, Adelaide, 1879.

Woolmer, George, *Riverland Aborigines of the past*, Barmera, 1976.

Woolmington, Jean, (ed.), *Aborigines in colonial society 1788–1850 from noble savage to rural pest*, Cassell Australia, Melbourne, 1973.

Woolmington, Jean, 'Early Christian missions to the Australian Aborigines: a study in failure', PhD thesis, University of New England, Armidale, 1980.

Index

Aboriginal agency, 67, 162; historical interpretation of, 162
Aboriginal ceremonial activity, 63, 67
Aboriginal ceremonies, 69, 71, 72, 76, 77, 84, 96, 97, 122, 126, 127, 131, 139, 148, 150
Aboriginal death rates, 15
Aboriginal Heritage Branch, 153
Aboriginal history, 6; interpretation of, 2
Aboriginal identity, 157
Aboriginal Lands Trust, 107, 153
Aboriginal Lands Trust Act, 1966, 19
Aboriginal languages spoken on west coast of South Australia, 64
Aboriginal reserves, 14
Aboriginal resistance, 2
Aboriginal school, 22, 23, 24, 25, 94; Adelaide, 26, 27, 28, 29, 31, 35; Albany (Mrs Camfield), 43; Lacepede Bay, 43; Native School Establishment, 24; Port Lincoln, 26, 35, 37, 80; closing of, 38; Walkerville, 24
Aboriginal survival, 3, 6
Aboriginal writers, 3
Aborigines: definition of, 17; education, 7; European perceptions of, 11, 15; labour, 7; missionary views of, 80; violence against, 12
Aborigines Act: exemption from, 17, 100, 106, 110, 133
Aborigines Act Amendment Act, 1939, 17
Aborigines Act, 1911, 16, 17, 82, 107
Aborigines Protection Board, 18, 93, 96,

104, 106, 109, 111, 116
acculturation, 4, 65
Adams, Bessie, 53
Adams, Esther, 53
Adams, Fanny, 53
Adams, Lewis, 53
Adams, Louisa, 53, 54
Adams, Maria, 52
Adams, Mary Ann, *see* Kudnarto
Adams, Thomas (snr), 51, 52, 53
Adams, Tim, 35, 50, 51-3, 55
Adams, Tom, 35, 48, 50, 51-3, 55, 59
Adelaide, 6, 21, 22, 23, 24, 31, 32, 43, 48, 54, 80, 94, 103, 125, 127, 145, 153, 159; Native Location, 23
Adelaide Gaol, 23
Adelaide Plains, 6, 7, 21, 22, 23, 160; Aboriginal population of, 21
Adnyamathanha, 6, 7, 121-54, 157, 158, 159, 161, 163, 164; accommodation to pastoralism, 130; adoption of new technology, 164; burial ceremonies, 151; burial grounds, 139; ceremonial leader, 146, ceremonial life, 131, 139; communal identity, 129; cultural identity, 153; daily life, 132; deaths, 130; end of ceremonies, 150; European views of, 130; identity, 152; impact of mission on, 152; initiation ceremonies, 149; 150; institutionalisation, experience of, 154; kinship system, 131; land, control of, 153; language, 152, 153, 161; living conditions, 145;

marriage, 151; matrilineal descent, 130; music, 153; mythology, 149, 152; request for school, 131; resistance, 124, 125, 126; saved from starvation, 140; sites recorded, 153; starving, 129, 138; working conditions, 144
Adnyamathanha genealogy, 146
Adnyamathanha rangers, 153
agriculture, 65, 79
Albany, 43
alcohol, 55, 99, 100, 106, 111; drinking of, 19; effects of, 22; legalisation of, 117, 160
American Indian history, 3
American Indians, 4, 5, 122, 158; European perceptions of, 11; Mandan, 5; Massachusetts, 5, 6; New England 'praying towns', 5, 6; Yacqui, 5, 122
Angas, George Fife, 23
Angepena, 122, 124, 128, 130, 132, 134, 146
anthropology, 3, 4
Antikarinja, 64
Appelt, Ernest, 92, 95
Arabana, 122
Aroona, 122, 126
Aroona Hills, 127
Artimore, 130
Artoowarrapunna Council, 153
assimilation, 4, 24, 115
assimilation policies, 3, 6, 11, 12, 17, 18, 116, 117, 153, 157; establishment of Poonindie, 25

Attwood, Bain, 156
Australian Bight, 63
Australian Constitution, 12
Australian Workers Union, 143
Axtell, James, 5, 6, 39, 158

Balcanoona, 132, 133, 134, 140
Ballarat, 54
Baptism, 71, 117
Barossa Valley, 21
Basedow, Herbert, 128
Bates, Daisy, 114
Baumann, Miss, 82
Beltana, 128, 129, 130, 133, 134, 144, 147
Beltana station, 126
Betts, Andrew, 99
Betts, Cecil, 99
Betts, Edward, 99, 100
Betts, Olga (née Free), 99, 100
Betts, Olive, 100
Betts, Reg, 99, 100
Betts, Robert, 91, 99, 163
Bilney, Lily, 78
Bishop, Captain, 28
Blanchetown, 44
Blinman, 128, 129, 130, 132, 134, 144, 147, 161
Boas, Franz, 3
Bookabie, 77, 97, 101, 103, 105, 112, 118
Boston Island, 24, 25, 28
Boundary Gate, 140, 146
Brachina Gorge, 127
Brisbane, 77
British Colonial Office, 14
Bromley, Captain, 23
Brown, Dudley, 117
Bruce, J. D., 50, 51, 52, 53, 54, 55, 56, 58
Bull, J. B., 124
Burr Well, 145
Burra, 21

camel depot, Mount Serle, 129, 130, 131, 132, 134
Carbine, William, 99
Ceduna, 1, 94, 97, 100, 101, 103, 104, 105, 106, 108, 111, 147, 158, 163, 164; hospital, 109; reserve, services upgraded, 105; reserve, lack of services, 104
Ceduna Council, 105, 106, 107
Ceduna School, 106, 107
Charlie, 31
Charra, 101
Chester, Clem, 116
Chief Commissioner of Police, 127
children, 23, 24, 39, 79, 82, 89, 92, 94, 103, 106, 112, 114, 118, 124, 133, 152, 157; arrested as neglected, 131; control of, 16, 17; marriage of, 24; mixed

descent sent to Poonindie, 26; of mixed descent, 51
Christianity, 5, 23, 39, 68, 96, 121, 148, 150, 158, 159, 160, 161; conversion to, 38; process of conversion, 71
Clare, 51
Coaby, Cyril, 114, 116
Colebrook Home, 145
Coleman, William, 99
Colona, 101
Colona Tom, 95, 162
colonialism, 71; responses to, 163
colonialisation, 5, 6, 11, 13, 14, 156; Aboriginal accommodation to, 37; British, 2
Commissioner of Crown Lands and Immigration, 34, 36
communal biographies, 162
Concordia College, 94
Coopers Creek, 126
Coorabie, 100, 111
Copley, 133, 138, 142, 144, 145, 146, 147, 161; living conditions, 147, 148
Copley, A. J., 116, 117
Coulthard, Andrew, 148
Coulthard, Dick, 146
Coulthard, Ted, 141, 146, 162
Coulthard, Walter, 148
Cox, Percy: family, 93
Crossland, J. M., 29
Crystal Brook, 51
Cummins, 100, 103

Davey, Dick, 95, 158; and family, 110
Demell, Claude, 134, 162
Demell, Emily, 132, 134
Demell, Ethel (née Ryan), 134
Demell, Nicholas, 132, 134
Denial Bay, 80, 95, 97, 101, 105, 164
Department of Aboriginal Affairs, 107, 115
Depot Springs, 132, 134
Dicks, Thomas, 31
dingo proof fence, 146
disease, 22, 23, 34, 44, 128; consumption, 32; measles, 129; smallpox, 23; whooping cough, 139
Diyari, 39, 122, 127, 128, 131, 134
Dolling, Dick, 95
donkeys, 146, 164
Donnelly, Emma, 46, 50
Dresden Mission Society, 23
drought, 79, 125, 126, 129, 130; breaking of, 89
Duck Ponds, 100, 107
Dudley, 95
Duguid, Charles, 105
Dutton, Francis S., 34

Eaton, Fred, 138, 141, 144, 145, 148, 149, 151

Eckermann, C. V., 96, 113, 115, 116, 117, 118
Edginton, G., 131, 132
education, 18, 22, 24, 25, 39, 82, 92, 94, 98, 100, 103, 106, 111, 116, 134, 144, 148, 162
Electricity Trust of South Australia, 128
Eliot, John, 5
Elkin, A. P., 4
employment, 27, 38, 47, 48, 49, 52, 55, 67, 76, 79, 83, 89, 90, 91, 96, 98, 101, 103, 104, 105, 106, 111, 112, 116, 128, 129, 130, 132, 134, 143, 144, 146, 147, 148, 153, 161, 162, 163; Aboriginal attitudes towards, 163; end of pastoral, 152; female, 49; scarce, 114
Encounter Bay, 23, 46
environment, 163
Ercowie, 126
Eucla, 63
Eyre Peninsula, 6, 8, 27, 43, 48, 51, 96, 100, 103, 108, 109, 110, 111, 131
Eyre, E. J., 23, 122

Far West Aboriginal Association, 107
Farina, 144
Federal government, 12
First World War: anti-German attitudes, 89
Fleurieu Peninsula, 53
Flinders Ranges, 6, 7, 122, 126, 128, 156, 163
Forbes, Jack, 144
Forbes, Mrs, 145
Fourmile, Henrietta, 162
Fowlers Bay, 64, 65, 66, 73, 75, 79, 82, 93, 95, 98, 103, 111, 160
Framlingham, 157
Franklin Harbour, 45, 53
Free, Flora, see Richards, Bertha Florence, 98
Free, Micky, 78, 97-8, 162
Free, Rose, 78, 98
Frome Charlie, 131
Frome Well, 128

Gaden, Hans, 96, 105
gambling, 99, 104
Gammon Ranges National Park, 153
Gawler Ranges, 63, 65, 66, 78, 93, 99, 103, 111, 160
Gawler, George, 23
Gersch's farm, 91
ghetto, 1, 2, 24, 91, 94, 163; Jewish, 2, 7
government policies and legislation, 11
government station, 3
Gray, Nellie, 73
Green, Harry, 138
guano, collection of, 58

Hale, Herbert, 131

Hale, Mathew, 6, 24, 25, 26, 27, 28, 29, 31, 35, 36, 37, 38, 39, 43, 50, 57, 58, 59, 68, 69, 84, 91, 159; diary, 32
Halfway Camp, 107
Hamilton, Andrew, 43, 49
Hammond, Octavius, 26, 35, 36, 37, 44, 53
Harbour, Tom, 51, 58
Hathaway, Bill, 141, 144, 152
Hawker, 144, 145, 146, 147
Hayward, J. F., 122, 124
Highfold, Jack, 77, 78
Highfold, John, see Highfold, Jack
Highfold, Melvina, 100
Hirschausen, Myrtle, 54
Hirschausen, Walter, 54
Hitchin, Edward, 34, 36
Hoff, C., 93, 95, 99
Holden, William, 37, 43, 44, 45, 49, 52
Hooper, Agnes, see Limberry, Mary
Hooper, Jack, 45
housing, 18
Howitt, A. W., 127
hunter-gatherers, 4
hunting, 129, 139

identity, defining of, 156
Ilkabindnie, James, 46
Inabuthina, 125, 127
Innamincka, 126
institutional experience, meaning of, 59
institutionalisation, 6, 7, 50, 159, 160, 165; process of, 157
integration policies, 19

Jabadee, 99
Jadliaura, 122
Jebydah, Jack, 78, 162
Jebydah, Nellie, 78
Johnson, Maurice, 148
Julburra speakers, see Wirangu

Kandwillan, 28, 29, 32, 38
kangaroo hunting, 65, 97, 112, 160
Kapunda, 21
Kaurna, 21, 23, 24, 35, 51, 59; impact of colonisation on, 23
Keeler, Doris (née Betts), 99, 100
Keure, 31, 33
Killalpaninna, 14, 39, 131
Kilpatko, 28
King Bob, see Mount Serle Bob
Kingston, 49, 53
kinship system, 160; moieties, 152
Kokatha, 7, 63, 64, 66, 78, 82, 121, 160, 165
Koonibba, 6, 7, 15, 63-118, 143, 147, 152, 153, 156, 158, 159, 160, 161, 162, 163, 164; Aboriginal camp, 81; Aboriginal ceremonies, 68; Aboriginal concern over farm sale, 91; accommodation, 85,

95, 101, shortage, 92; adoption of new technology, 165; baptisms, 79, 95, 96; camp life, 96; change from cattle to sheep farming, 90; change in employment policy, 90; change in mission policy, 91; Children's Home, 83, 89, 92, 93, 100, 108, 109, 111, 112, 114, 116, 118; admission policy, 93; closed, 117; opening of, 83; Christianity and 'civilising' mission, 160; Christianity, conversion to, 72; Christmas, 69, 71, 118; church, 84; Commission of investigation, 115; conversion rate, 70; daily life, 79; dedication of church, 73; dismissal from, 104, 113, 114; early life, 67; employment policy, 163; establishment of, 66; football team, 95; government takeover, 117; health services, 94; hospital, 94; living conditions, 94; mission landscape, 71, 84; mission policy, 68; missionary objectives, 79; motives for joining, 67; music, 68; number baptised, 89; petition relating to government takeover, 115; population, 66, 92, 117; proposed government takeover, 115; proposed sale of land, 90, 99; role of, 71, 117; school, 68, 69, 82, 94, 116, 117; Schulfest, 69, 77; share farming, 91; supply of clothing to Aborigines, 83; wages, 74, 77, 79, 90, 98, as incentive to baptism, 80; walk off, 114; water shortage, 67
Koonibba Football Club, 101
Koonibba Mission Board, 79, 93, 115
Koonibba rockhole, 67, 97
Kooringabie, 111
Kooris, 157
Kopperamana, 14, 77, 127
Kudnarto, 35, 51, 52, 53, 55
Kuyani, 122

Lacepede Bay, 43
Lake Bonney, 32
Lake Eyre, 127
Lake Hope, 126, 127
Lake Hope Aborigines, 126
land, 19, 52, 54, 66, 74, 97, 107, 117, 141, 147, 153, 159, 164; access to, 52; access to Poonindie land, 51; clearing of, 66, 68; relationship to, 39; under cultivation, 21
Larrikin Tom, 126
Lawrie, Albert J., 115
Lawrie, Willis Michael, see Free, Micky
Le Bois, Dickie, 101
Leigh Creek, 126, 133, 134, 147; Aborigines excluded, 144
Leigh Creek coalfields, 128, 144, 161
Leigh Creek South, 144
Limberry, Daniel, 44, 45-6, 59, 163

Limberry, Mary, 45-6, 59
Linton, Ralph, 4, 5
Lock, 100, 103
Louth Bay, 48
Lush, John, 44
Lutheran Church, 65, 91, 114, 116
Lutherans, 63, 89, 97
Lyndhurst, 146

Mannera, 32
Manyatko, 28, 29
Maralinga, 121
Mardala, see Wailpi, 127
Maria, 29, 31
marriage, 43, 51, 92, 113, 150; firestick, 151; Poonindie early residents, 29
Martins Well, 146
Mason, George, 35
McKenzie, Fred, 146
McKenzie, Jessie, 146
McKenzie, John, 146, 163
McKenzie, Pearl (née Wilton), 145, 146, 163
McKenzie, W., 66
McDennett, Amelia, 43
McTaggart, John, 124
Meintangk, 59
Melbourne, 112
Mempong, 31, 32
Milera, Frederick, 35, 52, 54
Milera, Jessie, 52, 54
Milera, John, 50, 52, 56
Milera, Louisa, see Adams, Louisa
military service, 89
Miller, Joe, 73, 74, 77
Miller Joe (white), 105, 112
Miller, Lena, 105, 106, 158, 163
Miller, Maggie, 105
Miller, Robert K., 115, 116
Miller Yari (Harry Russel), 105-6, 158, 163
Minerawuta, see Ram Paddock Gate
Mingia (Lucy Washington), 100
mining, 63, 128, 141, 144, 146
Minnipa, 93, 100, 103
missionaries, 6; German, 23, 24; Jesuit, 5
missions, 3, 6, 14, 18, 24, 65; advantages of, 157, 159, 165; Anglican, 6; decision to join, 157; dependency on, 157; disadvantages, 157; end of, 18; ethnohistory of, 5; Lutheran, 6; success of, 39, 158
Molina, Abbot, 78
Monaitya, 31
Moonabie, 45, 53
Moonya, 28
Moorhouse, Matthew, 22, 24, 25, 29, 32, 35
Moorundie, 23, 32
Mortlock, Matthew, 49
Mount Deception, 126

Mount Fitton, 133, 144
Mount Freeling, 126
Mount Lyndhurst, 122, 129, 132
Mount Remarkable, 125
Mount Serle, 124, 128, 129, 130, 131, 132, 133, 134, 145, 146, 153; ration depot, 128
Mount Serle Bob, 128, 146
Mount Serle police station, 126
Mountford, C. P., 131, 134, 149, 150; visits to Nepabunna, 148
Mudlong, 29, 33
Mueller, Albert, 95
Murat Bay, 79
Murna, Alice, 78
Murray River, 6, 7, 13, 21, 23, 32, 125, 159
Murray, A. B. C., 97, 98
Murray, G. W., 95

Nantawarrina, 153
Nantilla, 31
Narrung, 28, 29, 32, 33, 38
National Parks and Wildlife Service, 153
Nauo, 59, 63
Neechi, 28, 32
Nepabunna, 7, 82, 126, 133, 134, 138-54, 158, 161, 163; accommodation, 142; attitudes to ceremonies, 149; cemeteries, 151; church, 149; daily life, 142, 145; dormitory, 144; establishment of, 141; government takeover, 141, 153; health care, 145; missionaries, 148; movement away, 164; reasons for leaving, 162; school, 144, 148
New South Wales, 11, 12, 21, 100, 159
Newchurch, John, 48
Newchurch, Richard, 56
Newland, Mr, 45, 49, 53, 54
Ngalia, 63, 71, 77
Ngarrindjeri, 39
Ngullar ngullar, 32
Nhindina, Jack, see Yendinna Jack
Nilpena, 126
North Flinders Ranges, 122, 152; Aboriginal population, 128; drought, 129
North Shields, 45, 48
Northern Territory, 12, 100
Nukunu, 59
Nullarbor Plain, 63, 65, 98, 103, 111, 112
Nungas, 157
Nyungar, 157

ochre, 125, 126, 127; black, 132; mining, 127; mining of, 125, 127; myths associated with, 126
Old Colona station, 100
Old Yalata station, 101
Ooldea, 63, 64, 77, 93, 96, 114, 160
Ooldea Soak, 114
overlanders, 21

Owieandana, 122, 131
Owieandana Billy, 125, 127

Paddy Nandy (Lame Paddy), 78, 96
Page, Jim, 138, 141
Pangkala, 37, 39, 59, 63, 134
Pannach, J., 66, 67
Parachilna, 125, 126, 127
Parallana, 129
pastoral leases, 64, 65
pastoral stations, 111
pastoralism, 21, 122, 124, 160, 163
Pathera, 33
Peltungal, see Popjoy, 31
Penalumba, 103, 105, 112
Penhall, W. R., 93, 106, 107, 108, 109
Penong, 65, 73, 79, 80, 91, 97, 103, 111, 112
Pernunna, 124
Pilpane, 32
Pintaacla, 99
Pintumba, 77
Pirlatapa, 122
Pitjantjatjara, 64, 121, 157
Pitpowie, 33
pituri, 125
Playford, Thomas, 53
ploughing championships, national, 53
Point McLeay, 14, 17, 39, 43, 45, 53, 58, 59, 70, 95, 129
Point Pearce, 14, 17, 52, 53, 55, 58, 59, 75, 95, 103, 145
police, 1, 66, 104, 105, 108, 110, 111, 124, 125, 126, 127, 128, 129, 130, 131, 132, 133, 144, 145, 162; mounted, 23
Pompey, see Inabuthina
Poonindie, 6, 7, 14, 25, 68, 82, 84, 91, 134, 143, 152, 156, 158, 159, 160, 161, 162, 163, 164; administrative changes, 36; adoption of new technology, 165; advantages of, 37; baptisms by Bishop Short, 29; church, 54; closure, 55; conditions after Hale, 35; conversions to Christianity, 34; cricket and athletics, 48; daily life, 32, 33, 34, 46; death rate, 36, 159; disease, 34; dismissal, 44, 45, 46, 54; dispersal of the people, 57; epidemics, 44; establishment of, 26; establishment of farm, 32; farmwork, 47; government funding cut, 36; Hale's parting words, 36; Hale's recruitment policy, 26; land, 25; living conditions, 48; low morale, 55; Native Training Institution, 25, 58; operation of, 26; origin of early recruits, 35; petition to have institution closed, 55; petition to Protector of Aborigines, 51; petition to retain land, 56; population, 34, 43; ration depot, 27, 51; recruitment drive, Murray River, 43; recruitment from Western Austra-

lia, 43; recruitment policies, 26, 39; regulations, 46; self-supporting community, 47; shearing and ploughing competitions, 48; social experiment, 37, 38; Toolilee run, 36; wages, 49; working conditions, 39
Poonindie trustees, 57, 58
Popjoy, 31, 32
Port Augusta, 43, 46, 66, 145, 152, 153
Port Lincoln, 6, 25, 27, 28, 29, 32, 37, 44, 48, 51, 53, 54, 55, 59, 71, 80, 100, 103, 108, 110, 113, 158; Kirton Point, 111; living conditions, 111; Mallee Park, 111; school, 111
Port Lincoln district, 53, 57
Port Neill, 110
Power, Charles, 56
prostitution, 104, 111, 113
protection legislation, 16, 17
protection policies, 2, 12, 15, 91; end of, 19
Protector of Aborigines, 14, 16, 22, 23, 32, 39, 46, 51, 52, 82, 98, 105, 127, 129, 145, 148, 150; sub-protector, 23, 126; sub-protector Scott, 32; sub-protector Wellington, 35
Puiscumba, 31

Queensland, 12, 13, 100; Aboriginal Protection Act, 1897, 12, 16
Quorn, 134

rabbit trapping, 112, 143
racial terminology, 16
Ram Paddock Gate, 132, 133, 134, 138, 139, 140, 146, 151, 161; archeological survey, 139; daily life, 139; missionary arrives, 139
Ramahyuck, 156
Randall, Mrs, 45, 52
Rankine, Sam, 46
Rathoola, 35, 53
ration depot, 51, 64, 67, 80, 128, 129, 132, 138; Blinman, 129
rations, 23, 27, 37, 44, 45, 46, 48, 58, 59, 65, 66, 67, 79, 80, 114, 122, 125, 126, 128, 129, 133, 142, 145, 161; distribution of, 23; meat in, 80
referendum, national 1967, 12
reserve councils, 19
reserves, 25, 51, 54, 56, 59, 103, 104, 105, 107, 108, 109, 113, 148, 164; for farming, 164; lack of services, 103
Richards, Ada, 75-6
Richards, Arthur, 75-6
Richards, Bertha Florence, 98; baptism of, 76
Richards, Jimmy (Thomas), 67, 70, 71-5, 77, 162, 165; baptism, 73
Richards, Nellie (née Gray), 74
River Murray, 24, 31, 35, 43, 44, 159

River Torrens, 23
Roberts, Louisa, 35
Roberts, Louisa, see Adams, Louisa
Rovers Football Club, 101
Rowley, C. D., 156
Royal Commission on The Aborigines, 16, 89

Sahlins, Marshall, 6
Salvation Army, 46
Saunders, George, 73, 74, 77
Schebeck, B., 131
school, 131, 133, 142, 144, 146; Aboriginal children excluded, 103, 105
Schürmann, Clamor, 23, 26, 35, 37, 80
Secretary of the Aborigines Protection Board, 93, 105, 106, 108
Select Committee of the Legislative Council on the Aborigines, 14, 128
self-determination policies, 153
Shanahan, P. F., 127
Shaw, 50, 52
Short, Augustus, 24, 25, 28, 29, 31, 35
Skillogalee, see Skylogolee Creek
Skylogolee Creek, 51, 52
Smith, Molly, 100
Society for the Propagation of the Gospel, 25
Solomon, Daisy, 54
Solomon, Emanuel, 35, 53-5, 56, 58, 158, 162
Solomon, George, 35, 51, 53
Solomon, George (jnr), 35
Solomon, John, 35, 49, 53-5, 56, 58, 158, 162
Solomon, Lucy, 53, 54
South Australia, 1, 6, 11, 12, 13, 14, 18, 21, 23, 25, 51, 164; Aboriginal Affairs Act, 1962-8, 19; Aboriginal population of, 6; Foundation Act of, 13, 14; population of, 21; west coast, 63, 67, 89, 121
South Australian Colonisation Commission, 13, 14
South Australian Museum, 127
Spicer, E. H., 5, 122
sport, 48, 95, 101
St Peter's College, 48
Sterling, Amy, 43
Stirling, E. C., 127
Strathalbyn, 45
Streaky Bay, 65, 93, 100; hospital, 109
Stubbs, Amelia, 54
Stubbs, Benjamin, 132
Stubbs, Bill (Cecil), 132, 134
Stubbs, Mabel (née Johnson), 132
Stubbs, Sam, 44
Sturt, Charles, 13, 23
Surveyor-General, 54
survival, Aboriginal, 28, 59; assessment of, 44
Swan, W. R., 64

Tandatko, 28, 29
Taplin, George, 45
Tarcoola, 69, 82
Tartan, 29, 32, 33
Tchuna, Yarrie, 98, 162
technological change, 91
Teichelmann, Christian, 23
Tennant, John, 36
terra nullius, 2
Thevenard, 92, 97, 99, 101, 103, 104, 105, 113
Tindale, Norman, 77, 131
Tod River, 33, 48
Tod River pipeline, 100, 108, 109
Todbrook, 38, 50
Toodko, 28
Tooncatchin, 127
Traeger, R. H., 98, 104, 113, 118
Tucknott, 32

Umberatana, 128, 133
United Aborigines Mission, 82, 114, 121, 134, 138, 144, 148; process for conversion, 150

Varco, Ben, 50
Venus Bay, 43
Victoria, 12, 159
violence, 12, 23, 27, 124, 125, 127; threatened, 127

wages, 53, 96, 100, 101, 112, 139, 143, 163
Wailpi, 122, 127
Wandana, 91
Wanganeen, James, 35, 38
Wangka-Aranta, 122
Warburton Ranges, 98
Ware, Dick, 100
Ware, Edmund, 101, 116
Ware, Jessie, 100
Ware, Robert, 100
Waste Lands Act, 14
Watherston, Alexander, 36, 37
Wellington, 35
Wentworth, 44
Wertaloona, 132, 134, 146
Western Australia, 11, 12, 13, 43, 44, 53, 100, 159; Moore River Native Settlement, 163
Western Desert cultural bloc, 63
Wetra, 50
White Well, 95
Whitlam, E. G., 12
Wiebusch, C. A., 68, 69, 70, 71, 72, 73, 76, 80, 81, 82, 89, 92, 95, 98
Wiebusch, E. W., 115
Wilgena, 66
William, A., 132
Williams, Nellie, 49
Williams, R. M.: leather workshop, 141

Williamy, 33
Willoughby, 67
Wilton, Albert, 132, 145
Wilton, Ethel, 133
Wilton, Henry, 145, 146
Wilton, May, 145, 146
Wilton, Rufus, 132, 133, 163
Wilton, Susie, 131, 132
Wirangu, 7, 63, 64, 67, 96, 121, 160, 165
Wirrealpa, 133, 146
Wirrealpa Billy, 124
Wirrulla, 74, 99, 103, 108
Wirrup, 38
Witchelina, 144
women, 49, 81, 104, 106, 112, 124, 129, 130, 133, 144, 149, 150; employment, 81, 96, 113; protection of, 17, 18; sexual exploitation, 113; single, 113
Wooltana, 124, 132, 133
Wowinda, Fred, 46, 56
Wudinna, 100, 103, 108, 147; hospital, 108, 109; reserve, 109; living conditions, 109, 110; school, 108, 109
Wudinna council, 109
wurley natives, 27, 48
Wyatt, William, 23

Yadliyawara, see Jadliaura
Yalata, 64, 107, 114, 116, 160
Yankaninna, 132
Yantanaby, 93, 108
Yardea, 66, 93, 99
Yari Miller Hostel, 107
Yates, Charlotte, 54
Yates, Robert, 54
Yendinna Jack, 71, 77
Yorke Peninsula, 21, 26, 43, 46, 52, 53, 58
Yorrock, 32, 33
Yudnamatana mine, 128, 132
Yura, 157
Yura Ngawarla, 161